THE REBELLIOUS CEO

Also by Ralph Nader

Told You So: The Big Book of Weekly Columns

Getting Steamed to Overcome Corporatism

The Seventeen Solutions: Bold Ideas for Our American Future

"Only the Super Rich Can Save Us!" (political fiction)

The Seventeen Traditions: Lessons from an American Childhood

The Good Fight: Declare Your Independence and Close the Democracy Gap

In Pursuit of Justice: Collected Writings 2000–2003

*Crashing the Party: Taking On the Corporate
Government in an Age of Surrender*

No Contest: Corporate Lawyers and the Perversion of Justice in America

Winning the Insurance Game (with Wesley J. Smith)

*Unsafe at Any Speed: The Designed-In
Dangers of the American Automobile*

*To the Ramparts: How Bush and Obama Paved the Way for the Trump
Presidency, and Why It Isn't Too Late to Reverse Course*

Breaking Through Power: It's Easier Than We Think.

*Unstoppable: The Emerging Left–Right
Alliance to Dismantle the Corporate State*

THE
REBELLIOUS
CEO

---

12 LEADERS WHO DID IT RIGHT

RALPH
NADER

MELVILLE HOUSE

BROOKLYN · LONDON

The Rebellious CEO: 12 Leaders Who Did It Right

First published in 2023 by Melville House
Copyright © 2023 by Ralph Nader
All rights reserved
First Melville House Printing: September 2023

Melville House Publishing
46 John Street
Brooklyn, NY 11201
and
Melville House UK
Suite 2000
16/18 Woodford Road
London E7 0HA

mhpbooks.com
@melvillehouse

ISBN: 978-1-68589-107-7
ISBN: 978-1-68589-108-4 (eBook)

Library of Congress Control Number: 2023943080

Designed by Patrice Sheridan

Printed in the United States of America
1 3 5 7 9 10 8 6 4 2
A catalog record for this book is available from the Library of Congress

To the twelve CEOs, their best practices and
their families who assisted them and supported
their high standards through thick and thin and to
leading business responsibility advocate Mitch Rofsky
(1953–2023), champion of consumer cooperatives and
Founder CEO of the Better World Club offering
consumer and environmental services for motorists.

CONTENTS

INTRODUCTION

This book is an easy read for business students, current and future business leaders, and for a discouraged citizenry. During six decades of confronting CEOs in many different industries and lines of commerce, I have had, from time to time, one-on-one meetings with the heads of corporations. Some of these meetings were desirable; others were necessary. In some of these encounters, I found a few CEOs to be wonders of values and performance. These meetings turned out to be impressive, educational, and even encouraging concerning the state of what other CEOs could emulate. This book, the result of these encounters, selects twelve CEOs who exceeded my expectations. These are people whom I got to know and grew to admire. All but three have passed on. Their work generated forces that have made our economy better than it would have been. Whether their practices and accompanying wisdom continue to reverberate and resonate outside of their immediate circles is hard to say. Their lives and work provide examples that can benefit the present and future, if more people, more students, are able to learn about these leaders and examine how they overcame their challenges to deal with the human beings whose lives impacted or were impacted by them.

I met many other CEOs at various events, conferences, social gatherings, and even depositions. I found most of them to be prisoners on temporary leave from their top-down, authoritarian corporations. In more informal settings, they spoke as less fettered human beings.

Some cases in point. Paul Austin, a fellow Harvard Law alumnus and CEO of Coca-Cola, advised on a walk to lunch that, contrary to popular lore, large powerful corporations were, if put under certain pressures, fragile and vulnerable. I countered by asking him why he used his obvious talents in the service of a company that sold a non-nutritious, sugary drink all over the world, based on a secret formula locked somewhere in a safe in Atlanta, Georgia. He replied: "I don't see anything wrong with selling a refreshing drink."

Here's another instance of that informality. The CEO of Armco Steel once told me he took his board of directors on a "sensitivity trip" deep into a coal mine that the company owned. "They didn't want to stay there very long," he said. When they emerged above, he heard them mutter that they would never again say coal miners were overpaid.

When we had these exchanges, neither of these gentlemen was accompanied by advisors, assistants, or flaks. Each spoke candidly. Unfortunately, such relative openness was not often on display when they were operating in their normal realm, whether in an executive suite or shareholders meeting.

One reason for my choice of the people profiled here is that each displayed forthright candor, competence, and a recognition of the complexities of society that shape the bottom line. I want to say at the outset that if I didn't want to keep this book relatively short, other CEOs who were productively engaging in the community could have been added, whether, depending on the scope of their interventions, that be community writ large or small.

I might have chosen Peter B. Lewis, CEO of Progressive Insurance Company, who performed in exemplary ways as a philanthropist. He built the tiny company started by his father into the third largest auto insurance company in America. He was the largest contributor to the ACLU, funded progressive think tanks, and was one of a few billionaires, along with George Soros, to openly oppose wars of empire and press for peaceful diplomacy as a solution to global conflicts. He was my classmate at Princeton, where I remembered him as almost shy, nothing like the iconoclastic, bold, flamboyant head of his insurance company or the daring promoter of architectural and artistic projects that he became.

It took just one lunch with Peter for me to convince him to equip Progressive's large fleet of company cars with airbags. Only Travelers Insurance Company did this earlier and, dramatically, it was because of an airbag that saved an employee's life in a collision with a truck. Peter was a believer in insurance companies fostering "loss prevention," or safer products and conditions.

At my urging, Peter led Progressive to become the first auto insurance company to give their customers comparison rates so they could price Progressive policies in relation to those of their top competitors, such as Allstate and State Farm. This was done even though, in some localities, Progressive might not come in first. When I informed him about my plan to establish the first tort museum in the world, The American Museum of Tort Law in Winsted, Connecticut, he blurted a pithy description of what the place was all about when he exclaimed, "Tort law is quality control" for the insurance industry! However, he declined to become one of its numerous founders.

Peter took the Giving Pledge, promising to give away at least half of his fortune to good causes during his lifetime. Unfortunately for the many civic charities he was contributing to and for those on the drawing board, Peter died from a heart attack on November 23, 2013, at age eighty.

A many-splendored free spirit, with a keen appreciation for marijuana, which he first used as a pain reliever after part of his leg was amputated in 1998, he left many who met him with "off the wall" stories about his thoughts on "grass" and other matters. He once told me that when Princeton investigated him before nominating him to its Board of Trustees—he gave Princeton more than $200 million over the years—their report called him "a functional pothead."

Peter, like many of the best CEOs, understood that working to mitigate societal problems through his advocacy, philanthropy, and style of corporate leadership would benefit the world and his company.

In Joel Makower's optimistic book from the 1990s, *Beyond the Bottom Line: Putting Social Responsibility to Work for Your Business and the World*, he offers numerous examples of socially sensitive companies (Stride Rite, Levi Strauss, South Shore Bank, Ben & Jerry's, Stonyfield Farms, Just Desserts bakery, and others) led by progressive doers and thinkers. Some of these firms had elaborate, enlightened mission statements. All believed that a wider "arc" for their company made their firm, workers, and suppliers more productive and happier, leading to more satisfied customers and a more profitable bottom line.

Makower said such a corporate culture, one that took a wider perspective on civic culture and the environment, was reaping the "benefits of benevolence." However, if one looks with less rose-tinted glasses than the ones Makower wore, it's noticeable that some of his snapshots were of large divisions of companies like

Freddie Mac or Reebok International, divisions that were doing something commendable while the rest of the company operated in conventional, profit-seeking ways with all the liabilities that accompany such a narrow focus. Others that he justly praises went out of business or merged with larger corporations and lost much of their identity. Enthusiastic forecasts of a growing trend of corporate civic consciousness put forward by progressive business groups, such as Social Venture Network or Business for Social Responsibility, did not materialize as hoped.

Instead, we sometimes saw a contrary trend over the last few years. Indeed, companies emerging from Silicon Valley or those that are a part of the "gig economy," often took irresponsible steps backward, while the standbys, those companies that have always stood against a strong civic culture, such as banks and other giant financial intermediaries and the venerable, ever-more-entrenched "military-industrial complex" persist.

Among new corporate threats are "the triad of new technologies," described in Bill Joy's landmark *Wired* magazine article from 2000, "Why The Future Doesn't Need Us." He warned of the looming risks from artificial intelligence, biotechnology, and nanotechnology, which are proceeding full speed ahead, with no legal or ethical frameworks to restrain them. Rarely has such a portentous forecast been more on target and less heeded once its immediate shock value wore off, swept aside by recklessness or the headlong rush for more of the latest sensation—and profits. And that meant more corporate science and technology driven by ever narrower, monetized minds, regardless of consequences.

In contradistinction to the leaders at the head of this new wave of reaction, the chief executives portrayed in this book provide fertile and fascinating materials for study. They made ethical choices to promote civic culture and the natural environment—self-chosen behaviors not required by law nor industry practice or custom. They challenged stereotypes slapped on their line of commerce, stereotypes which saw them as made up solely of companies that put the bottom line above all. They chose higher, ethical behavior, declining to avail themselves of the routine excuses about duty to shareholders, competitive riskiness, government regulation or other pretexts most executives employ for explaining why they are not making beneficial changes. They were trailblazers whose own conduct and that of their companies shaped distinctive pathways toward excellence.

The executives profiled here stood against the gray crowd. They were all unique individuals, so meeting them could understandably lead one to conclude that they were all completely different in personality and style. Even so, they shared an astonishingly uniform set of characteristics. (The only one of these executives also depicted in Makower's upbeat treatment was Anita Roddick, founder of The Body Shop. That was his choice even though nine of the twelve of my selected CEOs were in full operation at that time.)

Curiously, though confident and upbeat, they did not, as Makower did, extrapolate their achievements as part of an upward, unstoppable trend. They shared a tough-minded pessimism. They were too realistic in their appraisal of the corporate resistance to change, no matter how much their forays into social responsiveness and internal company humanity were proven to benefit sales and profits.

Other innovators in the mid-nineties, the time Makower was writing his book, waxed euphorically about the future in the same way Makower did. As an example, Ben Cohen, the upbeat ice cream magnate, said that if business was smart, it had better "jump on the [progressive] bandwagon," because altruism was good for business and staying competitive. (From a glance at today's business climate, you can see how few that bandwagon picked up.)

Paul Fireman, CEO of Reebok International, was equally euphoric, saying about the same time, "I believe we're on the verge of what might be a genuine shift in our nation's priorities—and official end to the 'me' and 'greed' decade. We now know that the conditions of our business cannot be separated from the conditions of the society in which we operate." Another mistaken prediction. For most companies, the only difference in their control of society's institutions is that now companies have changed to reflect greater diversity in their hiring and promotions. Otherwise, their baleful influence continues in force, diversity notwithstanding.

The Twelve's similarities were striking. But on second glance, you can see these character traits were functional prerequisites for getting things done their way. Another trait was that they marched to their own drums. They couldn't care less what people thought of them. Restless Bob Townsend, who ran Avis through a turnaround (among other executive tasks), made his writing, speaking, and consulting career out of jolting contrarian thinking. Jeno Paulucci, who started many companies, mostly in the food and packaging business, discovered that to win the sale from his position as an underdog, he had to do brazen things as an upstart.

They all did the improbable.

Ray Anderson had to reinvent his large carpet-tile company, Interface, from the bottom up to make it environmentally responsive. John Bogle reinvented his industry by pioneering the low-fee Vanguard Group as a mutual company, not a stock company.

It is the message of Paul Hawken, the environmentalist and entrepreneur, who goes around the world preaching the gospel of reinvention, and showing corporations how they must somersault their operations to achieve sustainability before time runs out for the planet.

Another commonality among these leaders: They insisted on treating their workers and customers well.

All CEOs mouth that they are committed to their workers and customers, but it seldom goes beyond lip service. These CEOs meant it and delivered. Herb Kelleher, CEO of Southwest Airlines, fostered a family-caring culture in a firm that employs 66,000 people. His personal touch included reaching out to its workers to help them get through turmoil and tragedy. Employees I have talked to—I was a frequent flyer on this airline—tell me the caring standard of management toward workers is almost too good to be true. Kelleher put the well-being of workers first, even before that of customers, and he explained why. As for addressing their customers in a way that goes beyond expectations, speak to Yvon Chouinard's Patagonia customers and you'll see what I mean.

Idealistic as all these CEOs are, and no matter how many different good causes they and their companies pursued, they shared another trait. All these CEOs insisted that nothing would be possible if they didn't pay attention to profits.

Thus, they were heedful of the details of their businesses. Anita Roddick spared no effort in designing The Body Shop stores for an authentic, warm atmosphere while posting bold signs urging actions for justice. She was an environmentally aware person, who made clear to her environmentally conscious customers that she was detail-minded in relation to ecological concerns, which ran from her choice of suppliers in tropical forests to the reuse of bottles for the store's sales. While restaurateur Andy Shallal, as he continued his political activism, personally reviewed menus to make sure they were hitting his customers' taste buds. He created the artwork on his restaurant walls to ensure a positive atmosphere and made sure there was no censorship at his attached bookstores and public event rooms, so the bookstore and event patrons got a full perspective. Every Saturday, Bernard Rapoport of American

Income Life Insurance Company, telephoned his general agents one after the other for brief chats about the state of business.

However, none of them avoided speaking out against injustices for fear it would offend customers, cause political retaliation, or hurt the bottom line.

They refused to censor their political views; they named the political candidates they supported, without worrying that they might lose sales.

Sol Price, the Jewish founder of Price Club, condemned the functioning of grand juries and funded Palestinian job training and other charitable activities, to the consternation of some of his Jewish business colleagues.

Rapoport also championed labor unions as the CEO of a life insurance company. This stance was unheard of at the time in this staid, reactionary, non-unionized industry. Gordon Sherman of Midas Muffler offended Chicago's business upper crust with his open support of tough advocates who were working to rein in their chronic abuses.

I rarely heard any of them whine about government over-regulation. For one thing, they went beyond the regulations, doing more for environmental and civic betterment than was required by law, especially in the case of Patagonia and Interface. For another, they realized that corporations deserved to be regulated or broken up, given what most corporations were not doing about corruption and pollution, among other abuses. This is why Jeno Paulucci took those who wronged him to court, suing in all directions as one way to protest dishonest peers.

Most of them, too, were founders.

They had control and exerted it to get things done, to get the best out of people, to give their company meaning, and be concerned with issues beyond maximizing the company's profits and personal wealth. Kelleher was for years, by far, the lowest compensated executive among big airlines, even though he was running the country's most profitable airline. He was paid less than one million dollars a year. But he retired a wealthy man, because Southwest's stock greatly appreciated during his tenure. The company's wealth was spread around. Everyone at Southwest was awarded shares, a payback for their commitment and helpfulness. John Bogle of Vanguard made such priorities specific in his remarkable book, *Enough*, where he chastised fellow executives who made amassing money their number one goal.

As founders, the Twelve could imprint on their firms their own special character, personality, and vision, developing an expanding structure that they intimately shaped. Were they to have inherited a bureaucratic company, it would have been far more difficult to produce such accomplishments.

Most of the CEOs in this book are white men. Unfortunately, gender and racial equality in the corporate suites increases at a glacial pace. In 2021, 86 percent of Fortune 500 CEOs were white men. Only 1 percent of Fortune 500 CEOs were African Americans. In January of 2023, the percentage of women CEOs at Fortune 500 companies hit 10 percent.

Most of these twelve had stable families and showed care and compassion in their daily lives. They were generous with time and money toward others whom they encountered, whether in their family circles, their businesses, or their outside philanthropy. They set examples for their employees; they were hands-on people who were good at foreseeing and forestalling situations that might destabilize or harm their workforce. Kelleher never laid-off a single worker in the boom-and-bust airline industry. This is not to say they never made wrong decisions or took the wrong track.

Some made mistakes that shortened their tenures as controlling CEOs.

Anita and Gordon Roddick were persuaded that going public

would provide more resources to expand and help them do more of their remarkable, groundbreaking philanthropy and democratic institution building. It didn't work out. They lost control of their company. This cut short their exponential contributions to world betterment. This was particularly tragic because Anita, among all those profiled here, had the most all-encompassing grasp of how to turn the world around and shift power from the few to the many. She expounded her views in her four books, which are marvels of readable, visual, personal, no-holds-barred challenges to the present exploitations and environmental degradation, while clear-sightedly offering ways to democratize the world and fulfill human possibilities.

In another tragic case, Gordon Sherman challenged his angry, conservative father for control of Midas Muffler, which Gordon took from the tiny firm of his father's in Chicago to a company with hundreds of franchises around the world. He lost the share-holder struggle and was pushed out just when his momentum and the philanthropic Midas Foundation were getting underway in a peerless, bold fashion.

None of the CEOs profiled were interested in turning their companies into conglomerates, nor in themselves becoming preachers.

As to conglomeration, for one thing, they knew how difficult it would be to manage such corporate sprawl. It would dilute the high standards of their original business enterprises. When asked to franchise his restaurants, Andy Shallal shrugged his shoulders and said he doubts anyone could replicate his personal hybrid model. Only modestly were they interested in spreading their business gospel. They preferred to speak through their actions, though Ray Anderson, an exception, made hundreds of speeches in which he hammered home in technological detail the dire necessity of making sustainability the number one priority for business. He persuaded upper management in Walmart to reduce their excessive packaging and therefore reduce their costs. But aside from Anderson, this group of CEOs pretty much stuck to their tasks. They did not fear competition because their way of competing was so far ahead of their industry peers.

Let's turn the page on that destructive way of living and doing business conducted by today's corporate chiefs and look to the example outlined by these exemplars. I am going to divide them into two classes. Despite the commonalities I pointed out, I still see a division, one which will structure this book.

Some are *visionaries*, such as Anita Roddick with her environmental consciousness or Yvon Chouinard with his love for the wild, who had a crystal-clear vision of the way the world should be moving. They poured all their energy into their visions.

Others are *mavericks*. These are CEOs who were just all-around humanists. They didn't move in tune to a burning vision but simply acted in solidarity with the people and progressively to solve the problems that obstructed their paths. Here I place Jeno Paulucci, who, when he saw a mining company was illegally dumping in his own backyard, fought hard to stop it in its tracks. Also of this genre was Sol Price, who worked hard to improve educational and employment opportunities in his home base of San Diego, California.

The distinction I am making is a differentiation, not a judgment, for each set of leaders, in their own way, gave us a sense of what might have been and what still could be if business were rigorously framed as a process that was not only about making money and selling things, but about reducing damage and improving our social and natural world.

1

JOHN BOGLE

Founder of the Vanguard Group

Surprising as it may seem to most people, Americans are the greatest owners of wealth, not the one percent of the super-rich who own so much of the *private* wealth. What I'm referring to are such massive assets as the public lands—which together with adjacent offshore seabed territory constitute one third of the United States—the public airwaves, trillions of dollars in pension and mutual funds, and, least recognized, trillions of dollars in government research & development given away to build the major industries of our economy, including biotech, computer, internet, drug, aerospace, and nanotech companies, and many other enterprises. The problem is that the people do not *control* what they *own*. Corporations do, either directly or through their dominating influence over such government agencies as the Federal Communications Commission and the Departments of Agriculture, Interior, Defense, and Commerce.

No one has recognized this difference between ownership and control better than John C. Bogle—best known for founding the giant Vanguard Group (with over seven trillion dollars in assets) and pioneering low-cost, low-fee investing with mutual funds and stock market index funds. I wanted to invite Bogle to participate in an event at DAR Constitution Hall in DC devoted to "Breaking Through Power, a Historic Civic Mobilization." So, I put in a call to Mr. Bogle to invite him to be our keynote speaker on September 27, 2016, about "Fiduciary Duties as if Shareholders Mattered."

His tone was friendly but weary. He was in great demand by people hungry for the truth, at various levels, about corporate greed, the ripping-off of investors, especially individuals, and the excessive power of the Wall Street crowd. "Jack"—as he insisted on being called—was a big thinker and a relentless doer, a man whose integrity and steadiness contrasted with fast-talking speculators with fully monetized minds. Years earlier, admiring investors calling themselves Bogleheads combined to form clubs around the country. Everyone wanted a piece of Jack, and now, in his late eighties, I was asking for half a day of his time. He sighed and said that he might be able to shift a meeting that day and come down from Pennsylvania. He did and spoke before a rapt audience.

In 1951 he wrote his Princeton undergraduate thesis on this newfangled thing called a mutual fund. He was prophetic. And like most innovators, he was ahead of his time and therefore mocked or dismissed. Those were the days of high fixed commissions and few required disclosure about companies' financial conditions. The brokerage industry was a uniform, smug fortress against change and diverse offerings for investors.

It's hard to imagine what Jack Bogle had to endure and overcome as he threw himself into a life and career with an almost missionary zeal. He wrote ten books, ran a fast-evolving business, crossed swords with the staid and already established investment industry that often spread disinformation about him, raised six children with his wife, and educated himself in the classics, history, and poetry, all while maintaining a sense of humor. He possessed a level of generosity and understanding of people and places that amazed his friends.

He suffered his first heart attack in 1960 when he was thirty, and other heart attacks followed until he received a heart transplant at age sixty-six in 1996. When he was thirty-seven years old, his doctor urged him to retire, given his perilous condition. Jack simply thanked him and found another physician.

Erin Arvedlund and Art Carey of the *Philadelphia Inquirer* said after his passing at age eighty-nine in January 2019 that he "displayed the energy of men half his age, and his pace and ambition were the more remarkable because of his lifelong battle with heart disease, the result of a congenital defect that affected the heart's electrical current."

You just had to believe that he loved what he was doing so much that mortal risk was never high on his radar screen. He resumed playing squash and tennis after his transplant. A testimony to psychosomatic triumph, perhaps.

On his passing, Vanguard Chief Executive Officer Tim Buckley said that "Jack Bogle made an impact not only on the entire investment industry, but more importantly, on the lives of countless individuals saving for their futures or their children's futures."

"He democratized and simplified investing and made it affordable for the average American. He was the original industry disruptor," said Peter G. Fitzgerald, a former Republican US Senator from Illinois.

Author and investment manager William Bernstein, said "Jack could have been a multi-billionaire on par with Gates and Buffett." Instead, he turned his company into one owned by its mutual funds, and in turn their investors, to provide its customers the lowest price. "He basically chose to forgo an enormous fortune to do something right for millions of people. I don't know any other story like it in American business history."

At his death, Bogle's fortune was estimated to be eighty million dollars, while his counterparts at higher-fee Fidelity, are worth billions.

Rick Stengel, former managing editor of *Time*, worked with Bogle, who then was the chair of the National Constitution Center's board, and saw a different side of the man. "He was like the last honorable man, a complete straight-shooter." "Jack," he said, "used the phrase 'so-and-so is all hat and no cattle,' to describe a gas bag." Stengel said, "Jack was all cattle and not very much hat."

Mel Lindauer, a Boglehead leader and co-author of *The Boglehead's Guide to Investing,* had this to say: "What impressed me most about Jack was his humility and approachability. His zeal for his mission of helping investors get a 'fair shake' was legendary. He worked tirelessly toward that goal, and his message never changed with the investing climate. The world won't be the same without Jack. He was a true American hero."

Was that over the top—about the world not being the same again? If you define the world as the investing world in the United States, no one today has the credibility that "Jack" had, or indeed the record, the knowledge, the just-right admonishing tone, a complete sense of the specialized hypocrisy of his occupational peers for "rank speculation," reckless assumption of debt, "obscene" multi-million-dollar paychecks, and golden parachutes. Who else among that crowd then concluded that they had violated their duty as fiduciaries, as stewards, in favor of their self-enriching sales pitches? Who else would challenge the abuses of others in his field?

He wanted capitalism, finance, and fund management to return to the standards involved in one of his favorite words: "stewardship." Arthur Zeikel, former chairman of Merrill Lynch

Investment Management, who was a Bogle friend for many years, said: "He held our industry to a higher standard than it held itself, and I think a lot of people took umbrage at that."

Paul Miller, a longtime friend and an investment manager himself, noted that "he never failed to mention, in speech after speech and talk after talk, that money managers had failed miserably to earn their high fees . . . calling them 'croupiers' at the gambling table."

Going to Bogle's bedrock personality qualities, William Bernstein declared: "He cared enough about his clients to personally answer their letters; he cared enough about his employees to be on a first-name basis with thousands of them, and to pitch in at the phone banks when things got busy; and in the end, he cared enough about his country that he spent much of his last two decades away from home tirelessly crusading against an increasingly elephantine and dysfunctional financial system." At age seventy-six, Bogle reflected what Bernstein said when he wrote his fifth book, *The Battle for the Soul of Capitalism*. He was not a revolutionary—he was instead, as he put it, in "a lover's quarrel," with a capitalism run amuck on the backs of defenseless savers and investors. Though he served on advisory committees of the Securities and Exchange Commission (SEC), he was under no illusions about that captured agency nor the chances of ever being nominated to become SEC Chairman.

The furthest he reached and achieved was the mutual principle—namely that Vanguard was not to be a company owned by shareholders on the stock exchanges, like BlackRock. It became a structure owned by the investors in its funds—not by shareholders in a publicly traded company or a small group of institutional investors. That allowed Vanguard to run cheaply and efficiently, with minimum costs to the investors who brought many of its more than four-hundred mutual and index funds. No diversions and stratifications with stock price watching, options, executive compensations based on stock prices, stock buyouts, and all the rest of the plutocratic baggage ultimately and directly charged to the investors. Mutual Vanguard did not mean a fully open democratic structure. It was still top down, and the investors had little engagement in the governance of Vanguard. What "Mutual" did, however, was put important restraints on executive greed, executive manipulation, and executive conflicts of interest against their "owners."

As we shall see, Jack Bogle was far more than a one-note Charlie, gigantic as that one-note turned out to be. He cared about the injustices in the entire economy and the pathway for an obsessed commercial culture. At a gathering in Philadelphia with Governor Ed Rendell and President Bill Clinton, he observed of our economy, almost plaintively, that "the disparity in income is deeply regrettable. I don't know what we do about it exactly." When I heard Jack say this, I thought he must have known. He knew what Western Europe had known for decades, that a higher minimum wage, full health insurance, fairer tax systems, freer public services such as public transit and tuition-free college education (as was done for students after World War II from The City University of New York to the University of California) are ways to ameliorate income inequality.

Jack knew all these programs, but not the practical ways to achieve them through the one powerful institution that could deliver them—the US Congress, populated officially by five hundred and thirty-five people who need votes more than campaign cash. This gap affected other people written about in this volume. A simple explanation is that they didn't know how to get such proposals through Congress, mostly, I believe, because it was outside their expertise, too embroiling, and, especially draining on their time and the necessity to concentrate on their businesses. With Jack, it wasn't fear of controversy, it was the disruption of his concentration on what he chose as his life's work. Another way of putting it is that his plate was full with a creative routine that would have to confront an entirely new experience and master an array of talents not suited to his studied skills. As with an athlete whose muscles and reactions and temperaments are suited to his or her chosen sport—making it in another sport, even if he or she wants to do so, is a challenge. See: Michael Jordan.

What Jack did discover that was perfectly congenial to his talents and his self-described combativeness was the relentless and incremental displacement of his rival high-fee, poorer service competition. Hence Vanguard's low expenses benefited mutual fund investors and introduced them to the better performance index funds that he innovated. The arithmetic was decisive. But the routine that investors had to change was an uphill struggle. Just like switching banks, switching from one's investment advisors or conventional mutual funds requires overcoming apathy and procrastination and the bureaucratic hurdles erected by one's existing financial institutions. He went all over the country extolling Vanguard's better deal. He wrote everywhere, including best-selling books, about low expense, index-fund investing that spread the risk beyond specialized mutual funds. Suffice to say, Vanguard spotted the giant Fidelity mutual funds, slowly caught up to them and then, accelerating, raced past them just the way Walmart surpassed Sears, Roebuck.

Bogle was nothing if not persistent. Year after year his low fees and index funds approach gained ground, prompting the Nobel Prize laureate, economist Paul A. Samuelson, to write: "John Bogle has changed a basic industry in the optimal direction. Of very few this can be said."

His strategy is best called a "displacement" movement with three prongs, starting in 1975. First was his mutual form of governance by Vanguard fund investors. This eliminated daily conflicts of interests and allegiances by management toward what would have been outside shareholders. The investors in the various Vanguard mutual funds owned them. Second, he created stock indexing, meaning that, for safety, people could put their money in the famous Vanguard 500 Index Fund that consisted of 500 companies that is about as diversified as the overall market. Third, he cut fees and, in the process, educated investors on how very much they were losing in much higher exactions imposed and compounded over time by competitors like the giant Fidelity group of funds based in Boston. As *The New York Times* reported, "Vanguard's asset-weighted average fee has fallen in the past twenty years to 0.10% from 0.25% according to Morningstar, Inc., while many traditional funds will demand 1% or more." The large savings from such low-cost index funds were kept by the investors. Over time, Jack has proven that indexing produced better results overall than most actively managed mutual funds picking stocks. There were none of the perverse incentives that often came with traditional investment management companies.

That is why the super-investor and financier, Warren Buffett, told *The Wall Street Journal* in 2009 that "if all investors heeded his [Bogle's] ideas, they would be hundreds of billions of dollars better off than they are now." Buffett's Berkshire Hathaway—with so many subsidiaries—is a kind of diversified, modified index fund and, some may say, has proven Buffett's point. Even without paying a dividend.

Bogle wasn't always of this opinion. Writing in the *Financial Analysts Journal* in 1960 under a pen name, he rejected what later became index-fund investing. Doubling down, thirteen years later he said that "neither compensation of salesman nor profitability of broker-dealers and underwriters, is excessive." Being fired in 1974 from his top post at the Wellington Fund must have concentrated his attention on the fundamental questions of his premises and calculations and led to a dramatic revision of his thinking. By 1977, Vanguard eliminated sales commissions and middlemen and went "no-load." With a mutual ownership structure—that is, owned by its investors or customers—he avoided the demands of shareholders for ever-greater profits based on high fees, commissions, and churning.

The next decade, however, was hard going, as Bogle was ridiculed by his much larger competitors, like Fidelity, whose president scoffed at being satisfied with "average returns." "The name of the game is to be the best," he declared. One could almost hear the sneer in his voice.

But like the race between the hare and the tortoise, more and more investors began to wonder what they were getting for these very high fees, paying for essentially very little, and began to turn to Vanguard's assortment of mutual funds, with dramatically lower fees yet excellent service.

Then in 2018 Jack did it again. He warned that if the success of the giant index funds continued—Vanguard, BlackRock, and State Street Global comprised 17 percent of the total US stock market value—it could lead to the three giants dominating the market. By 2030 the "Big Three might own 30% or more of the US stock market—effective control." He then concluded, as only one Jack Bogle could dare to admit, that his booming progeny would lead to such concentration as not to "serve the national interest."

Have you ever heard the heads of the military weapons industry saying that too many weapons of mass destruction bought by the Pentagon would not serve the national interest? Or the heads of the drug industry saying that they're selling too many drugs and not serving the people's health? Or the giant oil, gas, and coal industry saying that they are producing and burning too much tonnage from their wells and mines?

As was his wont, Bogle went from warning to possible remedies. He urged (1) more timely public disclosure by index funds of their voting policies, (2) public documentation of each engagement with corporate managers, and, most importantly (3) legislation making crystal clear the fiduciary duty to the interests of the investors.

I always had one concern about Bogle's blanket statement that "index funds provide investors with the most effective stock market strategy of all time: buy American business and hold it forever, and do so at rock-bottom cost." But what if you need to cash out for living expenses or for a one-time huge medical expense or a home down payment? What if that need arose in 2008–2009, when index funds crashed along with the stock markets? When do you sell, sensing a rampage of speculative risk? You must have some strategy of timing—of when to get out when the signs of collapse are evident. Or you can only invest your savings for a few years and when you want to take advantage of a "hot sector" such as technology stocks. Not all investors can behave as worker pension funds who have longer time horizons.

When confronted with the reversal of Obama's fiduciary rule, scuttled by President Trump, Bogle once again optimistically said that investor demands and index-fund expansion are starting to force brokerage firms to practice "clients first" fiduciary principles regardless of any mandatory rule by the government.

Again and again, Bogle pointed out how his innovations were forcing the industry to do voluntarily what the SEC has been blocked from requiring. In 2011, the SEC allowed shareholders to propose to management that they, the shareholders, decide policies on the company's political spending—campaign contributions. Bogle saw this opening as a way to blunt the Supreme Court's opening the door wide for companies to make the unlimited independent political contributions for or against candidates for public office. He thought that "shareholders—not self-interested corporate managers [executives]—should, and can, decide policies on corporate political contributions." He wanted shareholders to insist on a resolution that the "corporations shall make no political contributions without the approval of the holders of at least 75% of its shares outstanding." No major corporation has done this.

He felt it urgent to do something to slow down the cash that is subverting "our political system." "Certainly," he declared, "the institutional shareholders have the power to make this and other reforms"—such as runaway executive compensation—happen. But, "with a handful of exceptions," the participation of our institutional money managers (including Vanguard, I might add) has been limited, reluctant, and unenthusiastic. Perhaps they feared angering the large corporate clients whose pension and thrift funds they manage—that is, the very corporations whose shares fill their investment portfolios. It is an obvious conflict of interest, however often denied.

That is not all. He decried that "most of the large mutual and pension funds are themselves owned or controlled by giant global financial conglomerates such as the Big Banks and insurance companies. Shares of these giants are held by the institutional investors resulting in a web that won't be easily untangled."

Still, Jack, who had a cheerful, optimistic disposition, held out hope that these big mutual and pension funds and university endowments would observe their fiduciary duty and put "the interest of the small investors in pension funds that are their clients before their own!" He wanted them to "bring democracy to corporate governance, recognize conflicts that arise from the interlocking interests of our corporate and financial systems, and take that first step along the road to reducing the dominant role that big money plays in our political system." A fine exhortation, but how is this to be done?

Organizing individual shareholders has been tried over the past fifty years and failed. It has been like the proverbial herding of cats. Trying to organize large institutional shareholders, like the "Big Three," has been met with no response or rhetorical concurrence about the proposed goals but with no action.

We had this experience when we sent letters to one hundred large money managers—mutual funds, pension funds, and university endowments—asking them to oppose out-of-control executive compensation of major corporations. Executives' pay has risen to more than 350 times the average workers' wages from about 28 in 1980. Sent twice, the letter was ignored by most of the funds. Those who answered did so with routine acknowledgments. About half a dozen, including BlackRock, invited us to meet with or contact them to discuss the matters further. This was done. We're still awaiting any follow-through.

But people like Jack Bogle are obviously more serious. Around 2014, I sent him my proposal, which I called "The Penny Brigade." It had occurred to me that a tiny fraction of 1 percent of the literally trillions of shares of the top 500 corporations could be self-assessed by their owners—say a penny a share a year—to provide enough funds to hire 500 experienced, full-time watchdogs over the 500 companies. Consider the arithmetic. Cisco alone has about 5 billion shares outstanding. If owners of a mere 10 billion shares from the trillions of shares of S&P 500 companies contributed a penny a share, there would be $100 million a year to retain a team of watchdogs coordinating with one another for the kinds of reforms, on behalf of investors, that Bogle, Bob Monks, Steve Silberstein, Steve Clifford, and a few other stalwart watchdogs of the financial world have been urging for decades. Imagine if the penny assessment covered 20 billion shares, a powerful investor-protection law firm could be established working on the SEC, Congress, and the opposing corporate lobbies. Mr. Bogle and others receiving this proposal wrote back favorably about the idea but did not offer to either raise funds or participate in its furtherance. It is lying fallow, notwithstanding that my initial foray with the Penny Brigade focusing on Cisco resulted in enough media coverage and penny pledges to persuade Cisco to announce the company's first dividend (2.9%) in its history—and to unload a little of the $45 billion in retained earnings assumed to be the management's piggy bank, instead of the owner-shareholders' money.

Over these years, particularly in the mid-1990s, Jack Bogle started to wonder how the mad rush for profits and executive pay at any price would impact not just the morale of corporate workers, but also the general citizenry. Violating customary mores, muscling Washington to further loosen long-established regulatory restraints, such as those on stock buybacks, and weakening the Great Depression's reforms could lead to rampant speculation with other people's money and have disastrous ramifications for the economy and in the public square. He could see better than most observers the multiple tiers of conflicts of interest by management against investors and even internally against one another. Neither boom nor bust provided any speed bumps. During the Silicon Valley boom and stock market bust, nothing changed. Earlier, the collapse of the savings and loan industry and the successful prosecution of over 800 culpable executives did not lead to any collective sobering pauses in the mad rush for super-wealth by the few. "Get it while you can" seems to be the operative motto.

The much larger collapse of the giant banks, brokerage firms, and some insurance behemoths during the 2007–2008 Wall Street collapse—the loss of 8 million jobs, the stripping of trillions of dollars in mutual and pension funds, and the massive resultant taxpayer bailout—produced only minor embarrassment for the reckless financiers. But by 2011, it was off to the races again. Bogle was taking all this in while his fast-growing Vanguard—from which he had retired in 2000—was continuing without significant losses and no overt scandals, unlike its hyper-commercialized counterparts. In fact, Vanguard was entering its fastest growth period ever.

Drawing on his lifetime of reading economics, philosophy, history, and poetry, he began to write a book, published in 2009 with the title—intriguing for a financier—of *Enough! True Measures of Money, Business, and Life.* Unlike most books of rumination by well-known people in the business world, this was far more than tales of success and other life engagements. Bogle was talking to his wide-ranging world of businesspeople and drawing them out of their cocoons—first as money makers and then as human beings with families and their possible civic lives connected to the future of their country.

The book took people like Arthur Levitt, former chairman of the Securities and Exchange Commission, further than Levitt's own addresses to investors about the world beyond obsession with bottom line behavior. He called *Enough* "must-reading for millions of US investors disenchanted by today's culture of greed, accounting distortions, corporate malfeasance, and oversight failure." Bogle made sure every Vanguard employee received a copy.

The Princetonian was really a good and clear writer. Maybe it was the air of the Adirondacks, where he spent his summers, that cleared his mind for contemplating reality over myth, for fundamental values over expedient rationalizations. His chapter titles are a master list of concise aphorisms that could be the outline of an indelible course in the nation's business schools—assuming they are capable of entertaining such reflections.

These chapter headings explain what I mean: (1) Too Much Cost, Not Enough Value; (2) Too Much Speculation, Not Enough

Investment; (3) Too Much Complexity, Not Enough Simplicity; (4) Too Much Counting, Not Enough Trust; (5) Too Much Business Conduct, Not Enough Professional Conduct; (6) Too Much Salesmanship, Not Enough Stewardship; (7) Too Much Management, Not Enough Leadership; (8) Too Much Focus on Things, Not Enough Focus on Commitment; (9) Too Many Twenty-First-Century Values, Not Enough Eighteenth-Century Values; (10) Too Much "Success," Not Enough Character.

Then, in the final section called "Wrapping Up: What's Enough?" he gives the Bogle treatment to: "What's Enough For Me? For You? For America?"

From even just what you know so far about this man from Malvern, Pennsylvania, wouldn't this trail of contemplation be a great webinar with thousands of people participating at a time? I'd like very much to be a moderator of such a dynamic extension of Jack Bogle into the future. This would be a good starting point in creating a legacy for Vanguard's Founder.

These provocative chapter headings, in their totality, represent Jack's professional and overall philosophy of life. His insights demonstrate that, "What is past is prologue."

The first paragraph in his introduction told the story of how he got the title of his now classic little volume of experience and wisdom. In his words:

At a party given by a billionaire on Shelter Island, Kurt Vonnegut informs his pal, Joseph Heller, that their host, a hedge fund manager, had made more money in a single day than Heller had earned from his wildly popular novel, *Catch 22*, over its whole history. Heller responds, "Yes, but I have something he will never have . . . Enough."

Note where Bogle takes that word, "Enough."

Joseph Heller captured in that powerful single word "enough" not only our worship of wealth and the growing corruption of our professional ethics but ultimately the subversion of our character and values.

Bogle decried chasing "the false rabbit of success . . . too often bowing down at the altar of the transitory and finally meaningless and fail[ing] to cherish what is beyond calculations, indeed eternal."

In his opening chapter, "Too Much Cost, Not Enough Value," Bogle points to a truth not often noted in Economics 101. He begins with a nineteenth-century English epigram.

Some men wrest a living from nature and with their hands, this is called work.

Some men wrest a living from those who wrest a living from those who wrest a living from nature and with their hands, this is called finance.

Apart from leaving out half the human race, which, at that time, produced great value at little cost to the men, this epigram meant that finance was a derivative business that was abstractly reliant on real production and exchanges of that production. Finance used to be a small part of the economy. But in recent decades, it has grown to be the single largest part of the US economy, making up about a third of all the profits of all the sectors of the economy, such as manufacturing, health care, technology, and energy. To Jack, there is a lot of snare and delusion enveloping investors who think they make more than they do because they do not subtract the annual costs deducted in a compounded way over the years from their packages, the 20 percent plus 2 percent of the hedge funds' gains leaving you absorbing all the losses. It is the drip, drip of "brokerage

commissions, management fees, sales loads, advisory fees, the costs
of all that advertising, lawyer's fees, and so on." Vanguard shows
the impact of such costs:

> Imagine you have $100,000 invested. If the account earned
> 6% a year for the next 25 years and had no costs or fees,
> you'd end up with about $430,000.

> If, on the other hand, you paid 2% a year in costs, after 25
> years you'd only have about $260,000.

> That's right: The 2% you paid every year would wipe out
> almost 40% of your final account value. 2% doesn't sound
> so small anymore, does it?

"Clearly," he writes, "the wonderful magic of compounding returns
has been overwhelmed by the powerful tyranny of compounding
costs." "On balance," he concludes, "our financial system
subtracts value from our society." In the aggregate, he warns that,
"Continuation of such a costly system will undermine the ability of
our citizens to accumulate savings for retirement."

Bogle's analysis of reckless speculation could apply equally to
gambling at the craps tables in Las Vegas. Sure, some people come
out winners every day, but overall, "in the aggregate," the gamblers
lose to the House.

Back to the epigram, he warns that until efficiency for the investor is the rule, "the financial economy will continue to subtract
inordinately from the value created by our productive businesses."
Which brings us to the next lesson, following distinguished
Jeremiahs, such as the British economist, John Maynard Keynes,
of "Too Much Speculation, Not Enough Investment." About
ninety years ago, Keynes described enterprise [investment] as

"forecasting the prospective yield of an asset over their whole life." "Speculation," he said, was "the activity of forecasting the psychology of the market."

What Supreme Court Justice Potter Stewart said about pornography, "I know it when I see it," also applies to speculation. First, the less-than-real assets of the economy are exchanged between buyer and seller—that is, the tangible goods and services that make up people's livelihoods, like land, motor vehicles, textiles, food, energy, housing, health care, etc.—and the more the exchange is that of intangibles, the more likely we are to expect speculation. For example, stocks and bonds are once removed from the real economy, options and puts, further removed as the bets they are, and even further removed are exchanges of complex derivatives. The latter, based on algorithms, are bets on bets on bets on bets and so on. Rank speculation. As one might guess, speculative activity in the stock market is usually much more short-term than investments. So rife with speculation are the stock markets that Bogle declared that "the stock market is a giant distraction from the business of investing."

Although speculation is quantitatively rampant in dollars and players, Bogle shows the arguments lead to "the obvious conclusion: Investors win, speculators lose. There is no way around it." Even the reserved Federal Deposit Insurance Corporation concluded, "As is typical of boom and bust cycles, this boom was characterized by loose credit, rampant speculation, and general exuberance in the outlook for the market—in this instance, the housing market." So the orgy of speculation we are witnessing today ill serves our market participant. It serves only Wall Street, and "the croupiers" in charge.

While he goes into great detail, Bogle's view, accepted by most of the nation's independent, astute observers of financial markets, is that unchecked, speculation starts driving out investment in the uses of money. One result is that large US companies have adopted much of the speculator mindset. Rubber-stamp corporate boards are using distorted metrics to set executive compensation. Massive stock buybacks, exercised at market heights, without shareholder approval, are associated with low levels of long-term investment in the real economy. Even many mergers and acquisitions—solemnly justified at news conferences as sublimely rational from an investment viewpoint—are speculation. That's one reason why most of them do not work out, other than to further concentrate markets and restrict choice. "There needs to be a much better balance between speculation and investment," he writes, noting some useful functions for speculators to clear markets. But now it is out of kilter. Bogle quotes Keynes, who saw this craziness and volatility coming some ninety years ago: "Speculators may do no harm as bubbles on a steady stream of enterprise. But the position is serious when enterprise becomes a bubble on a whirlpool of speculation. When the capital development of a country becomes a by-product of the activities of a casino, the job is likely to be ill done." Today, that means "corporate capitalism," not your ma-and-pa retail store.

Providing readers with some relief, Bogle's next essay dilates on the importance of simplicity over complexity. Is he paddling upstream? He credits his career successes "not to brilliance or complexity, but to common sense and simplicity," or, "the uncanny ability," as one observer said, "to recognize the obvious." Here his arguments are obvious and hard to refute. Bogle: "Innovation in finance is designed largely to benefit those who create the complex new products, rather than those who own them." Or, I might add, those who bear the brunt of periodic crashes. He cites "collateralized debt obligations" and their record of exploitative speculation. More need not be added but could be. They have in common an array of huge fees, ranging from what the banks charge to what the rating agencies gouge for giving top rankings to such deals while they collect from the deal makers; the latter then, of course, find many ways to pass the costs on to the innocent masses, including through their retirement plans.

Not surprisingly, his clinching comparison is the simplicity of the index fund with the huge array, here and abroad, of specially promoted funds—many fly-by-night in duration—allegedly tailored to your temperament and wish fulfillment. Or whatever happens to be hot right now, not yesterday or tomorrow.

The Oracle from Malvern displays confidence in his position by ever repeating it better and showing how the brightest free minds in investment—like Warren Buffett and David Swensen, chief investment officer of the Yale University Endowment—agree with him.

The last summary of Bogle's thinking and practicing:

> Mark me down, too, as an adversary of complexity, complexity that obfuscates and confuses, complexity that comes hand-in-hand with costs that serve its creators and marketers, even as those costs thwart the remote possibility that a rare, sound idea will serve those investors who own it.

He could make an even stronger case. Complexity means that fewer of those ripped-off can begin to grasp what is happening in order to object and correct. Complexity means cognitive dissonance or a very clever controlling process over its dependent victims who mostly stay and fervently hope they can continue to trust such untrustworthy gobbledygook. Such complexity is worthy indeed of psychiatry.

Working in a world of numbers led young Bogle to skepticism. He liked to refer to a sign Albert Einstein had on his desk at the Institute for Advanced Study at Princeton: "Not Everything That Counts Can Be Counted, and Not Everything That Can Be Counted Counts." It is laughable to think everything, even intangibles, can be measured, yet creators of those ever more intrusive, arrogant algorithms are laughing profitably; they are penetrating deeper recesses of human and natural life to make more and more of everything for sale. They are presuming to detect or measure what Jack calls the unmeasurable—"things like trust, wisdom, character, ethical values and the hearts and souls of the human beings who play the central role in all economic activity . . . Numbers are not reality. At best, they are a pale reflection of reality."

He refers to the ways the GDP and the unemployment rate are calculated. Somehow the benefits of a free checking account find their way into the GDP. But workers who want work but who have given up looking for a job, and those who work fewer than twenty hours per week, are *not* considered unemployed. Predictions, projections turning out false so frequently, and accounting redefinition of earnings are other examples of "Twistifications," in Jefferson's words, that people swallow as being reliable.

These numerical abuses and deceptions, such as the crazy hyping of assumed future returns of pension plans or the tyranny of short-term numbers imposed on corporate quarterly reports, have real-life consequences. A financial writer called this "the empire of numbers hope," that creates unrealistic expectations by stock analysts and leads corporate executives to cook the books to maintain this mirage. Judgment, common sense, and intuition are being degraded and sacrificed on the myopic altar of the numbers rackets and their chieftains. Jack calls repeatedly for a "healthier balance" between counting and trusting.

From trust, the transition to what it means to be a member of a profession is easy. Commercialism, meaning everything is for sale, profit at any cost, has invaded the professions of law, medicine, engineering, architecture, accounting, and publishing, and nearly destroyed their independence (most of these professionals are now employed by corporations) and their tradition of public service. Now they can be considered more as "traders"—expertise for hire—and leave their conscience at home to follow orders no matter what. Certainly, the stories of corporate crime, violence, and abuse have filled books and newspapers and spawned ethical whistleblowers who risked their jobs to tell the truths suppressed inside their companies. Notice their label—"whistleblowers"—that is the status they are accorded for merely being professional and challenging commercial imperatives with their expert knowledge and sense of duty to the defenseless public.

The replacement of ownership capitalism with managers who *control* what people and institutional shareholders *own* separates the sense of responsibility that ownership entails. Adam Smith recognized this disconnect 247 years ago. In the years up to and during the Wall Street crash of 2008–2009, corporate lawyers, accountants, and auditors were literally paid *not* to do their jobs. Those few who insisted on meeting professional standards found the exit door beckoning. The spiraling, staggering increase in executive compensation of major companies over three decades from some 28 times the average worker to 350 or more times nowadays mocks the pretense of any corporate governance involving the owners. The SEC's "business judgment" rule is so extreme that all major decisions, except for the sale of the company or a major merger, can occur without requiring shareholder approval. The decisions are made by two or three corporate monarchs at the top with their rubber-stamp board of directors.

Tim Cook, CEO of Apple, who in 2022 received compensation at the rate of $833 a minute over a forty-hour week, and a couple of his top officers made the unilateral decision seven years ago to buy back about $300 billion of company stock without shareholder approval. They decide, with a rubber stamp Board of Directors, whether it is well advised, how much is accorded to dividends or other investments in the longer-range interests of the company, or internally to its workers, and its often-underfunded pensions.

Of course, there is the other disconnect of the giant institutional shareholders, who almost always vote with management. They see their role as exiting or selling their shares, rather than voting against management, should they have a major, rare disagreement. Major corporation after major corporation have had their obscenely compensated executives run their companies into the ground with the institutional shareholders hanging on. Consider General Electric, General Motors, Citigroup, and AIG as illustrative of many other fallen Goliaths. Bogle shows how executive pay is really a self-setting process endlessly pushed upward by compensation consultants who use peer-group compensation and superficial managed metrics to head for the stratosphere. As far back as 1985, *Fortune Magazine* reflected how rigged the rise of executive pay had become with a cover story, "Why Executive's Pay Keeps Rising: How Executive Compensation Keeps Going Up and Why Nothing Can Be Done About It." Warren Buffett encapsulated this lucrative spiral as "Ratchet, Ratchet, and Bingo." Buffett sees enormous executive pay as a cause of distorted accounting in these companies.

Bogle summed up his concern over "the triumph of business over-reach over professional standards" by quoting Felix Rohatyn, former head of Lazard, who, citing "naked greed," told the *Wall Street Journal*: "Only capitalism can kill capitalism, but our system cannot stand much more abuse of the type we have witnessed recently." Oh yes it can, much more. Those words were written in 2003, and since then "naked greed" has grown, collapsed the economy in 2008–2009 with the "Great Recession," and risen again to new heights of "naked greed" and unaccountable power in all sectors of the economy beyond the financial. Now furthered by the Trump kleptocracy, giant corporations are exacting huge profits from the misery and deaths of the COVID-19 pandemic.

Like all business critics of large corporate non-governance, Bogle turns his attention to the large mutual funds, pension funds, and large university endowments that together own most of the shares of New York Stock Exchange companies and other major exchanges.

This is a quest where "hope springs eternal." Long before Jack entered Princeton, the celebrated corporate lawyer and author, Adolf Berle, raised the flag for what he called "pension fund capitalism." After documenting, with economist Gardiner Means, the separation of ownership from control of large companies in the famous 1932 book *The Modern Corporation and Private Property*, Berle foresaw the emergence of giant worker pension funds whose investments in the stock market could reach controlling status. Alas, smart and experienced as he was as a corporate attorney, Berle underestimated his own colleagues' ingenuity in developing many separations of shareholder-owners from management control and between the worker-investors and the well-paid managers of the pension funds. With few exceptions, despite some fine rhetoric, these trillions of dollars of public and private pension funds have had little effect; the plutocrats running these companies have fixed Washington—Congress, the White House, and the SEC—to have their back. Thus, in his chapter titled "Too Much Salesmanship, Not Enough Stewardship," Bogle spares no rod to excoriate this spoiled but immensely rich child he helped to grow. With degraded services, more complexity and deception, inscrutable statements to investors, and the conflict of interest between managers and their fund shareholders, Bogle points to a majority of the fifty largest fund organizations owned by global financial conglomerates. Thus, another tier with which to concentrate power and proliferate offerings, churning, draining, and exacting yet more fees.

He pointed to "our trade association, the Investment Company Institute (ICI)" for "never" highlighting "the gap between the returns reported by mutual funds and the returns actually received by fund shareholders, even as it claims to be the advocate for those very shareholders." ICI, he notes, doesn't report the huge profits secured by fund managers, regardless of whether the fund shareholders got any return at all.

In one of the most devastating examinations of an industry by a prominent insider, Jack unloads an excoriating analysis of self-seeking, abdication, short-termism, and colossal indifference to the precarious situation of underfunded public and private worker pension funds.

Then he asks us to share five dreams of reform that place stewardship over salesmanship. They are a "fair shake for investors in terms of cost; serving the investor for a lifetime, long-term investment horizons, serving long-term investors, and putting Fund Investors in the Driver's Seat of fund governance," instead of being managed to benefit investment advisors. Most concisely, he calls for an industry "that is of the shareholder, by the shareholder, and for the shareholder."

Jack Bogle was indeed a dreamer, and his dreams have not only been largely ignored, outside of the Vanguard mutual index fund model he developed, but federal and state regulations of the industry have gotten weaker as the abuses he documents have become more widespread. Neither wise counsel nor reckless crashes nor criminal behavior have provoked any adequate reforms, whether by government or the industry's trade or professional societies. They don't say it; they just act it daily—"Greed is Good." Jack's plea near the end of *Enough* is for a granular leadership to build the "great organization." Walk the walk and recognize that "human beings represent the key to business leadership." These concise pages on leadership need to be read for their important wisdom. It is obvious he thought a lot about what he did, what he saw, what he shared and what he learned. Suffering so many heart attacks must have refined his sense of the ephemeral steeped in simple data. Of the 500 large companies listed in the Fortune 500 in 1955, only 71 companies remained in 2009, and even fewer today.

In his later years, Jack became more and more a philosopher of life, drawing on the wisdom of the ages, over 2,500 years of recorded history, the ancient thinkers so relevant today, the venerable poets, writers of sagas and novels, pithy recollections of people in his youth whose few words or questions shook him toward maturity and a Benjamin Franklin–type of self-conscious improvement. Bogle should be read by all persons, young and older, mired and caught in the iPhone internet frenzy, so often looking down and not viewing the horizon. He is writing for them, if they could only know; he writes of "boldness, commitment to Family and Community, to Citizenship, and the wise thinkers of the Eighteenth Century—often called 'The Age of Reason.'"

The works of these philosophers and activists are largely unknown to ever-rising generations—some of them thinkers and doers like Thomas Jefferson and Thomas Paine, and, of course, the great, preeminent Benjamin Franklin.

Near the end of *Enough*, Bogle has you understanding what he means by "character and course" in one man's life without retirement right to the last days, a few months short of his ninetieth birthday. He shows his frames of reference—rare for any business executive—by asking and discussing the question "What's Enough for Me? For You? For America?"

Bogle finally winds down the book with a remarkable "Top Ten" list of what has motivated him to answer his own question, "Why Do I Bother to Battle?"—a profound question in a democracy in which only a small percent of the people bother answering the question "Why Bother?" as engaged citizens upholding our society's fair play and promise for prosperity.

Even the ever-cheerful, optimistic Bogle must have had his deep disappointments. After a half century of proving his point in the perceived monetary interests of investors—with a booming mutually organized Vanguard, which he left twenty years ago—the rest of the industry had to lower their fees. But they did not adopt the crucial mutual type of organization to prevent reversions to the old ways of gouging when given the opportunity. His displacement strategy only went so far—though far further than anyone else with the same inclinations. The roots of greed grow deep. Bogle warned, "In the years ahead, all of those interested in the future of investment management must join the fight against largely unsupported theories that would . . . destroy the single best option that our families have for investing to accumulate wealth: buying and holding shares in a broadly diversified, low-cost stock market index fund."

But there must have been an immensely greater disappointment that he kept to himself. It is the question he must have asked himself many times. How are all these tens of trillions of dollars of the people's savings being used, being invested? That is the grim world that Bogle and the Bogleheads did not enter—absorbed as they were persuading firms to treat investors fairly on their returns with minimum costs. Well, it is not a pretty picture. Vanguard is one of the ten largest investment management firms in the world. As of February 2023, Vanguard had $7.5 trillion in global assets under management. It can't help investing in companies that exploit sweatshop labor, like Apple, or hollow-out communities, like Amazon, or the many exploitations by the giant banks, drug companies, agribusiness, defense companies, mining companies, Facebook, Phillip Morris, and more. The interlocks with the global financial powers are inescapable. In this arena, Bogle values scarcely exist. With over $7.5 trillion looking for diversified returns, Vanguard is focused on helping long-term investors seeking to meet their financial goals. Bogle did express disappointment that his executive successors at Vanguard did not publicly weigh in on excessive executive compensation, self-serving stock buybacks, and speculation risking pension and other fiduciary obligations. But over and over again, he criticized the financial investment industry at large, without excluding Vanguard as an exception to the contrary. There are innumerable times when socially responsible investors and groups (such as those identified with religious orders) beseeched Vanguard and other funds to vote for resolutions opposed by corporate management. In the vast majority of cases, Vanguard sided with management, even regarding sky-high executive compensation packages, despite their corrosive effect on an entire company.

On Jack's behalf, he had no base of support among investors solely seeking good returns with minimum costs, period. As noted, investors and institutional fund managers are exceedingly difficult not only to organize, but to move to voluntarily reflect, in any significant numbers, higher horizons directed at the harmful, antisocial uses of these vast mountains of money. Such uses that keep a political economy down or fail to diminish injustice to or promote people-oriented productivity, eventually come back to erode the quality of life of these very same investors.

Professor Peter Phillips, introducing his recent, immense directory of "The Global Elite," of which Vanguard is number two among financial behemoths in size of assets after BlackRock, writes that "the concentration of protected wealth leads to a crisis of humanity, whereby poverty, war, starvation, mass alienation, media propaganda and environmental devastation are reaching a species level threat. We realize that human-kind is in danger of possible extinction and recognize that the Global Power Elites are probably the only ones capable of correcting the condition without major civil unrest, war and chaos . . . Their biggest problem is to find enough safe investment opportunities for a return on capital that allows for continued growth. Inadequate capital-placement opportunities lead to dangerous speculative investments, buying up public assets and permanent war spending."

Imagine if Providence were to give Jack Bogle another ninety years of a new life to devote to the uses and misuses of investment money by the concentrated few who control, but do not own, most of these trillions of dollars around the planet. With his background, principles, and human relations skills, can any imaginative author write realistic fables about what he would have accomplished in order to release our own imaginations toward an advanced humanity? That would be a most fitting tribute to a man who persisted with two hearts to give so much more than he kept for himself to so many. May his Foundation locate such a Fabulist.

2

ANITA RODDICK

The Many-Splendored Revolutionary:
Co-CEO of The Body Shop

If there has ever been a CEO of any global corporation remotely like Anita Roddick—the founder and co-CEO with her husband, Gordon Roddick, of The Body Shop—neither I nor anyone I know has ever heard of him or her. Anita was a "her," alright, a fervent, cool feminist believing, and herself proving by example, that women, by and large, could show more compassion, caring, and future vision for humans than men. But she went a step further than having a company whose staff was mostly women under thirty; she demanded that women take their presumed virtues and actively make a constant difference for a better world. Feminism for her—and she didn't dwell on this—was more than just equal, upward, occupational or professional mobility with men. It had to be a force for revolutionary change against the injustices of the community and the world. And did she ever mean it, as we shall all too briefly describe.

Something in her upbringing and early experience must have inoculated her against hypocrisy or saying what she doesn't mean.

Start with her chosen business—cosmetics. Here is how she
started her first book, published in 1991—*Body and Soul: Profits
with Principles*:

> I hate the beauty business. It is a monster industry selling
> unattainable dreams. It lies. It cheats. It exploits women.
> Its major product lines are packaging and garbage. It is no
> wonder that Elizabeth Arden once said that the cosmetic
> business was the nastiest in the world.
>
> To me, the whole notion of a "beauty" business is pro-
> foundly disturbing. What is beauty? I believe beauty is
> about vivaciousness and energy and commitment and
> self-esteem, rather than some ideal arrangement of limbs
> or facial features as celebrated in fashion magazines and
> beauty pageants.
>
> In my view the cosmetics industry should be promoting
> health and well-being; instead it hypes an outdated notion
> of glamour and sells false hopes and fantasy.
>
> What is even worse is that the industry seems to have abso-
> lutely no sense of social responsibility, and in its desperate
> need to chase profits . . . It is producing lipstick and eye
> shadow for children in a society where the spread of child
> pornography is causing increasing concern. It has even
> launched an expensive perfume for babies and toddlers—
> how decadent can you get?
>
> The essential dilemma for the cosmetics industry can be
> easily explained. The big growth area is not in fragrance
> or make-up, but in skin care products, yet the simple truth

is that such products can do nothing more than cleanse, polish and protect the skin and hair. That's it. Amen. End of story. There are no magic potions, no miracle cures, no rejuvenating creams. That is all hype and lies.

Perhaps it is just too much to expect a cosmetics house to tell the unvarnished truth: "Ladies, this cream is no better and no worse than any other cream on the market but we are asking you to pay a lot of money for it because it is in a very fancy bottle and a very nice box."

Anita Roddick was writing these words when The Body Shop had over 600 franchised stores in the United Kingdom and a dozen other countries. A sizable network, but not big enough to really challenge the big cosmetic companies. And since The Body Shop did not advertise, it could not reach the huge television audience daily fantasized by vendors of "hope," as one executive put it. Roddick's views were hardly an attempt to develop a maverick brand; she meant every word and more. "Thus are women," she wrote, "enslaved by the images of beauty and glamour gazing out at them from every advertising hoarding, every glossy magazine and every television commercial, enslaved to a never-ending struggle to attain some unattainable standard of perfection. By preying on women's fears—of lost youth, diminishing appeal and fading beauty—the false hopes offered by the cosmetic industry can only result in misery, demoralization in a deep-rooted sense of inadequacy."

Well, then, what in the world were she and Gordon doing in this business? She gives us the narrowest answer: "Nothing that The Body Shop sells pretends to do anything other than it says, 'Moisturizers moisturize, fresheners freshen and cleansers cleanse. End of story.'"

Except that was scarcely the end of her story. She started her first little Body Shop in 1976 in Brighton, England, as a matter of survival, she recalls. With two small daughters to support, and with Gordon fulfilling a life's dream riding a horse from Buenos Aires to New York right after selling their restaurant, she had no choice but to start a business to "survive and feed [her] kids" while also being a mother and homemaker.

Also, as a consumer, she hated having to pay such high prices for simple creams, cleansers, and fragrances. It wasn't easy at first. She made sure that the shop floor was a bright space, that only natural ingredients were used in the products she sold, swore off products tested on animals, and used the simplest bottles—plastics, refills, or bring your own bottles—to eliminate wasteful packaging. A few weeks into her venture, Gordon cut his trekking trip short after 2,000 miles and joined her modest effort. In 1991, after receiving the World Vision Award for Development Initiative, she told *Third Way* magazine:

> The original Body Shop was a series of brilliant accidents. It had a great smell. It had a funky name. It was positioned between two funeral parlors—that always caused controversy. It was incredibly sensuous. It was 1976—the year of the heat wave, so there was a lot of flesh around. We knew about storytelling then, so all the products had stories. We recycled everything, not because we were environmentally friendly, but because we didn't have enough bottles. It was a good idea. What was unique about it with no intent at all, no marketing nous, was that it was translated across cultures, across geographical barriers and social structures. It wasn't a sophisticated plan, it just happened like that.

Almost, but not quite. Nothing is new in the business success world—there always seems to be an unsung antecedent to an innovation. It seems that Anita got the idea of sensuous simplicity and natural products from Berkeley, California, where a store named The Body Shop opened in 1970 on Telegraph Avenue and expanded to seven stores and mail orders before the owner decided—no more, that's enough.

Planning for expansion into New York City by 1988, Anita found she couldn't use The Body Shop name. So, after much negotiation, she bought rights to the name for $3.5 million, and the Berkeley Body Shop changed its name to "Body Time." That was probably the only time anybody could charge the Roddicks' business with imitation. They charged forth upon the world with staggering diversified energy and purpose. To Anita, business was a means to seize every opportunity to do good in the world, whether through establishing critical charities in desperate zones of need or taking on giant corporations and governments for their structural injustices against the weak, vulnerable, and powerless.

Anyone reading Anita's four books might come away with the impression that her role was the "idea," the "impulse" to civic action. That was true, but it might have masked her meticulous attention to business details, to the aesthetics of The Body Shop interior designs, to the signs and placement of her five sizes of bottles, to the remarkable ways she recruited and motivated workers to think of themselves as low-pressure salespeople with the exhorted freedom to engage in civic causes on company time. She told them that, in the midst of their exciting campaigning for the good of humanity, animals, and the environment, they must not forget that only by making profits can there be the resources to make all this visible, pulsating, socially responsible activity possible.

Confessing that she never learned anything from the stodgy business world, or from the Harvard Business School or its MBAs, which she ridiculed, she did admit to being a "great trader." She once said she could sell anything to anyone. But, astonishingly, not through high-pressure sales techniques or advertising. Just by creating an atmosphere for the customers, gently suggesting that they make up their own formulations if they wish and letting them come to their purchase on their own terms. That is how they will become faithful repeat customers, she said.

Asked about her attitude toward labor unions, she said that unions are only needed when the "employers are bastards." Meaning that for The Body Shop, unions would be steps down and a bureaucratic distraction. From what? Hear her out.

> We both knew that the simple pursuit of ever-increasing profits was not going to be enough. We frankly were not that interested in money. However, we did recognize that a function of profits was to create jobs and provide security and prosperity for our employees. That was fine, but then what?

> We accepted that it was our inherent responsibility to motivate and involve our staff and franchise holders, to try and make the working week a pleasure instead of the living death . . . By education, by stretching their abilities and their imaginations. By involving them in issues of greater significance than selling a pot of skin cream.

She called her employees "soul traders." Almost from the beginning of The Body Shop, this intrepid, extroverted, people-loving, animal-safeguarding, nature-preserving business leader had far greater horizons in mind than selling responsibly made lotions, creams, and shampoos. She said out loud what makes the big bosses of Big Business cringe. Namely, that business, far more than organized religion and government, was the most powerful institution on Earth. Given that premise, it is intolerable that it only be judged by profits and bonuses. With such power, business had to actively assume its multiple responsibilities to society. She defined those obligations more broadly than the customary list of shareholders, customers, and workers in a narrow monetary stakeholder sense. Her parameters attached to whatever the business impacted directly and indirectly, personally, or impersonally. Even with a relatively small global company—which sold its entire business in 2006 to L'Oréal for less than $1.3 billion—the Roddicks exported The Body Shop's model of business responsibility across the entire globe. The Body Shop defined for businesses direct, bold charity and, more formidably, advocacy for justice.

Note the authentic passion behind her great aspirations (based on thinking she credited to being forged in the sixties):

The very notion of using a business as a crusader, of harnessing success to ideals, set my imagination on fire. From that moment The Body Shop ceased to exist, at least in my eyes, as just another trading business. It became a force for social change. It became a lobby group to campaign on environmental and human rights issues. It became a communicator and an educator.

When I read these purposeful words, I immediately recalled a lunch I had with Paul Austin, CEO of the giant Coca-Cola Company, at his request. Since we were both graduates of the Harvard Law School, there was significant informality for me to ask him: of all the work he could have done in his life, didn't he feel a little unfulfilled presiding over a global enterprise pushing, worldwide, the sale of a drink that had no nutrition, that had so much sugar, that was, with dubious promotions, replacing native drinks, such as Brazil's Guaraná, which were more nutritious? He didn't express any remorse.

Could Anita Roddick have been more opposite? She dripped with distaste when she spoke of her creams, soaps, fragrances, and lotions. What she took seriously about her products in over 2,000 stores were the sources of these ingredients and the rigor with which she selected some and rejected others based entirely on human rights and environmental values. Pursuing the most "perfect" natural ingredients possible, she journeyed all over the world, year after year, picking up all kinds of collateral causes for justice along the way. And in the most unlikely, forbidding tropical wilderness where a CEO would never have visited for any reason or reward.

In this ever-widening process, beyond suppliers, of facing more and more of the world's deprivations and horrors, she did not neglect the mundane rigors of running the business and its product development with care, compassion, finesse, and a very lucky choice of husband in Gordon—the stolid backroom business manager with steady and uncanny judgment.

So, it was not surprising that she always started her quests for humanity with her workers in the shops. She wanted them to be on the front line for justice. She told them that their daily job was not stimulating or fulfilling enough. She knew, she related, because she had done that boring work herself for years. She offered them an opportunity to enhance their work experience on company time by "working for the community, lobbying for social change and campaigning for the environment." She wanted to raise their consciousness, for them to have a much higher sense of their significance in the world.

Anita first joined with Greenpeace's campaign against dumping hazardous wastes in the North Sea and shortly thereafter with the drive to oppose the slaughter of the whales. This took the form of placing posters and displays in The Body Shops, educating the employees to speak out on the subject, if they wished, and publicizing the company's uses of jojoba oil in some of its products. Jojoba oil—a product from a desert plant used by the American Indians for centuries on their hair and skin—had very similar properties to the spermaceti, or sperm whale oil, used by the cosmetic industry in various creams. Since the jojoba plant was more renewable than the endangered sperm whales facing extinction, there was an excellent blend of product and public policy.

Some franchise holders began to talk about being seen as too "political." She didn't buy that, telling them the "Save the Whales" posters brightened up what was otherwise the "boring old bottles with green labels." Still, though the campaign did bring new members to Greenpeace, she cut ties to Greenpeace because of the permissions and "petty jealousies" that came in taking these campaigns to other countries. The next alliance was with Friends of the Earth (FOE) against acid rain. She insisted that a poster be displayed in the windows of every Body Shop showing a dead tree coming out of a decomposing human head against a background of smoking factory chimneys. It was terribly misinterpreted and didn't go over well. The next campaign with FOE was on the dangers to the Earth's ozone layer. Preaching what The Body Shop was practicing—using no CFCs in aerosols—deepened the company's approaches with what she demanded and should become every industry's ways.

As The Body Shop's profit began to broach $5 million a year, Anita began adding other yardsticks that, to her, mattered beyond more money. How did the company measure up in education, public communication, caring for its staff, and fulfilling its social responsibilities? She even posed the yardstick: "Where did we stand on the quirkiness scale?"

As The Body Shop grew rapidly, the stockbrokers and finan-cial analysts became more interested as she became less interested. They did take note that her publicized environmental campaigns replaced the need for paid advertisements and brought more con-sumers into the stores. They saw the heightened morale and moti-vation of people who worked for The Body Shop. These employees were given the respect that comes with involvement in "things that matter—pushing for social change, improving the lot of the underprivileged, helping to save the world."

Of course, the Roddicks had the kind of business that allowed for these exertions. Unlike factories or offices, where workers work straight through the eight-hour shift with few lunch and restroom breaks, Body Shop staff sell simple products and have considerable free time between customers.

I first met Anita Roddick at the annual meeting of the Social Venture Network. SVN was a collection of several dozen new com-panies, mostly still run by their idealistic founders, that was striving to redefine corporate practices in all directions inside and outside their operations, especially giving concrete meaning to social re-sponsibility, environmentalism, and workplace experience. You've heard of some of them—Patagonia, Ben & Jerry's Ice Cream, and Esprit. She and Gordon really hit it off with Ben Cohen of Ben & Jerry's. They shared similar penchants for flamboyance and the un-predictable. This led to projects with Cultural Survival, an anthro-pology group, active in Brazil's Amazon to protect the indigenous people and slow the destruction of the greatest rainforest on Earth. (Later The Body Shop became the first cosmetic company to hire a full-time anthropologist.) Ben created a "Rainforest Crunch" ice cream to publicize the Amazon venture and Anita developed a "Brazil nut conditioner."

As she journeyed through the region, Anita was determined not to exploit the Amazon natives or destabilize their culture by introducing money and gadgets that they did not want. The relationship and exchange were fraught with risks and sensitivities. Outside critics had to be very carefully treated—not to mention the continuing encroachments of logging, gold, and hard-rock mining, and cattle ranching companies. What outside company would have even considered negotiating on the Amazon tribes' own terms? Anita was nothing if not serious. She described the campaigns in the company's annual report, made of the simplest of recycled paper. Shareholders were put on full notice that the company would wade into public controversies because its managers believed that "service to humanity is fundamental to what life is about."

Beyond exhortation is the power of example. Anita believed that the corporate structure needed an Environmental Projects Department to watchdog Body Shop standards and principles and to expand links with environmental groups. It wasn't long before the Roddicks decided to go it alone, without formal alliances with such groups. "I particularly wanted to be free to take up issues in the news as they arose," she said, without having to make decisions with committees of Friends of the Earth, or other groups, that she found painful, laborious, and maddeningly cumbersome.

She gives this tragic episode as an example of how fast she wanted to be free to react: "When there was that terrible gale in the south of England in October of 1987, and 15 million trees were destroyed in a single night, we had collecting boxes for tree planting in every Body Shop within a couple of days—we could never have reacted so quickly if the decisions had to be taken by committee." It wasn't as if The Body Shop wouldn't work with the civic groups; it would, but it wouldn't wait for them to decide before Anita's people acted.

As the AIDS epidemic exploded, Anita sold condoms in her shops, but failed to convince other skittish retail establishments, including the funky ones, to do likewise. She complained that "it was as if the retail industry had nothing to do with the community—a concept completely at odds with my own views." Undeterred, she teamed up with Richard Branson—the flamboyant entrepreneur and airline founder—to set up The Healthcare Foundation to fight this disease.

Anita's middle name could have been *Now*; never delay doing something *Now* that should have been done months or years ago. She plunged into the human rights campaigns, publicizing Amnesty International posters and offering explanatory leaflets in the shops. Over a thousand new members joined Amnesty.

So many justice campaigns came out of Anita's sense of seamless moral purpose between business and the community that she formalized them into a "routine of running shop-window campaigns for two-week periods throughout the year, with posters acting as the focal point." The Body Shops were often located on busy streets, and bright window displays caught the eye of far more passersby than those who entered the stores. Displays presenting facts and figures to get people to recycle were often featured. There was also the added benefit of media coverage, especially when the campaign subject matter was truly seen as "what the heck" incongruous.

Pushback came from more than a few of the franchise holders when Anita committed The Body Shop to the Nuclear Freeze, the campaign against nuclear weapons. That campaign was too uncomfortable for some, who asserted that she shouldn't be speaking for them. The first reaction from Anita was, "If you support nuclear weapons, what the hell are you doing in one of my shops?" Then she realized she didn't have the right to speak for them or The Body Shop on every issue. But she admitted that she was never able to separate her personal values from that of The Body Shop.

It was easier to avoid this dilemma by providing financial support to such favorite groups as the Fund for the Replacement of

Animals in Medical Experiments and the Skin Treatment and Research Trust. In another publicity initiative, campaign slogans were printed on the company's paper bags, made from recycled material, challenging other companies and consumers to reduce waste and reuse materials. She would even include membership application forms for customers interested in joining civic groups.

Groups in the United States found this promotion very attractive when The Body Shop was opening shops there at a rapid clip. Imagine having a citizen group adopted by The Body Shop for a period by distributing membership application forms in its stores, on its bags, and online. During occasional meetings with Anita, while she visited the States, we shared her unusual understanding of the critical need to build new civic groups to confront new and old challenges. She was so taken by the concept of "building democracy while practicing democracy" that she funded the printing of our breakthrough classroom civic text by Katherine Isaac, titled *Civics for Democracy: A Journey for Teachers and Students*. This book was an effort to show the educational world that civic books did not need to be dull or deprived of the proper names of bad companies corroding American history. Reading traditional civics books was like eating a ton of sawdust without butter. Anita loved that metaphor.

The Body Shop's entry into the United States market started in 1988, on Broadway and 8th Street in New York City. This move across the Atlantic took great care, expense, and adaptation to US regulations, tort law, and workplace styles. That is why Body Shops had opened earlier in Chinese-speaking countries and the Middle East. Anita and her colleagues spent endless hours at the Food and Drug Administration (FDA) to make sure they were observing FDA regulations. So meticulous were they that they even irritated the FDA's regulators—they weren't used to such open and precise desires for corporate compliance. Cosmetic companies usually regarded the FDA as nothing to worry about since it had little authority over the cosmetic industry.

Another challenge was trying to generate the kind of enthusiasm for their work at The Body Shop's offices in New Jersey. All she could see were "workers bent over their desks and screens everywhere." This was in stark contrast with her offices in Littlehampton, offices that "sometimes [were] like walking into the Folies Bergère." If she had doubts about whether The Body Shop was going to succeed in the United States, they were dispelled by the reception given to that first company-owned store on Broadway. Clearly, its reputation had preceded its arrival. Opening day was packed, and, despite not a single advertisement, there was great media coverage. The media were intrigued "by our values and philosophies," said Anita. "Opening day was covered by all the major television networks and news magazines."

In the early nineties The Body Shops opened scores of stores in the United States, with a concentration on the East and West Coasts for greater receptivity and more likely exuberant, frisky staff. The more success, the more Anita wanted to dig in her heels and deepen the corporate cultural life of The Body Shop to shield this now public company from slipping into just another one of the "dreaded" multinational companies. She reminded young staffers and franchisees about how grounded she and Gordon were in the 1960s, when they formed their attitudes and values. "In the sixties," she related, "we learned about people power, about alternatives, about the futility of war, about challenge as an acceptable form of growth."

We learned that femininity and love were no longer dirty words, that financial profit was meaningless without spiritual profit, and that being successful did not necessarily mean being soulless.

Hard-headed corporate strategists and analysts probably would have predicted the seeds of self-destruction in any business enterprise so decentralized and loosely disciplined from above—all suffused with debilitating words such as "love" and "being spiritual." Such predictions missed several points. First, The Body Shop was not an auto shop, steel factory, a shipbuilding or aerospace company. It had completely different kinds of pressure, different competitive stresses and risks, deadlines, buyers, and supply chains. For example, eschewing advertising and getting people's attention through bold civic campaigns and Anita's daring ways of empowering workers and attracting consumers were major expense savings for her company. The big cosmetic companies were known to spend much of their revenues on advertising, more than ten times that spent by other industries. That *ipso facto* required higher prices for their products. But they were selling essentially the same products as The Body Shop. More traditional cosmetic companies had to pay for a deep imprint of their brand, and trivial differentiations in packaging, presentations, models, and other non-product enticements. Not paying for such advertising and promotions was a huge Body Shop savings in sheer dollars, which could be put into much more functional ways of expanding product sales and retail outlets. They could pay for the expenses of the campaigns and substantial training and motivating of staff. For example, they paid for The Body Shop Training School in the West End of London in 1985. The school "concentrated on human development and conscious-raising." As Anita liked to compare: "Conventional retailers trained for sale; we trained for knowledge. They trained with an eye on the balance sheet; we trained with an eye on the soul." She chose not to dwell on just how difficult that was to achieve in enough workers to make it worthwhile. The recruitment was selective, yet all the newcomers had grown up "corporate" on corporate advertisements since they were toddlers.

They were miseducated in schools to believe rather than to think, to obey rather than to challenge or dissent. Anita and Gordon had their hands full trying to reach a majority success rate with workers adopting the requisite "emotional intelligence," they were seeking, to go along with the necessary sales skills or other technical know-how for the non-salespeople. She was looking for her workers to have a "fire in their belly" over any injustice or moral outrage. They could choose their own civic engagement if they were not keen on the options floated by the company. In her many writings, Anita did not go into explanatory detail about the recalcitrance or indifference of those workers—who just wanted to do their job every day and be done with it. By way of balance, the Roddicks did not forget that the seed corn, the capital reservoir, came from the profits. That was the bottom line to make everything else possible directly and indirectly, including their desire to have the workers keep learning to expand their abilities to advance the common good. The difference between the Roddicks and corporate capitalists was that the price of profits had to be justice for everyone, not riches for the few and crumbs for the many. They gave a very different dimension and meaning to the phrase "the price of profits."

A major challenge to their dual business philosophy of doing well and doing good came in 1984, when they accepted the urgings of the City (London's Wall Street) and took the company public. Year after year, the financial brokers would tell them how hot The Body Shop stock would be, that they would have more of their assets in liquid form, should they need to personally make contributions, that it would be easier to raise capital for expansion (and, added Anita wryly, make fees for these brokers). It was a decision they came to regret in two stages. Regarding going public—the first stage—Anita writes rather cryptically:

Gordon and I both felt we had missed a great opportunity, in the months before we went public, to educate our staff on the implications of the flotation, the workings of the City and what it meant to be a shareholder [workers were given shares as part of their nonprofit sharing plan]. Share-owning was still very much a secret society at that time, and we really should've taken steps to break down the mystique for the people who worked for us. Unfortunately we never did anything about it, and we regret it to this day.

What did they mean? It could be they would have warned about the temptations of monetizing the staff's minds into increasingly viewing the company through its stock values. The Roddicks feared turning away from the real yardsticks, such as what The Body Shop was accomplishing regarding homelessness, aiding the elderly to give their wisdom, AIDS sufferers, "urban survival, drug and alcohol abuse, community action, unemployment and a whole range of environmental issues." Such yardsticks that might push other companies to consider emulation, because The Body Shop was getting rave media reviews, attracting fine workers, and making money along a pattern of continual growth. Anita kept her belief that work should be fun and interesting. So they gave the workers anecdotes and funny stories to relay to the customers. "We ran a course on 'Management By Humour,'" she loved to highlight. In one poster for employees, the big words, in yellow and red colors, were SMILE, DAMMIT SMILE! Then: "Think of your customers as guests, make them laugh. Acknowledge their presence within thirty-seconds: smile, make eye contact, say hello. Talk to them within the first three minutes. Offer product advice where appropriate. Always thank customers and invite them back . . . TREAT CUSTOMERS AS YOU'D LIKE TO BE

TREATED!" (In red color). Anyone reducing loneliness "either through their store or their marketing, will have a business that will thrive forever," declared Anita over and over again to any staffer with whom she spoke. Suggestion boxes were found in every store, and six full-time people cataloged their suggestions and replied to them. She set up regular forums for customers to attend and tell her what they liked or didn't like. I don't have space to describe all the ways the Roddicks were pushing staff and customers to be more candid, tell them what was on their minds, and to challenge the rules and status quo. They even created a Department of Damned Good Ideas to stimulate the submitting of solutions.

Some critics have said Anita's books and articles are redundant. They are right up to a point. But her redundancy was rarely tedious; she managed to say the same thing in new ways with new examples. Her ability to interface daily and personally with many more things that were going on in the UK and through her high velocity trips to other countries was unmatched. That she never tired of these new experiences, fresh outrages, prompting proposals to help and even to set up new institutions, to make these proposals constantly contributing, came from a belief she admitted only rarely. She said that when she got up every morning, she assumed that this was her last day on Earth. Other people have declared such an attitude. Few can show that they have meant it like the whirlwind manager of The Body Shop, the imaginative, do-it-now driver who set the pace and retained the authenticity.

Here is an example of how she rephrases one of her core beliefs—that business must be in the "Business of Caring." "Whenever we traded, we were an integral part of that community, with consequent responsibilities and duties that could not be ducked. It had always made me angry that most businesses, big and small, operated in almost total social isolation from their immediate surroundings. I think it is completely immoral for a shop to trade in the middle of a community, to take money and make profits from that community, and then ignore the existence of that community, its needs and problems."

Tell that to Detroit's giant auto industry reaping immense profits but for decades ignoring the steady decline and depopulation of that city to eventual decay and bankruptcy. Tell that to the oil industry giants whose profits come at the expense of safe drinking water, clean air, and stable communities. However, she seemed to have too little empathy for smaller shopkeepers who could barely keep the doors open in broken communities whose misery came through their doors every day, sometimes disruptively. There were shopkeepers who often did what they thought they could do by offering some charitable donations or giving away some of their products to the needy. The differences between the financial and operational resources of big business and small business are enormous.

The Body Shop would set up a Community Care Department encouraging community projects each shop could choose or select themselves "during the Shop's opening hours." From there it took a while to overcome community suspicion or cynicism that a business could be so charitable without a hidden agenda. But there were shops that persisted to an unheard-of extent. She gives these examples: "The Leicester Shop linked up with the Douglas Bader Center for the Physically Disabled, the Guilford Shop sent staff to work in the pediatric department of the local hospital, the Bath franchise got involved with the Avon Wildlife Trust helping to run a demonstration organic farm, in Edinburgh they went into the women's prison as therapists, educators, and, get this, instigators of fun."

In Brighton, where The Body Shop started, "we set up a pilot project with the Red Cross to send volunteers into hospitals and day-care centers to give facials and massages." They used Body Shop products rejected due to damaged packaging or inaccurate labels.

Overseas, she cited other examples. In Brantford, Canada, the staff, on company time, started a school for children with disabilities. In Victoria, Australia, The Body Shop staff worked with the homeless and organized 500 people to plant 250,000 trees.

This still didn't satisfy Anita, who often complained that the staff was not imaginative enough, not bold enough to go into the streets and protest, for instance, "the hamburger joint's garbage that was strewn on the streets." She wanted "agitprop," but Gordon would counsel her that the staff could be pushed only so far.

Before they gave up control of the business they started, The Body Shop had over 2,000 franchises in over fifty countries. I was impressed by how little conflict there was between franchisor and franchisees. Most franchise agreements in other economic sectors contained draconian fine print, mostly to the advantage of the franchisor. Law professors have called these one-sided restrictions and burdens a new kind of contract serfdom. (The full text of The Body Shop agreement was not publicly available, to my knowledge, but it probably was fairer, given such harmony.)

Practicing what they preach was almost gospel to Anita. One of her favorite examples was the establishment of a soap factory in 1988 in the very depressed Scottish town of Easterhouse, to the east of Glasgow. Her first visit there, suggested by a young community worker who came to one of her speeches in London, horrified even this gritty woman. With the closing of shipyards and steelworks, chronic unemployment had grown worse. Almost half the men were out of work, shops were boarded up, and substance abuse was rampant among the young people. She wrote about how impressed she was with the people, "their guts and friendliness," their "apparent determination not to be crushed by their circumstances." Within eight months the Soapworks opened to supply a third of the soap requirements for all The Body Shops worldwide. In two years, the factory had a payroll of one hundred workers. The Roddicks made a firm agreement to "donate 25% of future profits to a charitable trust for the benefit of the local community." She raised donations from The Body Shop franchises to build a playground for the impoverished children of Easterhouse.

The Roddicks' authority to move quickly on their initiatives was not the same as it was before the company went public.

Increasingly, through the 1990s into the early years of the twenty-first century, the Roddicks had to deal with the City— shorthand for the single-minded aggressive stock analysts who did not like controversial social justice issues affecting The Body Shop's share prices. Soft charities and media coverage was okay, but challenging political power, corporate power, and engaging disputatious international injustices was another matter. Anita was ferocious in preserving what she called the "human health and spiritual wealth" of the company, not just the monoculture of economic returns.

They did not want to be told that actions for justice were either weakening or contradictory to robust returns on the shareholder's investments, which, of course, included their hefty shares and those of their workers. They wanted the freedom to act fast in emergencies that affected their consciences.

An amazing expression of this moral concern presented itself in 1990 in response to a destitute, violence-wracked Romania after the fall of the communist regime. Anita could not take the horrific pictures of dying Romanian babies in orphanages receiving no help from better-off countries. She immediately traveled to the village of Hălăucești in Moldavia and, once inside a building that from a distance looked like a fairy-tale castle, "was almost knocked over by the stench of feces and urine. Children lying on filthy cots covered with scabs and mosquito bites or just sitting with blank looks rocking backwards and forwards." Swinging into action, she had the orphanage cleaned up and renovated in two weeks. Helping these Romanian children became an ongoing effort by the Roddicks that continued through a charitable foundation involving Anita's daughters, Justine and Samantha, and some of The Body Shop staff.

The further the Roddicks delved into the developing nations to find sustainable materials for conceivably everything that they sold, used, and threw away, the deeper they drove their company's level of independence and determination to blaze new frontiers in the redefinition of a global business enterprise. They had a distinct framework of "Trade Not Aid," to present themselves to the inevitable skeptics, vested interests, and the monetized minds hovering around the company from the City. Before her business life, Anita had worked at the International Labor Organization of the United Nations in Geneva, Switzerland. She saw the waste and abuse involved in aid programs. While the motto "Trade Not Aid" has become a cliché to cover harmful trade products (such as the junk food flooding these countries) and exploitative terms of trade between the West and the less-developed world, the Roddicks had their own developed definitions thirty years ago. The Body Shop's principles embodied in "Trade Not Aid" were as follows:

We respect all environments, cultures and religions

We utilize traditional skills and materials

We created three links that were not only successful but sustainable

We traded in replenishable natural materials

We encouraged small scale projects that could be easily duplicated

We provided a long-term commitment to our projects

Their goal was to go to the source, whether in India or the Amazon, cut out the middleman and trade directly with the people who made, grew, or harvested the needed ingredients. This was the real deal.

Sometimes, Anita and her coworkers got more than they bargained for in these distant regions. She journeyed to the Humla, a remote mountain region of Nepal, to visit the Nyinba tribe living 18,000 feet above sea level in the Himalayas. She was looking for native papermaking. A holy man, or a "Sadhu," visited them. He was stark naked and covered with ashes as part of a cleansing ritual. He was also heavily inebriated. He proposed to demonstrate his strength by balancing twelve bricks on his penis. Anita, fearing self-harm, negotiated the number down to eight. He did it and Anita has the photograph to prove it.

Crucial to Anita's way of business was being able to make what she called "snap decisions." Writing in 1991, she emphasized, during the next few years, searching "for the young people in The Body Shop who will be the custodians of our culture, who will preserve and protect our core values with the fervour that I preserve and protect them. I am not worried that it will all disappear after Gordon and I have gone. We have our Charter, we have a whole lot of young people who live and breathe The Body Shop, who will provide our moral backbone in the future and who will be able to take over for me . . . who will keep this company bubbling, enthusiastic, motivated and challenging."

For about a decade and a half the Roddicks kept the faith. By 1991, she helped create the magazine *The Big Issue*, which was put out by people experiencing homelessness. She established Children on the Edge, as charity for needy children in Europe and Asia and pledged to give away most of her fortune. In 1999, I saw her marching with masses of protesters in Seattle against the corporate-managed World Trade Organization meeting there. She went to a notorious prison—Angola—in Louisiana calling for the release of framed prisoners rotting in solitary confinement for decades. As one demonstrator who watched her plunge into numerous citizen and labor protests related, "Anita is the real thing twenty times over. You'd never know, marching and talking with her, that she was the CEO of anything." Her success, by the City's profit standard, provided the Queen of England with cover, assuming she wanted it, to make Anita "Dame Anita," which she gracefully accepted to help expand her audience. That year—2003—also brought an emerging calamity for her family and The Body Shop family. She was diagnosed with Hepatitis C—a malady that she believed to have contracted from a contaminated blood transfusion during the birth of her second daughter in 1971. Responding to press calls, Anita said, "it's a bit of a bummer but you groan and move on." Later she added, "What I can say is that having [the disease] means that I live with a sharp sense of my own mortality, which in many ways makes life more vivid and immediate. It makes me even more determined to just get on with things." Irrepressible Anita Roddick!

She had recently written her second substantive book, *Business as Unusual: My Entrepreneurial Journal, Profits with Principles*. This was followed in 2003 with *A Revolution in Kindness*. Then, she started working on her most visual experience of a collection of articles, features, photographs, and aphorisms to back up her prior exhortations to the business and political worlds to get moving. An earlier book was titled—typically—*Take It Personally: How to*

Make Conscious Choices to Change the World. Life in Anita's operating framework is all being interconnected.

Teaming up with Greenpeace in 2001, she led an international campaign against ExxonMobil, calling it the "No. 1 Global Warming Villain," and declaring, "This is the company that refuses to accept a direct link between the burning of fossil fuels and global warming, and that has turned its back on investing even a single penny on renewable alternatives, such as wind and solar." Even today with much more evidence—scientific and on the ground—that climate disruption and devastation are everywhere, there is no one with the ferocious passion of Dame Anita—CEO—on the ramparts confronting directly, by name, the big business community.

Anita's hepatitis condition worsened in 2004 and 2005. This might have contributed to the Roddicks' agreement to sell the company in 2006 to the cosmetics giant L'Oréal, in France. When asked how she could do this, she replied, "I'm not an apologist for them. I'm just excited that I can be like a Trojan horse and go into that huge business and talk about how we can buy ingredients like cocoa butter from Ghana and sesame oil from the Nicaraguan farmers and how we can do that in a kindly, joyful way, and that it is happening."

It turned out to be an optimistic forecast. In 2007, growth and profits of The Body Shop were slowing. Her illness was debilitating and tragically prevailed, with the passing at the youthful age of sixty-four of this great spirit of knowing, sensing, doing, and uplifting all who came into contact with her indefatigable "force field."

She started the Hepatitis C Trust as her way of redirecting self-indulgence and "protecting the human body." So too was her hands-on work giving out grants from the Anita Roddick Foundation. None of these many institutions raised much money. But her energy and those she galvanized made them have an out-sized impact on their declared objectives. Even The Body Shop was modest in size, given its impact.

It is not clear from the public record why the Roddicks' managerial, day-to-day role diminished. Anita stopped managing the company in 2002, though she and Gordon remained as "non-executive directors." What seems likely is that as the publicly traded Body Shop became more corporatized and short-term, bottom-line oriented, with slowing growth, the Board of Directors became more conventional in their "directions."

L'Oréal ran The Body Shop as a wholly owned lackluster subsidiary for just over a decade. In 2017 it sold The Body Shop to Natura, a large Brazilian company whose two founders were friends of Anita and shared her values.

Natura, it turns out, is not only Brazil's largest cosmetic company, but the two cofounders, Guilherme Leal and Antonio Luiz Seabra, said they "share the same DNA," adding they bought The Body Shop with its 3,200 stores in sixty-three countries because "the spirit of Anita Roddick is strong with us." Natura is a B Corporation. B Corporations create value for non-shareholding stakeholders, such as their employees, the local community, and the environment. B Lab, the nonprofit organization that certifies B Corporations says, "B Corps use the power of business to do more than seek profit. They use their profits and growth to positively impact their stakeholders—and the planet." Natura was built on using natural products from the Amazon and using community trade to protect the forests, and its indigenous people. Natura sells its products door to door in South America through a network of 1.8 million sales reps. They now have more than 3,000 retail stores. They intend to enlarge the earnings by reconnecting the formally intrepid company with its own soul and the vision of a pioneering leader.

Mr. Leal was a former Green Party candidate for Vice President of Brazil in 2010 and is well known in global business sustainability circles. Natura already has an active campaign to protect the world's largest rainforest—which had been under direct attack; Brazil's extreme right-wing president, Jair Bolsonaro, trumpeted the call for more rapid development before his rule ended in 2022.

Both men of Natura say they want to turn their huge number of direct sellers into tribunes of the company's values and that is "how we want our future to be designed." Because Natura has sourced from over thirty tribal communities the seeds and foods for the basis of its oil, soaps, and lotions, mostly from the Amazon, their concern over mass deforestation is more than a philanthropic one. For example, 600 families supply Natura with ucuuba fruit, whose trees are many times more valuable erect than if they were cut down to sell as wood. Natura helped to create Brazil's Biodiversity Regulatory Framework, where indigenous families get paid for the products they supply as well as for their know-how and investment in the necessary local infrastructure. Natura has started to install an environmental profit and loss accounting system (often referred to as triple bottom line accounting) for its operations. Anita would have liked Natura's encouragement of refillable bottles, including perfume bottles, for the past decade.

Whether this dream-like revival of the life work of Anita and Gordon Roddick stays on its declared trajectory is yet to be seen. The desires of Natura's determined executives will come up against the political savagery and overt racist contempt spewed for years by Bolsonaro and allied back-bench militaristic politicians in the Brazilian Congress. The portentous battle for the Amazon Forest—"the lungs of the world" among its other critical contributions to the globe's life-sustaining ecology—is underway. If only Anita were there to join arms with the resistance and share its hopes under Brazil's new president, Luiz Inácio Lula da Silva.

In the meantime, Gordon Roddick is a self-appointed ambassador-at-large for the struggle against man-made climate disaster.

He tells any business or civic group that wants to hear his message that time is running out before their very eyes as climate-driven mega-floods, droughts, and storms, glacier melting, and wildfires set new records year-by-year. He is running the Roddick Foundation and collaborating with other foundations and civic groups to leverage effectiveness. The areas worked on by this foundation network are social, labor, and environmental justice, education, and human rights.

Anita once said that her activism was the rent she pays to the planet. Gordon continues her and his work as good ancestors for generations to come.

3

RAY C. ANDERSON

Founder and Chairman of Interface Inc.

Something happened in the middle of August 1994 to a successful, Atlanta-based industrialist—call it a secular epiphany—that unleashed forces to transform a large company's way of manufacturing. Ray C. Anderson, the founder and CEO of Interface, the largest carpet-tile manufacturer in the world, with plants on four continents and doing business in one hundred countries, had to give a speech at the end of August to a task force coming from around the world. Interface's salespeople were getting the same question from the company's customers, be they hospitals, universities, office buildings, arenas—"What is Interface doing for the environment?" More than that, when the company received requests for bid quotations, it was asked to state its explicit environmental policies in its response.

Anderson was always a good listener, but in a very conventional context. As an engineering graduate from Georgia Tech, he started his company at age thirty-eight with a tight capital budget and an established method of converting petroleum products into new kinds of carpets, while pouring wastes and pollution into land dumps and into the air and water, just like his competitors had done for years. He was dutiful in complying with all the state and federal environmental laws as he turned his attention to rigorously fabricating an enormous tonnage of carpets in traditionally efficient ways.

His sales force ever more insistently was telling his managers that they wanted answers to these recurring questions from actual and potential buyers: "What is Interface doing for the environment? What are our environmental policies?" Two of his managers suggested convening a task force to begin to structure some responses. They wanted to hear from the boss.

Anderson was a life-long learner. When he did not know something, he admitted it and went about methodically studying the matter, just like a good engineer. Two weeks before August 31, 1994—the date of his address—he admitted that he did not have "a clue as to what to say." Compliance—sure, but that is not a vision. He admitted to "sweating."

By a coincidence that will go down in industrial history, "a book lands on my desk." It was sent to him by a sales manager whose daughter in Seattle bought it after hearing the author speak. The sales manager had been hearing from environmental consultants to large customers that "Interface just doesn't get it." To which Anderson would reply, "Interface doesn't get what?"

The book, now long famous and used at many business schools all over the country, is *The Ecology of Commerce*, by Paul Hawken, a successful businessman in his own right. Anderson had never heard of Hawken, unlike the environmental advocates who heralded him and invited him everywhere. "Pure serendipity," he would later recall.

He started to leaf through the pages, coming onto a chapter called "The Death of Birth," where he encountered terms he had never heard—"carrying capacity," "overshoot," "collapse," and "extinction." It's that ignorant wonderment that led him a few months later to describe himself as a "plunderer of the Earth," and henceforth a "recovering plunderer of the Earth" with determined vengeance.

As the precocious advocate, Hawken had further developed and refined his analysis in hundreds of articles, several books and thousands of speeches and advisories. Hawken's points were reduced to three parts by Anderson:

(1) The living systems and life support systems of Earth are in decline and we will lose the biosphere, which contains and supports all life; (2) the biggest culprit in this decline is the industrial system—the linear, take-make-waste industrial system, driven by fossil fuel—derived energy, wasteful and abusive; and (3), the only institution on Earth that is large enough, powerful enough, wealthy enough, pervasive enough, influential enough to lead humankind out of the mess it is making for itself, is the same institution that is doing the most damage, the institution of business and industry—my institution.

Note his choice of words. There is no use of "corporation," "company" or "multinational corporation." He uses the word "institution," with deep roots, because he accepts the responsibility to go far beyond any governmental regulatory standards. A short time later he would refine Hawken's third point more gravely: "Unless business and industry come aboard, our descendants will inherit a hellish world."

A few months earlier, in 1993, President Bill Clinton and Vice President Al Gore released a lengthy, multicolored report that warned about the coming devastation from "climate change" if recycling, renewable resources, and reduction of greenhouse gases did not take root. For the next eight years they did little to address what Al Gore, in a separate book, *Earth in the Balance*, called a menace to the world—the motor vehicle and its gas guzzling internal combustion engine. They were daunted by and indentured to those very "institutions of business and industry."

Clearly, Anderson was neither daunted nor indentured to his industry. As he told that small audience of seventeen Interface sales managers: "Unless somebody leads nobody will. Why not us?" He challenged them and himself to lead the company to sustainability, soon to be defined more intensively as taking "nothing from the Earth that is not naturally and rapidly renewable"—not another fresh drop of oil—"and to do no harm to the biosphere." Interface projected reaching this goal by 2020, in accelerating stages until the company reached "the top of Mount Sustainability," his bold metaphorical vision.

Before his magisterial life and mind were cut short by cancer in 2011, what he and his stalwart colleagues accomplished, over odds never before surmounted, toward their ambitious goal of "zero environmental impact," is why I called Ray Anderson "the greatest CEO in our country."

I first met him at a gathering in Washington, D.C., where a rapt audience was listening to what seemed like an environmental engineering professor. Anderson was a micro-to-macro person—as an advocate engineer thinks—not macro-to-micro as an advocate lawyer might think. The latter thinks of governmental missions and mandates pushing for change down at the level of production design, manufacture, and disposal. I took this approach in the 1960s, when a technologically stagnant, unsafe, polluting auto industry had to be charged into the opposite directions by the mandated rule of law. These were regulations forcing innovation and priorities formerly subordinated to the supremacy of

short-term profit maximization over engineering integrity. When
legal mandates are issued for installation of seat belts or airbags
or better braking or handling performances, there is a wholesale
adoption (assuming compliance) across the board for all affected
companies. Apart from his later advocacy for a carbon tax to force
higher prices for fossil fuels compared to renewables, Anderson
stuck to his "task." He knew any regulatory environmental standards are restricted by the existing levels of technologies, which
were nowhere near sufficient to reach sustainability. Only when
companies such as his raised the levels of breakthrough and cost-
effective technology could the federal or state standards mandate
them for all similar manufacturers. If one company can do it, and
profit, the law presumably could make all of them do it.

There were two concentric circles worked by Interface's CEO.
Day after day, his team sought to rationalize every step of the manufacturing continuum and then honestly measure the reductions in
harm to the biosphere. The details involved are staggering but they
did add up to ever-higher levels of sustainability that has given
Interface a manifold competitive edge. As Anderson explained this
market differentiator, "Our costs are down, our profits are up, and
our products are the best they've ever been. It has rewarded us with
more positive visibility and goodwill among our customers than
the slickest, most expensive advertising or marketing campaign
could possibly have generated. And a strong environmental ethic
has no equal for attracting and motivating good people, galvanizing them around a shared higher purpose, and having me say . . .
We're making history."

The other concentric circle is the entire globe. And did he ever
encompass that range for change. He was a tireless proselytizer
through his technical lectures, his interviews, his writings, and
through his personal persuasions. Remarkably enough, Walmart
was one of his converts for reducing packaging redundancy and

waste. Two teams headed by Mike Duke and Doug McMillon, both to become Walmart CEOs, visited Interface's factory in LaGrange, Georgia. Persuaded that reductions would cut costs and increase profits, they returned to Bentonville, Arkansas, and stipulated the new specification for their 60,000 suppliers.

Marshaling hard engineering evidence, shop floor experience, and a mastery of the profit and loss statement, all the while meeting that proverbial payroll, Anderson overwhelmed audiences used to hearing from free market, libertarian ideologues. How could they argue with him? He more than rebutted their pitiless abstractions; he transcended them. The arguments came as a cascading Niagara. To do justice to them, one must read his books, especially his last one, *Business Lessons from a Radical Industrialist* (2011). But here is just one ordinary, extraordinary sample:

> There is a flawed view that relies on the invisible hand of the market to be an honest broker, even though we know the market can be very dishonest. Does the price of a pack of cigarettes reflect the true cost? Not even close! . . . and the price of a barrel of oil? Last time I looked the oil companies weren't deploying armies or naval forces in the Middle East to protect the oil fields and tankers. You and I are doing that with our taxes. Our sons and daughters are doing it with their lives. The oil companies aren't paying the medical bills for all those folks breathing smog, either. Nor are they building the seawalls our coastal cities will need to keep the warming rising ocean from drowning them. Let all those be somebody else's problem. Talk about innocent third parties.

> Here's the thing. While a few of us might enjoy the fruits of what we think is a free market, we all suffer the consequences

of a rigged one, a market that is very good at setting prices but has no concept at all of costs. A market that's rigged to get someone else to pay the bills whenever and wherever a gullible or unwary public allows it to happen.

Amory Lovins, who, together with Paul Hawken and several of the "transformers" formed a special advisory committee to Interface, wrote: "Markets make good servants but bad masters."

What made Anderson, unfortunately, so special as a manufacturer was that he did not hesitate, after his August 1994 realization, to rethink everything anew. To do this he had to be able to learn anew, at age sixty-one, in immense pioneering and experimental detail while running a business for profit and holding on to its workers' livelihoods. He had to read, read, read, absorb, absorb, absorb, apply, apply, apply, revise, revise, revise, aggregate, aggregate, aggregate, test, test, test, and finally produce, produce, produce for needs. Then recycle everything possible.

Seeds of ideas sprouted in his fertile, motivating mind. Here is one big example. In late 1994, a colleague casually mentioned how strange it is to call factories "plants." They neither look like plants and they don't work like plants. A plant runs with the sun, rain and soil—all renewable. Its dropped leaves are fully biodegradable. Some other plants and organisms use its "waste" as food and on and on. He asked, "What if our plants worked more like that?"

Thus was planted the pursuit of biomimicry as a conversion analogy for what Interface wanted to become. "Consider," he wrote, "the technology of how a healthy tree works, how a healthy forest works, and emulate those myriad symbiotic processes and relationships in the way we do business. I think we'll be on the right track to a healthy corporation, a healthy industrial system and a sustainable world."

Anytime other CEOs did the right thing, Anderson was quick

to praise them, thinking that they would feed a stronger momentum for other lagging companies to emulate. He would be optimistic, cheerleading ways of change that use known technologies. "The good news is that we can do it one small, smart step at a time, each paying its own way, all laying the groundwork for the next." Then the real Anderson emerges—worrying that we are running out of time and maybe one-step-at-a-time is too late. He asked, "What do we waste?" And then replies:

> Right now, if you measured honestly, you'd discover the overall efficiency of American industry is plain pathetic. How bad is it? Ninety-seven percent of all the energy and material that goes into manufacturing our society's products is wasted. Mountains of tailings pile up at the mines. Energy goes up the smokestack, leaks out the wires, and ends up as waste heat. Year-after-year we send a tsunami of scrap to inundate our landfills. Only about 3% ends up a finished product that still has any value six months later.

Three percent!

And he didn't even get to the finished product—such as the huge waste of energy by the internal combustion engine. He called our industrial system "first and foremost, a waste making machine."

What? The "overall efficiency of American industry is plain pathetic." Is not the productivity per worker the envy of the world? It has more than doubled in the last thirty years. What is Ray talking about? He's talking about different and more accurate yardsticks for productivity. Notice the keywords "overall efficiency," which includes the extensive, enduring damage to the air, water, land, and the health and safety of people well outside the plant, as well as the impact of toxics upon the workers. Corporations may have gotten away with these "externalities," in the bloodless jargon of economists, because they controlled the "yardsticks" until the advent of the environmental movement started to challenge them. Anderson was moving to displace these yardsticks while showing that doing so is good for business and all concerned with that business.

In his awakening, the Interface founder found multiple motivations. True, he was a numbers man—he never forgot he had to sell his products to make a profit—and we'll get to the reductions in "plundering" the Earth by Interface on its way up Mount Sustainability. Because he was such a daily heavy reader ("near total immersion"), he was driven by the pictures and stories about humankind's many assaults on the Earth's finite habitats. To get these images, he poses this question:

> How would a living planet—the rarest and most precious thing in the universe—lose its biosphere, i.e., its existential livability. We take it for granted and don't want to believe losing it is even possible. But if it happens, it will have happened insidiously.

At this point in his public presentations, Anderson shows that he is possibly the greatest of communicating engineers. In his words, he gives so many ways the Earth is being destroyed that listeners and readers are bound to identify personally with one or more—something less likely to happen from a barrage of lethal statistics:

– One silted or a polluted stream at a time;

– One collapsing fish stock at a time;

– One dying coral reef at a time;

– One acidified or entrophied lake at a time;

– One over-fertilized farm at a time, leading to one algae bloom at a time;

– One eroded ton of topsoil at a time;

– One developed wetland at a time;

– One disrupted animal migration corridor at a time;

– One butchered tree at a time;

– One corrupt politician at a time;

– One new open-pit coal mine in a pristine valley at a time;

– One decimated old growth forest at a time;

– One lost habitat at a time;

– One disappearing acre of rainforest at a time;

– One political pay-off at a time, resulting in one regulatory roll-back at a time;

– One leaching landfill at a time;

– One belching smokestack or exhaust pipe at a time;

– One depleted or polluted aquifer at a time;

– One desertified farm at a time;

– One over-grazed field at a time;

– One toxic release at a time;

– One oil spill at a time;

– One breath of fouled air at a time;

– One-tenth of a degree of global warming at a time;

– One exotic disease vector at a time;

– One new disease at a time;

– One invasive species at a time;

– One perchlorate contaminated head of lettuce at a time (Perchlorate is a rocket fuel, and it is in the groundwater of the fertile San Joaquin Valley of California, thanks to Aerojet General)

– One chloro-fluoridated or methyl-brominated molecule of ozone at a time, creating a deadly hole in the ozone ultraviolet radiation shield;

– One thoughtlessly designed building or building interior at a time;

– One poorly designed carpet at a time;

– One misplaced kilogram of plutonium at a time;

– One more ton of spent nuclear fuel at a time, looking for a safe and secure home for 240,000 (!) years;

– One advance of urban sprawl at a time;

– One insensitive or uninformed architect, or interior designer, or facility manager, or manufacturer at a time;

– One songbird at a time;

– One PCB-laced orca, one whale, one dolphin, one trumpeter swan, one mountain gorilla, one polar bear, one leatherneck turtle at a time;

– One entire world species at a time; and

– One poverty-stricken, starving, diseased, or exploited human being at a time.

That is how it would have happened, and we know that it is happening already just that way—so many ways! You could make your own list, just as long without any duplication. It is a long, long slippery slope, and we are on it . . . If we do come to our senses in time, that will happen one changed mind at a time.

Has the printed word ever displayed that ecological threat to the world in a more compressed pictorial way? Can anyone with a bit of sensitivity not look inward or not look at powerful corporations, their corporate law firms, and corporate captured legislators to be confronted in a different way? He was not giving anyone a free pass. But obviously he was placing greater responsibility on those generating the most damage. To reverse trends, he asserts, requires movement at the early design level spurred by a developing sense of environmental ethics—by companies, architects, engineers, government-driven system changes—"a vast redesign triggered by an equally vast mind-shift one mind, one organization, one technology at a time."

To reach such a historical goal in the evolution of this resilient but vulnerable planet, Anderson applies steps at a time to his company's declared mission of zero-impact on the environment. The seven paths to sustainability that Interface is working on to reach that "Mount Sustainability" cannot be paraphrased and need exactitude as follows:

Moving towards zero waste;

Increasingly benign emissions, working up the supply chain;

Increasing efficiency and using more and more renewable energy;

Closed-loop recycling, copying nature's way of turning waste into food;

Resource-efficient transportation, from commuting to logistics in plant siting;

Sensitivity hook-up, changing minds and getting employees, suppliers, customers, and our own communities on the same page, creating a corporate "ecosystem," to

borrow a term from nature, with cooperation replacing
confrontation;

Redesigning commerce, teaching a new Economics 101
that puts it all together and assesses accurate costs, sets
real prices, and maximizes resource-efficiency.

"These are the seven faces of Mount Sustainability to reach Mission
Zero, [which] is hard, hard work," Anderson notes, "It is not a
'program of the month.' And nobody is making us do it. We're
under no pressure from our competitors to achieve sustainability.
Actually, I think they are the ones who feel a competitive pressure
from us."

Nor is it some unfunded mandate from the government.
We're doing it because it is smart, because it is right. And
when we succeed we'll never need another drop of oil . . .
We'll be doing very well by doing good.

If this all sounds like generalized wishful thinking, Anderson
proceeds to devote an entire chapter to each of the steps. Certainly,
he is a many-splendored, self-motivated philosopher, but he is an
engineer first. In combination, his range is sweepingly vast yet
grounded in practical discovery and application. Which explains
why there has never been any CEO, at least in the United States,
to match his comprehensive embrace of this tormented Earth's
necessities for survival. One can see what he leaves out—a
much greater role for far-seeing government, the nuclear arms
race, and nuclear war driven by robotics, and looming global
epidemics, for example. But he is choosing laser-beam focus on
what he believes to be both the source of the destruction and

the solution due to the omnipresence of industry and commerce and its overweening economic technological power to obstruct or construct.

At the ten-year mark, in 2004, Anderson published the metrics—audited by independent third parties. Interface is intimately aware of what will happen to their reputation and public mission should any figures be fudged. He reported these advances or reductions at a conference in Nova Scotia, Canada:

- Waste—US $262 million saved (cumulative) more than paying for the entire mountain climb

- Net GHG Emissions—52% (absolute tonnage), 35% (efficiencies and renewables), 17% (off-sets)

- Non-Renewable, fossil energy (carpet operations)—43% (relative to sales)

- Water usage—66% (relative to sales)

- Smokestacks—40% closed

- Effluent pipes—53% abandoned

- Trees for Travel, over 52,000 planted (off-setting 78+ million passenger miles)

These recitations—basic as they are to prove the forward progress of Interface's Zero 2020 Mission—are not excitable for mass media. Carpet manufacturing is not as exciting as the Silicon Valley internet companies and their apps. Anderson never came close to being very rich or booming a stock on the stock exchanges. Nor was he as flashy with the phrases as Chrysler's Lee Iacocca or some CEO rogues. He received scores of awards and honorary degrees, served on the boards of avant-garde environmental groups such as the Rocky Mountain Institute, the David Suzuki Foundation and The Georgia Conservancy, yet these and other connections did not propel him to be a regular on the big TV shows. His influencing other larger corporations to attempt pieces of the transformation he pressed for was not front-burner material. He did not brag and wanted fervently for people and companies to think through themselves the pathways to zero impact. That way it becomes part of their purpose in life and not easily dislodged.

After he died from cancer in 2011, having planned his choice of successors from within the company, observers questioned whether he was so much a practical Renaissance man that no one could replicate such a performance. From manufacturing to marketing to visionary motivating the best from his employees and anyone who would listen to his rigorous analysis, he was a CEO yet to be equaled or surpassed.

In an article from GreenBiz, Joel Makower declared, "There will never be another Ray Anderson. He was a unique individual with a unique circumstance at a unique time." Then he began to think about the characteristics another "Ray Anderson" would have to possess to make that grade. He came up with six:

An Entrepreneur's Vision. Being a founder and in control of the board of directors of his stock exchange-listed corporation helps. He held a vision regardless of what anyone in and outside his company felt. At the beginning of his declared mission in 1994, one of his colleagues had to tell him that some of his colleagues "had thought he lost his mind."

A Passion for Learning, Reading and Talking to People. A quick learner due to a bright mind able to listen and not be a know-it-all. He worked very hard, even when taking his family for a week at the beach.

Missionary Zeal. This meant he wasn't just interested in setting Interface as a model to be emulated. He reached out everywhere, shucking proprietary shields, to transform all industry. He was self-critical publicly, which liberated his mind from set ways of defensiveness. He would say that he hoped there would come a time when CEOs plundering the Earth, the way he did, would be criminally prosecuted and jailed. The legal charge would be "stealing our children's future." In this way he so identified with Rachel Carson, "that great and brilliant woman."

Conviction and Control. A Board member, Dillon Ridley, who served on President Clinton's Council on Sustainable Development, which Anderson co-chaired, observed that Anderson "was startled at the levels of resistance [by other CEOs], stunned but ever more resolved of the rightness and necessity of his mission. He stuck to his guns, sometimes at considerable risk to his company."

Willingness to Rethink Everything. This was critical and minimized him getting stuck in his own brilliant concepts or mode. He made sure he invited revisions by the Composition of his Echo Dream Team—a dozen big thinkers and doers who are always challenging, rethinking and fearlessly willing to revise when facing difficulties. You would not last an hour in a room with this optimistic skeptic if you were not intellectually curious.

Relentless Storytelling. He spoke to all kinds of groups and conventions—probably over 1,000 throughout the country and the world. He was a master storyteller, but he always stayed on message about how his company was breaking through the impossible or improbable as they increase sales and profits, while cutting costs year in and year out. However, he always started with the big picture, the "Why's" before the "How's." Always ending being the salesman for carpets—"Would you like to buy some?"

I would like to add two other characteristics:

(7) A Strong Family Life. The stability of a strong family life encouraged Ray. His wife Pat Adams Anderson and daughters and their children were part of his *raison d'etre*, for they were the inheritors of either disaster or ecological salvation.

(8) Character and Personality. The ancient Greek philosopher Heraclitus wrote "character is destiny," and I should add that "personality is decisive." He had both in spades and was in sync and in full control of his company mission.

As you add all eight factors that become Ray Anderson, possible emulators become fewer and fewer in number. But as the urgency of climate disruption congeals all the plundering of the Earth in massive demonstrations of nature's reckonings from centuries of abuse, leaders should be coming forward. After all, whenever there are emergencies in communities, the most unlikely people brave-up and lead themselves to heroics.

Judge Benjamin N. Cardozo, an Associate Justice of the US Supreme Court from 1932 until his death in 1938, once wrote in a judicial opinion that "danger invites rescue," which implies that the greatest danger will invite the greatest rescuers. But will it be in time?

Anderson had a southern style of graciousness. He was quick to give credit—the sure sign of a leader who could have grabbed such credit for himself. He dedicated his final book and his heartfelt appreciation "to each of my fellow 'mountain climbers.' Without them, all this radical industrialist would be out on a thin ledge all by himself."

In his TED Talk delivered in 2009, Anderson updated the results as of 2007:

We have measured our process very rigorously . . . Net greenhouse gas emissions down 82% in absolute tonnage. Over the same span of time, sales have increased by two-thirds and profits have doubled. So an 82% absolute reduction translates into a 90% reduction in greenhouse gas intensity relative to sales. This is the magnitude of the reduction the entire global technosphere must realize by 2050 to avoid catastrophic climate disruption—so the scientists are telling us.

He continued:

Fossil fuel usage is down 60% per unit of production, due to efficiencies in renewables . . . Water usage is down 75% in our worldwide carpet tile business. [Water is] down

40% in our broadloom carpet business . . . which we acquired in 1993 right here in California . . . where water is
so precious. Renewable or recyclable material materials are
25% of the total of Interface products, and growing rapidly.
Renewable energy is 27% of our total, going for 100%. We
have diverted 148 million pounds—that is 74,000 tons—
of used carpet from landfills, closing the loop on material
flows through reverse logistics and post-customer recycling technologies that did not exist when we started 14
years ago.

My interaction with Ray was limited, which I regret. Once
in Atlanta, I called to visit but he was, not surprisingly, out of
town lecturing or motivating or showing how. When we needed
manufacturers to pledge that they would buy industrial hemp
for their products so that Congress would repeal the ignorant
prohibition and allow American farmers to grow this amazing
long-fiber with 5,000 uses going back to ancient China—George
Washington and Thomas Jefferson planted it—he promptly sent us
an affirmative letter.

We made Interface, Inc. a founder of the American Museum of
Tort Law—the only law museum in the world, located in Winsted,
Connecticut—for generously implementing Ray's promise to have
the floors covered with their carpet tiles. Visitors remark on their
beauty and durability.

Ray ended his TED Talk in one of the most memorable finales
of all TED Talks. He was speaking of all of us leading human-
kind away from the abyss because with the continued unchecked
decline of the biosphere, a very dear person is at risk here . . .

Who is that person? Not you. Not I. But let me introduce
you to the one who is most at risk here. On a Tuesday

morning in March of 1996, I was talking to people, as I did at every opportunity back then, bringing them along and often not knowing whether I was connecting. But about five days later back in Atlanta, I received an email from Glen Thomas, one of my people at the California meeting. He was sending me an original poem that he had composed after our Tuesday meeting together . . . Here is what Glen wrote. And here is that person, most at risk. Please meet "Tomorrow's Child."

Without a name, and unseen face, and not knowing your time or place,

Tomorrow's child, though yet unborn. I met you first last Tuesday morning.

A wise friend introduced us two. And through his sobering point of view.

I saw a day that you would see, a day for you but not for me.

Knowing you has changed my thinking. For I never had an inkling.

That perhaps the things I do might someday, somehow threaten you.

Tomorrow's child, my daughter, son,

I'm afraid I've just begun to think of you and of your good

Though always having known I should.

Begin, I will.

The way the cost of what I squander what is lost.

If I ever forget that you will someday come and live here too.

Our Founding Fathers used to call that "respect for posterity." The famous anthropologist, Margaret Mead, would have been very proud of Ray Anderson's galvanizing horizons. He concluded his *Ted* remarks: "We are, each and every one, a part of the web of life . . . We have a choice to make during our brief, brief visit to this beautiful blue and green planet: to hurt it or to help it. For you, it's your call."

The remarkable Lester Brown, president of Earth Policy Institute, told the *Washington Post* obituarist, Emily Langer, that, "I don't think any other corporation has come close to doing what he has done."

What has happened to Interface since Anderson's loss? They were about ten years from their deadline and the reductions were, expectedly, becoming more and more difficult, since the low-hanging fruit had been plucked. The company lost its great driving force. Were the directions he led, such as full leasing of carpets for recycling, sufficiently institutionalized?

It seems the answer is yes! Addressing the Global Climate Action Summit in San Francisco in September 2018, Interface CEO Jay Gould announced that its target 2020 Mission Zero initiative has been accomplished—no negative environmental impact. What's more, Mr. Gould spoke toward an even more ambitious goal of becoming carbon negative by 2040. That is, from Interface's supply chain to its direct production, to actually take out more carbon from the environment than it generates. "Zero is not enough," said Gould, adding, "What Ray Anderson helped us recognize is that our commitments and our ambitions must be bold, and that we have to go beyond zero. We are committed to take back our climate and to transform our business once again."

Then he declared what Anderson would have said: If Interface can do it, any company can do it, and if any company can do it, every company should do it. Zero is not only possible, it's profitable. In September of 2021, Interface announced that it had been certified as a "Carbon Neutral Enterprise." Laurel Hurd, the new Interface CEO said, "We have worked tirelessly to radically decarbonize, tapping into our culture of innovation and design, resulting in what we believe are the lowest cradle-to-gate carbon footprint carpet tile products on the market, even before applying offsets."

Not enough has been written about Interface's workforce, which turns Anderson's vision and precisions into reality. He made recruitment easier because the applicants, knowing of and where Interface was going, came with a higher-than-normal estimate of their own significance in this pioneering company.

Early in the COVID pandemic, Interface designed the workplace with meticulous care and comfort and respected the workers' judgment as to when they needed to work from home. The company has a respectful culture for all its workers.

In 2017, the company unveiled the carbon-negative carpet tile prototype. The Atlanta-based company calls its new mission "Climate Take Back" to bring carbon home and reverse climate change."

One would think that this historic breakthrough would have dominated headlines that lead to follow-up stories for days, with reporters calling other similarly inclined companies, such as Unilever and Patagonia, which are driving toward similar zero emissions. Not at all. Our society has a penchant of publicizing flash, outrageous bragging, hype (see self-driving car company boosters), and regularly reporting the corporate yardsticks of numerical sales, profits, and executive compensation that beckon global doom rather than the carpet yards of sustainable production that can avert it. This obsession is not conducive to survival. It demands relentless collective introspection, including by the business media.

Anderson liked to talk about biomimicry—how nature reuses everything so efficiently in an intricate web of life. Subhuman animals are said to survive through instinct. The squirrel can almost magically leap from twig to twig between tall trees and almost never miss and fall. The squirrel can differentiate between acorns and immediately eat those that will not be edible through the entire winter. In recent years, geologists are describing such acute self-interest as "animal intelligence" and not just genetically fostered.

I think Anderson acquired knowledge and transformed it into a kind of instinct. His mission was so deeply rooted that it was described as "messianic," or rooted in almost religious fervor. It was an attitude that brooked no delays from procrastination. He was a precrastinator—doing as early as possible. This is an accrued form of "human instinct." Humans are not there yet. True, they need no knowledge or coaching to flee or to try to put out an approaching fire or to escape rising floodwaters. They know what will happen to them physically, to their pain levels, if they do not take such reflexive actions. But unlike subhumans, humans create perils that are beyond their immediate sensory directions. Radiation, carbon monoxide, or lead, for instance, cannot be seen, felt, tasted, or heard. Until they reach critical mass, they build up without our own physiology's alarm going off.

We extend our inherited senses with detection equipment which, of course, is not everywhere and affordable. How, then, can we expand our aversion to these oncoming forms of silent violence to us, to both the inanimate and animate embodiment of the planet? We have technologies to displace these perils with sustainable tools such as renewable energy, resource efficiency, and the protection of forests, oceans, and lands. Indeed, we have far more of these kinds of solutions than we apply or are available to use in daily living. That is the gap. I have called it the democracy gap—for the few, immediate profits and the power to decide for the many of us who pay the price in health, safety, longevity, and descendants' dollars.

So how do we behave toward the silent violence—global warming, climate disruption—before irreversibility arrives? We have the knowledge and can obtain more to set the redirections. But it has not deeply rooted itself as "instinct" in the human brain. Fear produces instinctual fast bodily reactions. We really should not have to *think* about our response to perceived dangers. General George S. Patton defined battlefield coverage as "fear plus five minutes," but this does not work well for the silent violent threats that are multiplying—nuclear, chemical, and biological war, robots or losing control of human intelligence to artificial intelligence, increased probability of global pandemics and viral and bacterial mutations. We must instinctualize—out of deference to our posterity—our brains to foresee and forestall these non-anthropomorphic results of human, corporate, dictatorial follies. Just as the Buddhist strives for Nirvana, we must strive for Anderson's level of cranial or brain instinct—so the mind feels a resolve as deeply as the body does to fast oncoming, observable dangers. Some people thought Interface's visionary was impelled by a kind of religious passion. Call it what you will. If the anticipating mind does not detect what the body cannot yet recoil against, Interface's example will find few corporate leaders or governmental representatives engaged in such a comprehensive emulation. Call it civic and political engagement, call it realistic education and serious media, call it a religious movement for planetary stewardship; if the horrors of the fast-looming future do not grip our minds into first and foremost dimensions of action, you can call what is swarming toward us *omnicide*!

4

HERB KELLEHER

Co-founder & CEO of Southwest Airlines

Before the pandemic I flew Southwest Airlines whenever I could. Often, walking into the airplane off the jetway, I exclaim, "best airline in the country, and that's because Herb Kelleher started it that way." The beaming flight attendants and occasionally a pilot standing there beamed too. They know, no matter their age, that Herb was their main founder who retired from his CEO position in 2007. They know this man, the former practicing lawyer, because his imprint, his stamp on one of the nation's largest airlines was deep—professionally, behaviorally, tangibly, intangibly, and even spiritually. Whenever his successor, CEO Gary Kelly, was tempted to stray from the Southwest Way for a quick Delta-like profitable passenger fee, he was deterred by these traditions—except for one. In September 2018, Southwest's culinary mascot—the famous blue flag of free peanuts—was chucked, allegedly because of peanut allergies by a tiny number of afflicted passengers. (More on that later).

I never met Herb Kelleher personally. A couple of times, when I was to be in the Dallas area, I'd call for a meeting, but he was otherwise occupied or away. However, he was a good correspondent and was known to answer his own telephone calls. I absorbed some of the flavor of the man through these media and saw how quick he was to send a complaining passenger a box of peanuts with a letter of "sorry, it won't happen again" language.

Kelleher turned the airline industry more than a little upside down. When he started the airline with three Boeing 737s in 1971, after overcoming agonizing years of opposition and lawsuits from his smug competitors, he took advantage of a loophole in the federal cartel-like regulation. The federal jurisdiction did not extend to an airline that flew intrastate—like the successful Pacific Southwest Airlines in California. Flying from Dallas to Houston and San Antonio with lower fares and smaller, less utilized but more convenient airports, Kelleher got a foothold that enabled him to start flying routes outside of Texas. There was no stopping this airline. It now has over 700 Boeing jets, four-thousand flights a day, flying to over 121 airports in the US and airports in 11 other countries, with more than 66,000 employees, serving over 130 million passengers a year. Before the COVID pandemic, it had never had a losing year and never had to ask for the subsidies handed out at times to its major competitors—United, Delta, and American airlines—and has also placed first in financial stability. Needless to say, unlike other large airlines that follow gross mismanagement and excessive compensation largesse, Southwest has not come close to reorganizing bankruptcy style or going deeply in debt. Kelleher was always paid well under $1 million a year, a great deal less in direct compensation than his competitor executives. He did believe in stock options for himself and everyone else working with the airline. In short, the lowest paid CEO in the industry ran the most consistently profitable company while the other giants, with their vastly overpaid bosses, were hemorrhaging huge amounts of red ink.

Another crucial way the wisecracking, humorous, irreverent Kelleher departed from the conventional model of airline executives who say their often-disappointed shareholders come first, ahead of their workers and customers, was to put his employees—his profit-sharing workers—first! "What?" his early critics declared. Kelleher loved to rebut them in so many ways. Before an audience of University of Texas's McCombs School of Business students and business leaders in 2003, Kelleher put it concisely:

> I always felt that our people come first. Some of the business schools regarded that as a conundrum. They would say, which comes first, your people, your customers, or your shareholders? And I would say, it's not a conundrum. Your people come first, and if you treat them right, they'll treat the customers right, and the customers will come back, and that will make the shareholders happy.

That got me thinking anew since my response would have been that consumers should come first, since that is the whole purpose of and source of the company's profits and well-being. I've also experienced companies where the workers are well paid but surly toward their customers, with, of course, exceptions. But notice that Herb did not use the words "workers" or "staff," or "employees." He was not engaging in verbal ruse, as Walmart uses the word "associates" to refer to their low-paid, low-benefits employees. He referred to the full-fledged definition of people whether at work or outside of work.

Here, an explanation is essential to understanding the Southwest Airlines culture. It is not just an inside game; it reflects itself down the aisles of each Southwest airplane, loaded with passengers sitting in their unassigned seats and not paying extra for their knee space. And beyond!

First, Southwest is the most heavily unionized airline in the industry, dealing with eight different unions. The company has never
had an involuntary furlough for any of its "people." It has never had
a strike, though pandemic economic pressures almost bucked that
record. After all, the "people" have a part of the shareholder-owner
community built into their union contracts.

As for safety, Southwest has caused two avoidable fatalities
since 1971—one a small boy in a car when a Southwest airplane
skidded off the runway and slammed into the vehicle. The other
in 2017, when a passenger in a window seat was struck by engine
fragments in flight. Southwest has had maintenance problems in
recent years that have alarmed its executives, who strive for zero
such failures large or small. Without spooking them or its passengers, so far Southwest has a formidable safety record and no "feeder
airlines" with their more frequent safety problems.

Kelleher was a chronic storyteller, even though he was not a
Texas native. He was born in Camden, New Jersey, in 1931 and
"emigrated" to Texas as a young lawyer with his bride, Joan Negley,
in the early 1960s. Referring to the profit-sharing plan (the first
in the airline industry), he illustrated how very aware "our people"
are about being owners. Once, flying to San Antonio, he was taken
aside by Connie, who was into her fifteenth year at the airline.
"Herb," she asked, "can I talk to you alone?" "Sure," he said. She
told him that her stocks went down to $1.2 million and asked what
he was going to do about that. He related the case of a just-retired
pilot who "took with him $8 million in profit sharing, not includ-
ing his 401(k)." Which, by the way, the company matches dollar
for dollar.

He really came alive when talking about the standards he put
in place for treating Southwest workers. He cited an exchange
with Southwest's "fabulous Austin advertising agency, GSD&M—
otherwise known as Greed, Sex, Drugs and Money." The agency

asked him, right after deregulation, since any little airline can fly
to any place, "what's so special about Southwest Airlines?" Herb
replied, "Our people," which inspired the "Spirit of Southwest
Airlines Campaign." Herb continued:

> Now that's a big risk, because you know what you're do-
> ing in the newspapers? In the magazines? On television,
> on radio? You're telling all your prospective customers:
> Our people are the best. They're warm. They're hospitable.
> They're happy to see you. They want to help you. If you're
> wrong, you slit your own throat.

Then another story:

> A guy calls our Dallas reservation center from St. Louis
> from which his 85-year-old mother was supposed to fly,
> and that he's very concerned about her coming over to
> Love Field [Dallas] after having to make an intermediate
> connection in Tulsa. So the reservation agent says: 'I'm go-
> ing to be off in five minutes. I'll pick her up at DFW, drive
> her to Love Field, and fly with her to St. Louis to make
> sure she gets there okay.' That's the kind of devotion I'm
> talking about.

It's easy for an airline CEO to find an example like that and
claim that it is broadly representative of the company's culture.
Proving it by common concurrence of workers and customers
is quite another challenge. I speak to many people about their
airlines' experience. I read the annual customer satisfaction
surveys. Southwest Airlines consistently does very well. A central
reason, I believe, is that Southwest Airlines "people" are given
the discretion to adjust or respond to the specific circumstances

of airline passenger needs. They are trusted by their managers. Other airlines make their staff react "by the book," which often has them curtly saying an automatic "no," when Southwest's people are more likely to say an immediate "yes" to the needs and desires of their passengers—whether on the plane or at the airport. This discretion leads to greater satisfaction in their job, which has uniforms but not uniform minds. Sometimes the flight attendant speaking to passengers, after the door closes, with the customary FAA stipulations, can make funny, even edgy jokes. (Southwest has a bevy of short jokes that lead to anxiety-reducing chuckles.) Other attendants and announcers eschew the humor and formerly convey their safety instructions.

Kelleher liked to say that "everybody is a leader, no matter what your job is, we want you to focus on customer service." He alluded to the company's "People Department," not calling it "Human Resources," which he said, "sounds like something from a Stalin-five-year plan."

I sometimes ask flight attendants how the company interviews for new recruits. They smile and say—lots of interviewing before one passes "Go." Herb elaborated: "Confronting a complaint from the recruiting agent that they have interviewed 34 people for a ramp-agent position in Amarillo with no luck. I reply, if you have to interview 134 people to find the appropriate person to be the ramp-agent in Amarillo, do it. Because the most important thing is to get the right people, and if you get the wrong ones, they start poisoning everybody else." Maybe that's why Herb always said, "What we are looking for first and foremost is a sense of humor." He put the premium on temperament, adding, "You can always teach skills." This is profound in his business.

When I exit from a Southwest plane, I say to the flight attendants "good job" and then tell them to thank the pilots, just before walking into the jetway, where I say to the staff gripping wheelchairs and the new crew of flight attendants—"Best airline in the country." It has to brighten their day because they know it's true and not just coming from a person who received a Jack Daniels from the attendant who "forgot" to collect the free coupon, so it can be used the next time.

Even with stock options, the 401(k) plans and the labor union–negotiated salaries, Kelleher never thought that compensation was the primary motivator of his "People." Daringly, he said that "If somebody was working just to be compensated, we probably didn't want them at Southwest Airlines. We want them working in order to do something in an excellent way. And to serve people." "This is a cause," he told them, "This isn't just an ordinary corporation. And, you're doing a lot of good for everybody. We're proud of you, and we want you to have psychic satisfaction when you come to work." Another favorite exchange: "A ramp-agent from Oklahoma wrote me one time and said, 'Herb, I'm onto what you're doing!' He said, 'You're making work fun—and home . . . work.'"

Of course, everybody in the company called him "Herb." He's the boss who occasionally would work the aisle as a flight attendant for a few moments or work behind the ticket counter for a bit just to get the feel of the environment—and not knowingly—to have the passengers and staff get the feel of their caring founding entrepreneur. Overall, Herb was much more than good PR, he was as sincere with his concern for people as one can expect in a commercial, for-profit, big business.

"We've always tried to be sensitive to the needs of our people," said Herb, "and recognize the things that are important to them in their personal lives." He continued: "At Southwest Airlines, you can't have a baby without being recognized—getting communication from the general office. You can't have a death in your family without hearing from us. If you're out with a serious illness, we're in touch with you every two weeks to see how you were doing. Southwest keeps in touch with the retirees to show we value them as individuals, not just as workers." "Part of the *esprit de corps*," he exuded.

Humor is a part of the *esprit de corps*. Besides the flight attendant announcing the FAA rules at the onset of flights, the whole crew seems to laugh, smile, and joke more than those of other airlines. It all started, as with so many later Southwest ways of being and doing, with that improbable lawyer from Dallas. Herb related so many jokes that it is a wonder no one has collected them for a paperback. It would certainly become a best seller inside and outside of the Southwest Airlines community.

One asked, "What was your GPA in college, Herb?" He disingenuously replied: "Let me put it this way. At Love Field (Dallas), just the other day, when they gave me the B boarding pass, I said, you know what, I'm going to call my mother and tell her I finally got a B." (He graduated with honors.)

Or, on moving to Texas from New Jersey to practice law: "I was going to try cases, so I was constantly practicing [talking like a] Texan. [At the] gas station: 'Howdy! You mind filling 'er up?' I knew I had made it when I was at a buffet at the University of Texas and the fellow behind me said: 'I know where you're from.' And I thought: 'Oh shit!' And he said: 'West Texas, right?'"

Or, he related a story about a letter he received from a Texas congressman. The congressman told Herb that he was going to ruin Southwest Airlines if it flew beyond the boundaries of Texas. Herb wrote back reminding him "that man, not God, created the boundaries of Texas." The congressman responded: "Dear Herb, are you sure?"

When work and non-work life are meant to be joyous, Herb's comedic sense produced one- or two-liners from a wide variety of human-to-human experiences. Came to him naturally, effortlessly and . . . well . . . joyously. Yet with such an incisive, alert, foreshadowing mind, no one attempted to give him the moniker "Happy Herb"!

Astutely knowing that humor and geniality can become part of a company's brand, Herb began passing out little free bags of peanuts to passengers as soon as the airline got underway. And not just one bag—you could ask for two and the flight attendant would give you three or four. You could ask for a big bag of the little packages for a kid's party you're going to and voila, the attendant would reappear moments later with just what you asked for. Because Southwest started out as a low-price airline, undercutting its large competitors, Herb wanted his low prices to be associated with prices that were "peanuts." It worked until September 2018, when peanuts were discontinued. I wrote CEO Gary Kelly, with a copy to Herb, asking for the rationale. This approach worked well for years. Kelly wrote back saying, "Well, it took too much time of the flight attendants to adjust when they had other duties to perform." I related Kelly's response to a Southwest pilot who chuckled, saying, "No way, it's just cheaper to offer pretzels."

I sent a copy of my letter of objections to America's most famous "peanut farmer"—former President Jimmy Carter. He sent a copy of my letter back with a clear handwritten comment on my restoration request: "I fully concur, Jimmy Carter." Given all the problems of this tormented world, the peanuts service and associated banter were something of a solace to look forward to when buying passage on a Southwest plane.

Once in a telephone conversation with Herb, I cautioned that his chronic tobacco smoking was jeopardizing the key economic asset of the airline. I suggested it may be necessary for me and others to buy Southwest shares, put a resolution to the vote of the shareholders demanding that he stop smoking. Like a true cigarette addict, he didn't jump on the idea.

Nor did he respond favorably to another idea I put forth. Airlines need better and more prompt feedback from passengers when something starts to go wrong. They occasionally do pass out suggestion cards to passengers to fill out and give to the flight attendant at the plane's exit. I proposed a customer advisory committee to Southwest and other airlines, at no cost to the company, that would assemble, from varieties of sources and experience, specific recommendations for improvement. No way. Well, every CEO has his limits. He didn't explain, but he surely had his reasons. It could be that he was more than willing to hear from complaining passengers speaking out one at a time, but not from an advisory council that may have its own agenda getting publicity. Besides, he was probably thinking he had enough on his mind handling the long-range goals and the daily emergencies of a growing airline.

Put yourself, for a moment, in Herb's place. He spent more than four years before the courts and assorted agencies striving to break through the airline cartel to start, at first, a Texas-based airline. He had to hold together his financiers or investors, keep his board of directors from shutting down the company in despair by offering more of his own money to tide over a crisis, to get three planes of Southwest flying its small, regular schedule. As Southwest branched out beyond Texas into more and more states, he had to negotiate for highly contested slot space at big airports, fly into secondary airports near cities (like Chicago's Midway), avoid the "hub-and-spoke" scheduling system, then seen as the prudent way of building traffic, and maintain an almost perfect safety record with the highest customer satisfaction rating for most years. In the midst of all these decisions, thousands of flights are taking off and landing daily in all kinds of weather, in all kinds of airport congestion and all kinds of pressure from the armchair Wall Street analysts badgering him for being too much the maverick instead of the conventional, like the other, often failing, airline CEOs.

Of course, Herb could do all this—he was the one held responsible—because of the executive and working force he established through an exquisite recruitment and retention system without peer. Moreover, his wife Joan Negley and he were raising four children and they did not neglect either a social life or their charitable duties.

Herb took his many awards as prods to never let lag all the things that made the airline a success. When your company is named again and again as one of the five most-admired corporations in America by *Fortune* magazine's annual poll, falling off that list would make news—bad news. He set the example, never giving himself a raise or a bonus (he believed in honest, performance-based stock options), being there when the managers were having difficulties, but staying "out of their way when things were going well." To him, leadership was not about power ("power" should be reserved for weightlifting and boats, he jokes) but about responsibility. He once turned down 500,000 stock options on the grounds that it was too much and did not set a good example "for our people." Asked by a *Fortune* reporter whether he has a plane, Kelleher replied, "No. Heavens no. As a matter of fact, I established a policy that we should never have a corporate plane. I said, that's rather unbecoming for an airline. I charter, but I pay for it personally—not the company—when I do it."

In part, Kelleher managed by simplicity, so far as is possible. Southwest, under him, stuck to running an airline and not buying hotels, rental car companies, and other unrelated businesses, as some other airlines have. That sweeps aside all the temptations, proposed deals, failing cross-subsidies to failing subsidiaries, debt loads, and endless distractions. He told a reporter,

I don't want you to yawn when I say this. But I've always thought that having a simple set of values for a company

was also a very efficient and expedient way to go. And I'll
tell you why. Because if somebody makes a proposal and it
infringes on those values, you don't study it for two years.
You just say, "no, we don't do that." And you go on quickly.
So I think that contributes to efficiency.

Here is where Herb was so humble that full candor is not
forthcoming. Herb, distinctly unlike other airline top executives,
was not greedy. He was building an airline from a sense of mission—
first, better service at lower fares than the stodgy airlines were
providing, and then to show that the workplace can be a pleasant,
even enjoyable place to go every day, and even later to demonstrate
that this Southwest sub-society is a profitable, reliable investment
for thousands of shareholders. (Before the COVID pandemic,
the company had run forty-seven straight years of profit.) Had
Herb begun his quest to secure ever-limitless riches for himself,
the entire moral authority, solidarity, and commitment that he
made possible would never have gotten off the ground. The entire
Southwest community knew that for Herb—despite being quite
the character—it was never about Herb; it was about them in ever-
widening concentric circles of "our people." Not surprisingly, with
this managerial extroversion, Herb became wealthy enough, thank
you. His estimated wealth in 2007 was $2.5 billion!

Although now deceased, Herb Kelleher's philosophical omnipresence hovers over the Southwest culture as a form of business
practice sustainability. That's why the imprint on the paper napkins
handed out with drinks to passengers reads not as a quip but as a
serious standard of service—"In a world full of No, we're a plane
full of Yes." I've seen a few passengers asking flight attendants for
something *special*, waving the napkin with an expedient smile in
the air. They were not disappointed.

In a book titled *The Southwest Airlines Way*, by Jody Hoffer Gittell, published in 2005, the author cites its high-performance relationships as an enormous competitive advantage in "motivation, teamwork, and coordination among employees." Hoffer Gittell then skates on thinner ice when she attempts to show how any company can foster such labor productivity and keep the personal touch. The airline business uses its share of automation to be sure, but it is still an intensely person-to-person experience along the entire continuum, starting from how you're treated when you call or email for a reservation, or have to change one, all the way to the often-chaotic baggage claim sections. Not many businesses can miscue and not trigger personal emotions and despair. Author, Kevin Freiberg, of *Nuts! Southwest Airlines' Crazy Recipe for Business and Personal Success*, assesses the hurdles to be overcome by other businesses striving to duplicate this business model. The comparative circumstances are really the same. Kelleher was blessed by a stubborn bunch of competitors who didn't want or know how to compete in a deregulated environment. They were so used to the Civil Aeronautics Board (CAB) protecting their cartel and, for many years, until 1980, blocking any new airline competition. Moreover, Kelleher had a different way of raising and keeping labor productivity. Southwest didn't adopt a tough, disciplinary, dog-eat-dog working environment, like Walmart's, which strategically uses the prospect of high turnover for desperate, surveilled people at the lower run of the income ladder. Instead, by setting an example at the top, being easy and humorous in the saddle, Kelleher and his recruiters saved themselves gobs of trouble down the line by hiring people motivated by personality and character to serve their customers, to use their own best judgments instead of being beholden to rule books and inflexible company policies when a quick decision to assist had to be made.

Here is a situation I personally witnessed. We were flying from Oakland to Hartford's Bradley International Airport, stopping en route at Chicago's Midway and BWI in Baltimore. Landing at Midway, the announcer urged the people going to Hartford to stay in their seats, while the BWI passengers were exiting to another aircraft. "What?" we said. "This plane is going to Hartford? Can we be allowed to stay put and get to our destination much earlier?" Normally, the flight attendant would have told us we would have to get off with our luggage and stand in line by the gate if we were lucky enough to get a ticket transfer at the ticket counter. In other words, we were on our own and free to try. Not at Southwest. The flight attendant took our tickets, pulled out her phone and found out there were available seats in this plane and switched our reservations. After landing she went to the ticket counter and got our newly printed boarding passes. Because we were flying Southwest, and not Delta, American Airlines, or United Airlines, we weren't charged a $150 or $200 reservation change fee. What is there not to like! Did she go by the book? In a way she did. She went by the book of personal kindness, a little going out of her way and showing that she was in a "plane full of Yes!" (She would have done it for anybody—known or unknown.)

A commentator on the Hoffer Gittell book elaborates the emphasis by Southwest on "relational competence":

When it comes to employee reviews, they value learning over accountability. They are always trying to improve their employees as opposed to punishing them. In a day when test scores are used to judge teachers, I hope we can learn from that one. Analysts have scratched their heads wondering how Southwest—the most highly unionized airline in the US airline industry—keeps making money in good and bad times . . . valuing their employees as much as possible.

The Southwest Way is not without its temptations to stray from that way. I sometimes talk with pilots after landing when they're having a cup of coffee and ask whether Gary Kelly and his executive team are readying to depart from a Southwest company motto I once suggested to an agreeable Kelleher—"We do not imitate." They do have some worries. They tell me that Kelly wants to be sure that no-fee policies (for baggage and reservation changes) are attracting passengers from other airlines or adding new passengers due to affordability. If not, he may succumb to charging passengers a couple of billion dollars yearly, just as Delta Airlines imposes on its compliant customers. They worried that the reservation phones don't get personally answered the way they used to—a voice tells you how many minutes it will be before an operator comes to you, though they'll call you back if you wish so you don't have to stay on hold. Southwest's legroom shortened a little when the airline put another row of seats on its new Boeing 737s. Then there is a little more tightening of management-labor relationships, recently made more so with the pandemic's reduction of travel and the disruptions caused by Boeing's defective 737 MAX planes, two of which crashed— one in Indonesia, and one in Ethiopia, taking 346 lives in 2018 and 2019.

I like the open seat assignment, but that is diminishing with advance reservations paying more to secure a seat in the A Section. In years past, I really liked dialing Southwest for information and having a human being answer in four or five rings with know-how and an unruffled persona. I would tell people that dialing American Airlines would keep you on hold for a certain kind of music recital. A different kind of music would entertain me while waiting for United Airlines operators. While US Airways (now part of American Airlines) kept you on hold for relentless advertising of their special fares and trips.

The most beloved Southwest executive next to Herb was the intuitive Colleen Barrett, who succeeded Herb as President. Rising from a position as Executive Secretary to Herb, Colleen was chosen above many aspirants because, in Herb's words, "she knows how to love people to success." A wide-ranging conversation between Barrett and Ken Blanchard, author of the irresistible *The One Minute Manager* fills much of the book they co-authored, *Lead with LUV: A Different Way to Create Real Success.* Colleen Barrett retired in 2008, proving the worth of this golden rule in her management. It was still very hard work to be this airline's president, but at least by "leading with love," she didn't make it harder for herself as do so many hard-driving bosses in other corporations and industries. Her official responsibilities were Marketing, Corporate Communications, People (Human Resources), Customer Relations, and Rapid Rewards (which do not expire), Labor & Employee Relations, Reservations, Corporate Security, Culture Activities, and the Executive Office, in addition to being on various task forces, the company's Executive Planning Committee, and the company's Board of Directors. I list these dreary titles to assure readers that leading with LUV is far, far more than being an on-stage motivational speaker for Team Southwest.

For such an innovative, extroverted airline company, Southwest's monthly magazine *Southwest* hews pretty much to the standard menu and piled advertisements as other airline's company magazines inserted into your seat's pouch. True, I find some articles there that would not be printed in the ultra-cautious publications of the other big airlines. Imagine a feature about why Southwest and other airlines outsource their critical maintenance operations to low-wage Central American or Asian countries. Alas, Southwest and other airline magazines would reject out of hand any reporting critical of the airline industry. The in-flight magazines all wallow in too much boosterism.

Again and again, writers and journalists who specialize in covering the airline industry tear into United, American, and Delta for their anti-consumer policies, without prominently noting that Southwest empathetically does not engage in such practices, such as fees for services that were once, by industry standard, free, or mind-numbing charges for different seat placements, or charging for putting baggage in the bins above your seats. Passengers who don't often travel by Southwest need to know these comparative details. So, I wrote Gary Kelly, admonishing the company's excessive acceptance of such journalistic oversight, urging them to present Southwest's fine record to columnist/reporters, or send letters-to-the-editor rectifying the omissions. The Vice President for Public Relations wrote me a personal letter, wringing her hands in frustration, promising to do better and thanking me "from the bottom of my heart" for making this point. I've received letters from corporate officials over the years, some with personal language, but never did any of them say "from the bottom of my heart."

Kelleher had other interests—he took a keen interest in promoting cheaper natural gas for the consumer over coal and oil, but he was not as aware as he should have been about the toxic mess of fracking and the huge greenhouse gas multiplier—that escaping methane—which is not included in ordinary studies comparing natural gas with coal. It is also surprising that Kelleher wasn't chosen to be a director of the Federal Reserve Bank of Dallas. As a top graduate of Wesleyan University and New York University Law School, steeped in English and philosophy majors, there were inner Herbs that emerged after he retired from Southwest. These apparently didn't include changes in his tobacco addiction and imperviousness to his "doctor's orders." He still made fun of them. He told a reporter in 2013: "I've always tried to look a little bit ahead, at least when I'm sober—and when not, I look *way ahead.*"

This is the vintage Herb, in addition to his many management home runs, that made him such a lovable leader by his "people." After Herb ascended to the heavens on January 3, 2019, the family had a private funeral in San Antonio, but they promised a more public get-together on January 21, 2019, at the large Kay Bailey Hutchison Convention Center in Dallas. So many people wanted to attend and say "happy trails" to Herb that Southwest had to limit the audience to the extended Southwest "family" and invited guests. When the doors opened at 9 a.m., the line was as long as a football field. Five thousand people came for this final salute in a sentimental, intimate atmosphere that one person described as feeling "like a high school reunion."

The *Dallas Morning News* noted that at the head of the line were flight attendants who had more than thirty-eight years of joyous labor with Southwest. "The throng of celebrants," reported the *News*, came in Southwest uniforms, logo wear, bright company colors or Herb-esque attire. Blue jeans far outnumbered ties. For this "Herb Kelleher Celebration of Life," attached to the program were small Kleenex packs labeled "Summon Your Strength." However, it was not a time for tears, though some wept; it was a time for concise encomiums and spontaneous reactions.

Southwest CEO, Gary Kelly, Herb's hand picked successor, summed his thoughts: "Herb described Southwest as a mosaic of a thousand little things. Separately they might not seem like much, but put them together and they create a culture and a work environment that is the envy of corporate America." Kelly reiterated Kelleher's business philosophy as: "Put your people first. Empower them. Love them. Respect them and take very good care of them. And then, and only then, can you deliver on your promise to deliver to your customers really good products." I'll warrant that Herb would have added, "And make sure you stay fully unionized!"

Then Kelleher's son-in-law, John Agather, spoke and, in the name of the Kelleher family, rendered a toast to "all of you at Southwest and lift a bit of Wild Turkey [Herb's favorite whiskey] to you."

Two standing ovations responded to the arrival of Colleen Barrett, Southwest's president emerita who for years was the human touch, the spirit of the airline's culture. She told stories that regaled the assemblage. Then Broadway star and country musician Gary Morris sang "Wind Beneath My Wings" and, with the audience, sang "America the Beautiful." Morris had to note that Southwest was the first airline to permit musicians to carry their instruments onboard in the overhead bins.

Adding a sobering reminder that Southwest's emergence was not easy, Ron Ricks, former legal and regulatory officer, declared that "for twelve consecutive years, there would not be one year, one month, one week, one day, or one minute when Southwest's very existence was not at stake . . . For over 4,000 consecutive days, Herb suffered relentless tests and trials, crushing pressure and never-ending toil."

Why did he go through all this? Because the airline companies were trying to destroy this upstart, real competitor and Herb simply said he was not going to let them do it.

The all-too-rare intangibles of multi-layered leadership were wrapped up in this clenched-jaw, easy-in-the-saddle, overtime thinker, empathetic, resilient, life-enjoying, people-loving, laughing CEO. Herb proved that putting people first is good for the workers, the customers, and the shareholders, in that order.

What other major CEO would receive such a liftoff to eternity?
Almost a year after Herb passed away, Gary Kelly paid the
second tribute to him in *Southwest* magazine. Mr. Kelly obviously
carried Kelleher's executive skills and strategic moves with him
as a guiding post of daily reference. It is possible to believe that
he asks regularly, "What would Herb do?" Especially during the
tumultuous year of 2019. As CEO Kelly put it: "This has been arguably one of our company's most challenging years . . . a string of
unprecedented storms, a government shutdown, and the ground-
ing of the Boeing 737 MAX."

Many people in Southwest Airlines also must be searching for
what Herb Kelleher—who was a large buyer of Boeing 737s from
Boeing—would be thinking. How would he be handling this grave
deception and gross engineering negligence by Boeing's bosses.
After the disruption to Southwest (and many other airlines), what
demands, contractually and technically for the 737 MAXs, would
he be making as a condition of continuing relations with the mismanaged giant aircraft manufacturer? How much of his criticism
and demands would he make in public?

Obviously, Kelly and his top colleagues know privately a great
deal about how Herb dealt with Boeing during past strained relations with what has been Southwest Airlines' exclusive aircraft
vendor. With the 737 MAX being Southwest's most serious crisis in its long relationship with the Boeing company, they may
be looking deeper than ever to retrieve whatever insights, tactics,
bargaining chips and personal approaches they can from their
founder's guiding light. There are serious stakes involved, not just
for Southwest and other airlines, but for the future of trust of many
millions of airline passengers. Remember the determined, grieving
families of those 346 innocents lost in those preventable Indonesia
and Ethiopia crashes.

In December of 2022 Southwest Airlines was making news again, but not the kind that any airline wants. A nationwide storm left thousands of passengers stranded and resulted in the cancellation of more than 16,000 flights. The current Southwest CEO Bob Jordan says he is making changes to prevent such meltdowns from occurring in the future. Time will tell if he can truly lead as capably and with as much foresight as Herb Kelleher.

5

JENO PAULUCCI

Founder of over Seventy Companies

One day in 1973, I took a call from someone named Jeno Paulucci, who said he was from Duluth, Minnesota. He was calling to support my article slamming Reserve Mining Company for daily dumping tons of their taconite tailings (after extracting iron ore from the sedimentary rock) into what once were the pure waters of that great body of fresh water—Lake Superior. He identified himself briefly, saying he was the leading vendor of prepared Chinese food sold in supermarkets all over the country. He wanted to encourage my opposition of such dumping which, among other harms, contaminated Duluth's drinking water with "amphibole asbestos fibers."

It was not often that supportive business executives called me, especially ones who articulated his agreement in such a decisive and personal manner. Paulucci noted that he had supported six major tax breaks through the Minnesota legislature for the beleaguered taconite industry in the "Iron Range" country of northeastern Minnesota. But now he did not like what was happening to his hometown's drinking water. Eventually, pressed incessantly by a heroic citizen—Arlene Ione Lehto—the federal EPA won its lawsuit and forced the company—a joint venture between Armco and Republic Steel—to dump its tailings into land pits. That was what other similar mining companies were doing.

That call from Paulucci introduced me to the challenges, controversies, and influence of this unique and almost supersonic entrepreneur. He has astonished me for over thirty-five years. He was unlike any other major business CEO in some very important respects—to put it mildly. A proud Italian American, to which he attributed his famous temper and aversion to being in awe of anyone, he was quick and direct in his many public confrontations.

Given his wide array of achievements and outrageous derring-do, Jeno had a lucky start. He was born dirt poor of Italian immigrants in a three-room house on the edge of a mine pit in Aurora, Minnesota. His father came there in 1912 to work in the world-famous, back-breaking, dangerous, underground iron mines that gave northeastern Minnesota its name—"The Iron Range." Early on in school, he and his older sister, Elizabeth, endured discrimination and ridicule. As with all adversities in his long life of ninety-three years, Jeno became stronger as a result. As a seven-year-old schoolboy, he decided to change his last name from Paolucci to Paulucci to make it "look a little more American and liked by others who viewed my family as 'Dirty Dagos.'" From the start, Jeno—as everyone called him—neither minced his words nor referred to bad or bigoted words with only their first capitalized initial followed by _____. In trying to understand his personality characteristics, I conjecture that his profanity was a way he avoided procrastination. Impulses toward decisional confrontation and strong marketing skills led him to move fast and, in his wholesale and retail business, the rewards went to the fleet of foot.

With this intrepid, get-up-and-go human dynamo, suppositions were not much required. He laid it out in his 2005 autobiography, six years before he passed away in 2011, *Jeno: The Power of the Peddler.* It's a raw autobiography like no other I've ever read. You can see right away what is coming in the next 550 pages. "I've always hated the idea of an autobiography," he begins. "Who needs another book that could be titled 'How I Got Rich and Became a Pompous Ass?'" So he ducked the word by saying it's mostly "a collection of stories" full of fascinating details of how he overcame the obstacles he faced and succeeded. Details indeed there are, and since Jeno always kept good sales and product records, we know how he priced, how much and where he shipped, and his high-intensity negotiating strategies and tactics.

The year before publication of *Jeno*, Paulucci received arguably the most prestigious of his many awards. He was given the Ernst & Young International Lifetime Achievement Award for Activism, Entrepreneurship, and Leadership, which allowed his friends to say that made him the number one overall entrepreneur in the world. Jeno was without a sliver of bashfulness. He collected more "blurbs" on his career from more leading politicians, CEOs, and prominent others than perhaps anybody in the world. Some of them were placed at the beginning and throughout the book. Yet he chose to publish it privately and fast with thick paper and very readable large print.

After receiving an autographed copy from him, I called and told him: "Jeno, this is an engrossing, educational, thought-provoking, and revealing book with news about your exchanges with US presidents and other historic figures. Why didn't you go for a leading publisher that could turn it into a best-seller, like the Lee Iacocca best-seller?"

He replied simply—that he didn't want to wait a year, didn't want any editor messing with his prose and, just like his business start-ups, "wanted to do it his way." "Okay," I said, "now that it's out, why don't you get a publisher who will give it much bigger readership than the hundreds of books you're sending out one by one?" "Who cares," he said, "I wrote it for my family, friends, and anyone eager to get and learn from it." End of conversation. Click.

As a result, this heavy thud of a book landed without leaving much of a mark in the business schools, the business press, or the overall business community that still comprises a sizable part of readers who buy books. As far as the author was concerned, you want the book, order it from Paulucci International in Sanford, Florida, just like any of the many food products sold by the more than seventy companies that Jeno started.

Today's businesspeople or aspiring business students could read how Jeno Paulucci confounded the odds against him and how counterintuitive his business practices and values were from conventional wisdom on a wide scale.

Remarkably, his book started out declaring that if he were writing a book about success, then why not give "success" his own definition? His sense of "success" was quite conventional, except his methods to achieve it were far more eyebrow lifting. Success to Jeno was not the accumulation of wealth, though "that is just one of the ways to keep score. Success is how you play the game, not resorting to cheating to win, a way of living your life, and if it is so blessed, in raising a family in a manner of which you can be proud. Success is just doing that which you want to do, but being happy with it—by being yourself."

"Success is being able to 'spit in the eye' of those who stand in your way by being honest to the point that you are untouchable when they seek revenge." Then comes the lofty Jeno—"success is seeing to it that you do some good for your community, your state, your nation, and above all, your fellow man . . . The key to it all is providing jobs, the most valuable commodity on Earth." What's remarkable about the above descriptions of success is that he filled in the blanks of these goals again and again with sometimes spectacular flair—getting there and proving it.

Except for his quietly assertive wife, Lois Mae Trepanier, Jeno did not like or allow anyone to tell him what to do. That's not to say he didn't recognize and learn from his mistakes. No CEO put more of these mistakes and failures in the public sunlight than he did. But he didn't like government or bigger business to tell him what to do. By the same token, he didn't like powerless people to be bullied or commanded by the raw power of their overseers. This belief made him a better man, as we shall note. But it is a belief driven home by what he learned and observed about why Iron Rangers were, in his words, "so ultra-liberal in their thinking— some say even socialistic."

He expands:

> Well, it probably has something to do with the fact that these people—my people—were oppressed as few Americans have ever been oppressed. They'll never forget what the iron mining industry did to their fathers and grandfathers and great-grandfathers.

> Insurance for injuries? No, not a penny from any mining company. And if any worker talked union, he would be fired on the spot and his name added to the blacklist circulated among the other mining companies so he couldn't work anywhere. The work was 13 hours a day, six days a week.

Jeno's father made 35 cents an hour, or $4.20 a day. Even adjusted by inflation, the pay was very low.

The lesson from Jeno was that "out of all that labor and deprivation, came strength—it started with a fire in my gut that's never been extinguished—and a host of leaders in all fields of endeavor." The spirit reflected the old saying, "When the going gets rough, the tough get going." He lists as Iron Rangers leading political figures and judges, plus Judy Garland, Roger Maris, Bob Dylan, Jessica Lange, and Gus Hall, who was head of the Communist Party in the United States and a perennial presidential candidate.

Unlike so many people who grew up hardscrabble and made good, Jeno never forgot where he came from—the hardships and grit continued to shape his personality and character as nothing else did. Starting out in a grocery store and odd jobs, young Paulucci started peddling and never stopped. Never mind fancy words like "entrepreneur," he just wanted to be called a "Peddler" all his life. "When you think about it," he mused, "we're all peddling something, whether it's goods, services, real estate, our resumes, or deeply felt political or religious convictions . . . But all peddlers are not the same," he wrote, obviously introducing himself.

When his father, Ettore Paolucci, was laid off, Jeno's mother stepped into the breach by bootlegging good red wine during the Prohibition period, when selling alcohol was illegal. Mother Michelina, from Italy, where the wine flowed unimpeded, had to feed the family. She was so good at producing superior wine, assisted by eleven-year-old Jeno, that she took in four times what his father took in when he was working in the mines.

Federal agents raided repeatedly and destroyed her facilities and finally forced the family from their home. They moved and started again. Jeno adds, "Sometimes we'd hold the Feds off with payoffs to the police and other officials who helped themselves to a few gallons of wine . . . and Michelina's pasta dishes from her catering business." She was one of many little bootleggers desperate for survival in depressed areas. She finally gave up and opened a small grocery store in 1932. It was open seven days a week from 7 a.m. to 11 p.m. The family were hard workers for sure.

It was at another grocery store—The Daylight Economy Market, in Hibbing—that Jeno learned what *not* to do in order to succeed at $3 a week, while going to school. For instance, the owner told his employees that they were to cover their wages from ripping off the customers either by manipulating the scales or adding machines! Jeno learned that he was "working among a gang of thieves." It taught him to "think on his feet," but it also firmly turned him off crooked business. You may get away with it once or twice, but eventually it will catch up with you and destroy whatever business you are pursuing.

At age sixteen, he became "a barker for fruits and vegetables," finding himself very suitable for such a calling. He would stand in front of the door at a long table loaded with produce about to become overripe and holler "at the top of my lungs: Watermelons, 49 cents each! Half bushel of tomatoes, 69 cents! Bushel of spinach, 40 cents!" He invented gimmicks, such as shouting "Strawberries . . . fifteen-minute sale!" while placing an old alarm clock next to him. While working long hours in many pick-up jobs here and there until midnight, Jeno was still in high school. In 1935 Jeno started taking pre-law classes at Hibbing Junior College. He wanted to become a lawyer, but that didn't happen because he knew that he was "destined to be the prince of peddlers." He took a chance, quitting his "monotonous" pre-law classes, to take a job with the Minnesota Market as a wholesale grocery traveling salesman on straight 5 percent commission, paying all his expenses, but with the "skies the limit" potential. At age seventeen he was up at 5 a.m., going here and there all around northeastern Minnesota and always hustling, hustling, hustling. He took some foolhardy risks. He would drive across the frozen Lake Superior between Duluth and Superior, Wisconsin, to save the 10-cent charge on "that damn toll bridge." Recalling his youthful exuberance, "I'd take the chance of my 1929 Ford sinking into the bay, if the ice was too thin, just to save a dime." He slept in his car, shaved in gas stations, lived off lunches of tinned salmon and by his sixth week, he was selling at the unheard level of $1,000 a week. He learned to improvise in little shady ways to entice his retail buyers—sending telegrams to himself reporting forthcoming higher prices for salmon or produce, for example, convincing his buyers to place larger orders to avoid higher prices later. He would deliver more cases than ordered and the busy clerk would sign off without looking. He admitted he might have been "a little too devious at times," but they were sales techniques, not selling bad or rotting produce.

Other times he just was more alert than his competitors. He developed a phone order system so purchasers wouldn't have to wait for his monthly visit. When owners, for whom he was selling, tried to cheat him, he started his long tradition of suing in court. Jeno believed in vindicating his rights in court, for which he acquired a just reputation. Given his temper at any injustice, deploying litigation kept him out of another kind of trouble—direct retribution.

He soon decided to get into business for himself, seizing what he called "the chance of a lifetime" peddling "dehydrated garlic." There followed periods of boom or bust, with heartbreaking spoilage of his fresh foods, such as bean sprouts. He would swing from peddler to garage-style production or processing, from being broke to rising up again and making even more money—never giving up.

It was when he started getting lots of orders for his bushels of fresh bean sprouts from Chinese American food processors that he first saw the emerging potential for becoming really big time. Before that could happen, he had to deal with the erratic delivery schedule of Railway Express Agency, delivery schedules led to the bean sprouts arriving in deteriorating conditions. He contracted to fill the bottom of the rail cars with a mixture of salt and ice to preserve the sprouts. He broke into the big time when General

Foods, reacting to rising demand, put in an order for an entire railroad boxcar of his products. A first for Jeno, the order flopped because of deterioration from a deficient cooking process. That was General Foods' only order. To Jeno, failure was only another opportunity to bounce back.

What about canning the sprouts? With his partner, he quickly created a letterhead grandiosely titled "The Bean Sprout Growers Association" and went to a canned peas company in Wisconsin. The owner said he could do it, but he couldn't get the cans. They were in the middle of World War II, and metal was rationed for military purposes. Two days later he called Jeno to say Continental Can would sell him metal—slightly scratched or marred but fully intact—called "reject plate." With this material, enough for 500,000 cans, the Wisconsin factory owner agreed to turn them into cans if Jeno could get approval from the War Products Board in Washington, D.C., immediately.

Jeno went to Washington and won the okay by arguing that a negative decision would cost lots of jobs. More obstacles, more hustle to overcome and he returned home with an official letter authorizing the immediate release of 500,000 of those cans to the "now prestigious Bean Sprout Growers Association of America."

Crucially, Jeno had that *nth factor* of energy, problem-solving, and determination, to get it done right away that made him a rarity in his business. He wouldn't give up along the way, just like a champion mountain climber.

He knew how to dart, how to surprise with unusual demands, how to hurtle up his adversary's corporate hierarchy to reach the top man, how to bluff, how to outwork almost everyone by working at dawn, at night, on weekends. He was lucky also in having a wife and family who didn't complain about his long absences, in part because he was such a family man once he got home. His wife Lois knew him and his emotional intelligence so well that she encouraged him at every fork in the road and admonished him when he was flying off the handle. However, she found his resort to the courts a little much, even accusing him of "suing Mickey Mouse," when he sued Disney.

He chose to do the hard things himself—confronting top CEOs over their companies' bungling, getting the difficult approvals and licenses from governments, and taking charge personally and abruptly when his associates couldn't break through on a deal or a delivery.

With the Continental Can supply, Jeno plunged into the Chinese food market, which was finding more and more people developing a taste for that cuisine. Chun King—the first and most lasting brand—found its way onto most supermarket shelves in America. As the business grew into more fields, Jeno taught himself to avoid complacency. "As a lifelong peddler, one thing I've learned is that just when things are all going right, they're about to go all wrong." That's when the real test comes. Do you have the fortitude, the gumption, the street smarts, to turn misfortune into fortune? All of us must find that out about ourselves. Bouncing from one crisis after another—whether it was the wrong kind of packaging that discolored the food or total loss fires, weather storms, or losing a trial because the business plaintiff knew the judge and most of the jurors—nothing seemed to faze him. On the contrary, it made him stronger, more determined, wealthier, more standing out as a man you could trust, good to his word.

Besides his business philosophy of having a quality product providing good value for the price and loving your work so that you won't mind working so hard, Jeno believed that wasn't enough. "Sweat," he said, "is no substitute for brains." "You also have to find a way of standing out, running your business differently from everyone else. Zigging where others zag. Eventually you'll build the business of your dreams—which is time to think about selling it and going on to something else." Which he did dozens of times right into his nineties! He admitted to not being "suited to be involved in the businesses . . . even when I own 'em." He kept close watch on costs, spent very little time at meetings (that's why he kept his hat on inside) and burned through telephone calls fast. None of my conversations with him lasted more than five minutes.

One day I called him about my effort to get the giant *AARP: The Magazine* (over 18 million subscribers) to do a cover story on him. Here he was in his eighties starting and selling businesses, tough, alert, active and just what AARP's older readers should find interesting, if not motivating. The editors didn't accept my arguments; they were putting people in their fifties who looked forty on the cover so as not to depress the readers. I had told them, that was just wrong—their readers were not getting younger, and they needed to see examples of vigorous, successful people older than they were as something to anticipate. Still, no sale. After listening to this, Jeno thanked me and said goodbye. He was not that interested in being promoted for such a profile. If they were interested, they knew where to find him. The editors never were that curious.

His slicing costs off celery stalks, by involving celery fields in Florida, is a classic of how far he'd go to reduce his expenses for a staple in all Chinese food and beat his competitors who were buying fresh celery from California.

For his diversifying business into any fruits and vegetables that would make money, Jeno went back to the land, buying land to grow Minnesota wild rice, which came down with "wheat rust" and failed. The winter weather doomed his growing cauliflower, potatoes, and mushrooms; an angry Jeno drove a big engine Chrysler back and forth over the already destroyed rows of crops to vent his anger.

Another enterprise was packing his mother Michelina's "great spaghetti sauce" in cans. He built the promotion coast to coast, offering supermarkets Fiat cars if they bought 10,000 cases, Vespa scooters for one truckload of 2,000 cases, and so on down the line. After saturating supermarkets, there "emerged a wee bit of a problem. The public wouldn't buy spaghetti sauce in cans. They were too accustomed to buying it in jars." Back came almost all the cases he had shipped to the supermarkets of his "delicious, authentic, Italiano sauce."

Like no other entrepreneur, Jeno seemed to revel in publicly admitting his mistakes and failures, as if to suck energy and the resolve to be better out of these experiences. This was very unusual for a strong personality. Over the years he diversified into the restaurant business. In his book, he lists each of his restaurants, starting in 1957, from Florida to Minnesota. Most failed ("failure due to poor location," "failure due to Jeno's stubbornness and stupidity," "due to incompetent managers, etc."). He even started a restaurant franchise he called Pasta Lovers, which got underway before it ended with twenty lawsuits. "To hell with franchising," he observed. After thirty-seven years of striving, one eatery—Luigino's Pasta and Steak House—finally did succeed. It happened to be in Heathrow, Florida, the new town built by the Paulucci family—led, of course, by Jeno.

In all the thousands of workers and hundreds of workplaces making up Jeno Paulucci's enterprises, there has never been a strike. Not one day, over decades, he asserted, was lost due to a labor disruption. How come? I turn to Jeno's explanations:

> For some reason, demanding SOB that I am, people like to work for me. Probably has something to do with the fact that they can earn a lot of money doing it . . . Executives and managers get above-average salaries, with generous bonuses for those who deserve them, and a variety of other financial extras but no perks.

Perks, he believed, can lead to troubling distractions and envy. "Play politics and you're out. No play, play, play with your laptop. Work a full day or get out."

Continuing, "People in factories, on the canning lines, and those performing all the routine work that is the heart of any business . . . are represented by strong unions."

"I believe in unions, and they're entitled to negotiate every last dollar they can get out of me—though the negotiations may be tough."

Jeno argued the case for unions by telling people what it was like when workers didn't have any. He started with the iron mine owners who would fire and blacklist anyone even mentioning the word "union," even in his uncle's native Italian. Uncle Rinaldo was fired after one day and blacklisted from all the mines in the Iron Range because he mentioned unions in passing his first day on the job. Then Jeno would argue for unions from the employers' or owners' interest—negotiate union contracts and make sure both sides stick to it for maximum productivity.

Jeno bargained with the Retail Clerks and Food Handlers, the United Packinghouse, Food and Allied Workers, the Amalgamated Meat Cutters and Butcher Workmen of North America, the Steam Fitters, the Laborers union, and even the famous District 50 of John L. Lewis's United Mine Workers. His recounting of negotiating sessions was often hilarious—Jeno-hilarious. As when, before a National Labor Relations Board hearing, an official asking the negotiator for the United Mine Workers, "Tell me, Mr. Sandy, what in hell's business does a coal miners' union have to do with organizing a Chinese food packer?" "Just as much," Sandy replied, "as that Italian Paulucci, has in owning it." Jeno's comment: "That's what America is all about, and rightfully so." Take *that*, politically correct people.

His favorite technique in face-to-face negotiations with union reps was, "Just shut up and let the other guy negotiate with himself; a lesson I often used."

After Jeno had set up a trucking company called the Orient Express to ship finished products from his plants to their customers and then bring back raw materials, the Teamsters Union began representing all the drivers of his fifty-tractor fleet. Soon thereafter, the Teamsters notified him that they wanted to replace the Food Handlers and Meat Cutters unions' contracts with the workers at the Duluth, Jackson, and Cambridge plants in Minnesota. Jeno replied, "No way am I violating our contracts with the other unions." So the Teamsters brought their boss, Jimmy Hoffa, for a morning showdown meeting at Hotel Duluth.

Here is Jeno's recollection: "Paulucci," Hoffa said, "I've heard you're resisting our people taking over your plants. Now, I'm not going to take a lot of time to tell you what's what."

He lifted his arm, bent it, and clenched his fist. He showed me his muscle, tapped it with his hand, and said, "You see this, Paulucci? That's what we've got. Muscle. Now I'm going to give you 20 minutes to make up your mind and dance to our music. If you don't turn over your plants to us, we will secondarily boycott your plants and products all over the country, legal or not. You got that?"

Jeno replied: "If you know so much about me, why don't you ask our mutual friend, Abner Wolf, of Detroit, about me?"

(Abner was a good customer of mine with Abner Wolf Wholesale and I knew he was a good friend of Hoffa's.) Anyone will tell you that I am the only union organized packer of Chinese food in the US, and I'm honest and I treat my people right . . . and I don't run scared for anyone."

Apparently, this impressed Hoffa who said that he would talk with Abner, "but if you're lying, God help you!" Two weeks later,

Hoffa called him and said Abner vouched for him as predicted. "Paulucci," Hoffa said in closing, "we will never bother you again."

"After," Jeno related, "countless negotiations with unions of all kinds for almost sixty years, I'm proud of my record of employing tens of thousands of union people and never having suffered through one hour of work stoppage or strike . . . anywhere . . . ever."

But Jeno is best known as a brilliant salesman. How so? He didn't like to advertise to the general public, preferring to help supermarkets with in-store promotions, passing to them the savings in the form of lower prices for shoppers. Still, he felt the pressure from his large competitors who were advertising in newspapers and on radio and TV. He did agree to join with other Chinese food companies to put 1 percent of total sales in a fund for national advertising and promotions. It took three years for the wrangling between the parties to break up this joint effort.

Always searching, Jeno made contact with Stan Freberg, a free-thinking young advertising genius in Los Angeles. Freburg developed some ads that were supposed to be funny but off-the-wall.

Here was one TV ad: "Nine out of ten doctors recommend you eat chow mein for dinner." The camera opened to ten men in white coats, then panned slowly over the smiling medical corps. Nine of the ten doctors were Chinese. Stan bet Jeno that the ad would increase sales up to 25 percent. If not, he would personally pull Jeno in a rickshaw down La Cienega Boulevard in Los Angeles, past restaurant row. "You're on!" roared Jeno, "And if sales go up, I'll pull you."

Turned out Jeno had to pull Freberg—so relayed in a rickshaw before a mass of press up the Boulevard. For in "the target audiences, sales went up 30%." Jeno did many stunts and eye-grabbing promotions, even though he and Lois often had their reservations, born of their strict upbringing.

He had no hesitation heaping ridicule on big companies with giant executive salaries, loaded with limousines, gulfstream jets, country club memberships, long vacations, big offices, and "when they fail, they pick up their golden parachutes and inflated pensions." He was always championing small entrepreneurial firms that keep growing in performing and outmaneuvering these giant corporations until they are gobbled up by their giants who often run them into the ground.

He confessed that he didn't feel comfortable with high finance, creating conglomerates—too managerially cumbersome, too bureaucratic, too computer-driven decision making—and all the rest that went with staying with the trend of the big getting bigger. As he often said, "I build companies to sell 'em, not to go to bed with 'em." "What it comes down to . . . is that I don't like to run big companies. I like to create, to build and then sell, sell, sell . . . first the products of my creation and then eventually the companies . . . That's the fun in my game of life."

There are other reasons for his preferences. Jeno ran his businesses hands on, low on the corporate abstraction ladder. He liked to be informed but not briefed. He wanted to do things his own way—without all the formalisms and petty turf battles inherent in a giant hierarchical corporation. He set records for hiring workers with disabilities, ex-convicts who had served their time, and, remarkably, working over the decades to get over one hundred unjustly imprisoned inmates out of prison—one at a time.

He told executives of companies that were actually or potentially dealing with his businesses what he thought of them in no uncertain phraseology, especially when rejecting takeover offers. He mocked the trivial questions asked by shareholders attending annual meetings of publicly owned companies. He preferred to finance his companies himself and stay private and . . . *free*. He succumbed once—selling his Chun King company to R. J. Reynolds for $65 million in cash in 1962. In return the company created a new division with Jeno, at age forty-eight, as its working chairman. He and Lois were so pleased that they turned around and gave $2 million in tax-free gifts to Chun King employees at the time of the sale.

Over the years, Jeno compiled a series of what he called "Pointers from the Peddler." This was the pointer he delivered during his many "thank yous" to people at Chun King: "If you're a successful entrepreneur and you think you did it all on your own, you've lost touch with reality. You were just lucky as hell to have the people around you who boosted you on the ladder to success and give you an extra nudge when you stumbled."

Moving to New York City, Jeno started filling his role as the new chairman of R. J. Reynolds Foods. Not surprisingly, he didn't fit in from day one. Listen to his description: "I'm still wondering how in hell Reynolds or any other New York company ever got anything done in those days. [He omitted noting the biggest moneymaker for Reynolds was selling addicting cigarettes—a fairly easy selling persuasion.] Productivity was nil. I did see employees come in at nine or nine-thirty, take off their coats, then down the elevator to get coffee and a roll. Maybe they'd start work about ten o'clock or so. Around eleven or noon, down all would go for lunch. They come back between one and three o'clock. Around four-thirty, down they'd go again to catch the commuter train, or the subway, or maybe another martini. Jesus! What a way to run a business."

He hated working in New York City, but he stayed on until he put his division on track and left, with a noncompete agreement. The one exception—which he used to start, in Duluth, of course—was one of his most successful products, the pizza roll.

About this time in 1960, Paulucci was becoming more interested in life as a civic activist. He wanted to grow more jobs in the depressed Iron Range country of his birth. The high-grade iron ore was exhausted and the unemployment rate there was in double digits. Mining taconite—a flint-like deposit with enough iron ore content to be commercially processed—was seen as a future basis for recovery, but the extracting plants that had to be built were very expensive. He put together a coalition of important people in politics, business, and labor and hammered out an amendment to the Minnesota Constitution providing tax breaks for companies building these plants over some twenty to twenty-five years without any other audience concessions, in his words. In 1963, help came from President John F. Kennedy, whom Jeno buttonholed during his visit to Duluth. The legislature passed the amendment. Then came the dispute over what level of production per ton tax was going to be imposed on the industry. He and others got a tax through the legislature that pegged the tax to the price of steel. It ranged from 2 to 3 dollars per ton. The proceeds, in a trust fund, went to protect the environment, to diversify employment, and to provide assistance to the towns for job-creating projects.

The industry did not like what Jeno was pushing for in taxes. The Reserve Mining Company also didn't like Jeno's next project to diminish dumping taconite tailings into Lake Superior, where he grew up fishing, swimming, and drinking its pure waters. From these controversies came a "Jeno's Credo": "Who the hell cares if I make enemies . . . as long as I serve the common cause."

The sale of Chun King, for what Jeno figured was worth almost $1 billion in today's dollars, made him suddenly "rich and fairly famous . . . Amazing how my image suddenly changed, especially in the eyes of the elite of Duluth . . . Until then, they had regarded me as a Dago ruffian from the Iron Range who should go back to the mines and dig. But after the sale, I got telegrams of congratulations from them. I was the angel of northeastern Minnesota." He asked advice from many specialists and friends about what to do with the money. It reflected another "Jeno's Credo": "Look beyond the horizon. Today is already old. The new is tomorrow's . . . But don't be an expert too soon."

When he started investing his millions in the stock market, it was a new experience. Some investment experts put him into options and soon $10 million shrunk to $5 million. Jeno was outraged. He called the brokerage firm of Donaldson, Lufkin and Jenrette (DLJ) and demanded "my $10 million back." Never hearing about such a thing, Bill Donaldson tried to tell him about market risk. Nothing is guaranteed, especially about options. Jeno was undeterred, and he learned that DLJ was about to take the firm public and that one of the lead partners was about to go to work for the president of the United States. He reasoned that the last thing they wanted was a brawl with Jeno and a complaint to the Securities and Exchange Commission. He alerted Donaldson and suggested that they journey up to Duluth with a check for $10 million!

What followed illustrates perfectly the unbridled brass that was Jeno's approach to winning and going where no one has ever tread. Donaldson flew to Minneapolis to meet with him. He started to calmly convey the rules of the stock market game—sometimes you win, sometimes you lose. What followed, in Jeno's rendition, was first a "strategic loss" of Jeno's famous temper.

Bill Donaldson stood up to it, to his credit. He said something like, "Don't take that attitude with me. I've seen irate people before."

"That may be true," I said, "but you've never had one goddamn mad Wop on your hands."

I finally looked him in the eye and said, "Listen, do you want to settle this thing now and see to it that we get the full 10 million, and we forget about doing business together but part as friends? Or do you want me to go to the SEC tomorrow?

That's really all I had to say. Bill realized that if I did go to the SEC, there was every possibility that their plans to offer stock would be skewed or delayed.

Then the unheard of on Wall Street happened. Jeno again: "The $10 million was transferred to me within twenty-four hours."

On another similar occasion, DLJ recommended a stock investment in the Cornelius Company—a manufacturer of soft drink dispensing units for Coke and Pepsi for bars and restaurants. He put in $3 million, or 5 percent of the company stock, and soon the stock started spiraling down. Jeno demanded his money back before the company's executive committee or he would "sue your combined asses in court." A banker friend on the committee calmed him down, advising Jeno that the company had serious problems, could go bankrupt and leave him with nothing. He suggested Jeno join the board of the Minneapolis-based company and help them turn the company around. Jeno said "okay," and rolled up his sleeves, scrutinized the company's wasteful worldwide operations, turned it around and sold the restructured company for a family profit of about $25 million. Reflecting on it, Jeno wished he had never gotten into that mess in the first place, but "it was fun." Vintage Jeno. Jeno didn't just win through his form of bluster and intimidation. He won battles because he went into the details of matters.

Another "Pointer from the Peddler": "When you draw up a

contract, pay close attention to the fine print. The devil is in the details. And make sure that fine print is yours." Then, the details are not the devil, but the portals to victory.

Please do not take away the impression that Mr. Paulucci was a braggadocio. Right after his narration of the foregoing "wins," he devoted a chapter to how he muffed a once-in-a-lifetime chance to buy the NFL's Miami Dolphins in 1967 for only $4 million. Somehow, he was persuaded that Miami was a big-time college football town (the University of Miami Hurricanes) and would not patronize a professional football team. He turned down the offer. By 2005 the Dolphins were worth 100 to 200 times more than that $4 million installment loan by the seller would have cost.

Jeno's personality was such that he didn't spend much time regretting. He had a balanced life—worked very hard, then went fishing and hunting in the wilderness areas of northern Minnesota and northern Ontario. (He called the latter complex "Wilderness Village.") He had docks and cabins in these areas, where he entertained major political and business friends. His many stories about such social adventures displayed a deeply ironic, sometimes edgy, and self-deprecating sense of humor.

Knowing of Jeno's willingness to sue for justice—he was involved by his count in sixty major lawsuits in sixty years—I sent him a description of our planned American Museum of Tort Law. He was delighted—sending me back on fine, thick paper a message that is compelling enough to quote in its entirety.

> I am very pleased to hear that there is going to be a law museum, there sure as hell is a need for one. That brings to mind the quotation from President John Adams, which was in his autobiography concerning the law and lawsuits, which is as follows:

"Now to what higher object, to what greater character, can any mortal aspire than to be possessed of all this knowledge, well digested and ready at command, to assist the feeble and friendless, to discountenance the haughty and lawless, to procure redress to wrongs, the advancement of right, to assert and maintain liberty and virtue, to discourage and abolish tyranny and vice?"

In other words, Ralph, "sue their asses!"

He simply learned in his long career that "going to court, or threatening to go to court: it's just a normal part of being in business." Sometimes you win, sometimes you lose, sometimes you compromise . . . Never hesitate to use the power of the law to back up your beliefs!

Self-taught lawyer Paulucci (remember, he did a brief stint with pre-law courses at junior college) divided his lawsuits into two categories—"PCs (proved correct) and PIAs (pains in the ass)." "Some of them were a combination of PC and PIA . . . Lawsuits can be short and sweet, or long and tedious. They can also be fun . . . no kidding. I guess that friend of mine was right when he said, 'Jeno, you're more litigious than religious.'"

His lawsuits were almost always against bigger fish or misbehaving competitors, suppliers, or large customers. He did not use lawsuits to bully his workers or intimidate defendants who could not afford to defend themselves. He also stayed right along with his lawyers in the filed cases so that he could keep them from straying from his purpose or overcharging him.

Because he believed in treating his business circle fairly and openly, Jeno became ferociously bold when he felt cheated or misled, or stonewalled waiting for a decision. He relates one improbable case that is believable only because Jeno has the kind of gall and immediacy that could pull it off.

It started with his company package designer coming up with an eye-catching red aluminum foil package for its Chinese frozen food brand. In three months, the brand reached nation-wide distribution. Then the disaster started. The special red ink was rubbing off the foil packaging and smearing everything, including the shoppers' clothes. The brokers, supermarkets, and consumers were complaining loudly. Jeno demanded compensation from the culpable Indiana supplier, who offered a measly $30,000 for the ruined packaging and dry-cleaning bills for the stained shoppers.

Jeno's response: "Bullshit, I have 4 million cases of frozen food packages selling for 5 dollars a case that I'll have to make good on at a cost of $2 million." The man said that's all he could offer, and, since the supplier was a division of Continental Can, Jeno would have to take it up with retired general Lucius Clay, the CEO from whose office the $30,000 offer emanated. Jeno knew that General Clay was the hero of the Berlin Airlift, so he flew to New York insisting on meeting with him. Not surprisingly, on arriving he was told that General Clay was not available but his executive assistant, also ex-military, would receive him.

The veteran officer took Jeno out to lunch at a nearby five-star restaurant on top of the Chrysler building where all the staff swarmed around them, eager to serve. Jeno called him "Lt. General Wiseguy," because he tried to patronize and impress Jeno with this place, the view, and how he could leave tickets at the box office to catch a Broadway show or two.

Jeno threw down his napkin and blew up, telling him he was there to collect compensation. The military man raised the offer to $50,000. Again, Jeno's narrative:

"I'd say, screw it. If that's your idea of a reasonable settlement, what I'd like to do is shove your military ass right off
the roof of this penthouse clip joint."

"Don't talk to me like that," the executive assistant replied.

"I just did," Jeno retorted.

"Well, what is it you want?"

Jeno wanted $900,000. Pulling out his trump card, General Clay's
right-hand man lowered his voice and said the company's hands
were tied by a restrictive consent decree imposed by the US Justice
Department preventing the company from preferring one valued
customer over another. Now who would make this astonishing
next move, besides Jeno?

Getting up from the table, he took a cab straight to LaGuardia
Airport and his Aero Commander. "File for Washington, D.C.,"
he told his pilot, Virgil. He arrived at the US Justice Department
at 3 p.m., went to a payphone, and dialed General Lucius Clay,
getting past the secretarial screen by telling her that he was down
at the Justice Department and wanted the name of the official
in charge of the consent decree that he was told about at lunch.
Suddenly General Clay was not so busy and got on the phone.
"Jeno, are you really down there," he asked. "Yes, please tell me the
official's name so I can plead my case directly."

General Clay paused for a moment and said he would give
the matter further thought and asked Jeno to be at his office the
next morning. At 9:30 the next morning, still without meeting
CEO Clay, Jeno walked out with a check for $900,000, without
signing any release from further liability. Jeno seemed to have

had trouble with his packagers—bad smells, things falling apart, smears—and he always went to the top to get compensated for his losses.

Paulucci privately owned all his companies; there were no public shareholders or listings on the stock exchange. He relished self-reliance. He disliked going into private debt. When he opened up a plant with jobs, he negotiated public assistance in the form of loans and bonds from the city, county, or state. None of the loans cost these public entities any money, he asserted, because he claimed they were all repaid from the profits of these new enterprises. That, in Jeno's work mind, would not qualify as corporate welfare, though it saved him from having to invest any of his money to get underway. On the other hand, he fought against a sweetheart corporate-welfare-cum-eminent-domain giveaway involving a new Lake Superior company in Duluth that cost him a site for his food-processing plant. He called it "the rape of the taxpayer." Out came another of "Jeno's Credo": "Greed is like a jackal. Sometimes it eats its own guts!"

Wearing many self-described hats, Jeno savored the one of "Jeno the Activist." As was typical, he had to define it. "What the hell is an activist? Just somebody who is willing to devote time and energy and ideas—and money—to get things done that you know damn well should be done. My activism roamed from Alaska and Canada to Italy and elsewhere, but it started in Duluth."

From the beginning of his career, he was determined to employ what he called "the unemployables." Long before the disability rights movement was stirring. Whether they were "physically or mentally handicapped or recovering from addiction and needed a new start in life," he refused to call his special sensitivity "philanthropy." It was good for business as well as for those misnamed "unemployables." Hear Jeno out:

These folks, who get the same union wages and benefits and chance for advancement as anyone else, are a good investment. They work hard; they are low on absenteeism and high on loyalty. In fact, they often set an example for the 'normal' people working alongside them.

He also had a "special feeling" for imprisoned convicts, explaining that "but for the grace of God . . ." alluding to some of his close calls resulting from his youthful drinking and temper outbursts in the streets. This led to his noticing and helping, one by one, over one hundred convicts and addicts out of jail. It took hard work, money, and attention to get their cases reopened and secure paroles, new trials, or their immediate outright release. Some of those aggrieved people whom he thought he could rehabilitate were released in his care. In his book, he describes about a dozen of these cases in enough detail to invoke sheer wonder at the emotional toll they must've taken on him as he dealt with the interminable prison and judicial procedures—all the while tending to his business, political, and family relationships.

He should have told us how he managed to use his time so efficiently over his lifetime the way Benjamin Franklin chose to do back in the eighteenth century. Amazing! While I'm discussing his "shoulds," how did he manage to get such worthy workers and managers—other than paying them and bonuses for their performance? Maybe that was enough, together with the examples he set as the boss.

Jeno also had a hard-headed sympathy for the first Native Americans. He assisted with repairs of a crucial fish processing barge at the home of the Yu'pik Eskimos in Alaska, he helped the Chippewa near the Canadian border, and embarked on a failed mission to the heartrending, impoverished Oglala Sioux's Pine Ridge Reservation in South Dakota.

In between, there were some harrowing rescue missions that

Jeno participated in with his private plane full of essential foods and water. On the Sioux Reservation, the disintegration of lives, the deadly addictions, the pervasive unemployment stunned the man from the Iron Range who has seen his share of deprived people in deep hardship. Jeno writes: "So this is what we have done to these Native Americans, we foreigners, we barbarians who stole their land, broke their spirit, and took away their self-respect." He went twice to the Bureau of Indian Affairs in Washington for small business grants but got nowhere with that bureaucracy. He spent $100,000 of his own money and gave up in sheer frustration.

Around 1976, Jeno decided to spread his wings and start the National Italian American Foundation (NIAF). That none of the many well-placed, accomplished and celebrity Italian Americans from Washington, D.C.'s, political heights to Hollywood's entertainers and executives, plus everywhere in between, had already done this is a commentary on another one of Jeno's traits. He knew that 25 million Italian Americans needed such an ethnic association celebrating their achievements in equal rights in a discriminatory society. Yes, Jeno had his own stories and those of others about bigotry and slurs on his ethnicity. But he had always decried "the sickening and stupid" waves of bigotry, prejudice, or discrimination sweeping war-like across the globe century after century. He adds: "All too often, the root of warfare is religion. Despite all the good that religion has done for individual souls, religious dogma, in my opinion, has been a plague since the Middle Ages."

For himself, he especially hated being suspected of having some connection to the Mafia, simply due to his wealth. He located NIAF in Washington, D.C., because thirty members of the Italian American Congressional delegation were there, including some with serious seniority and power, such as Peter Rodino, then chair of the House Judiciary Committee. Thus, began that stage in

Jeno's life where he would network with a dizzying array of politicians, celebrities, and the high and mighty asking for their time and name for various projects like the NIAF.

NIAF was almost an instant success. He enlisted Jack Valenti, the extremely well-connected president of the Motion Picture Association of America and former key aide to President Lyndon Johnson. It turned out that prominent Italian Americans had been waiting for such a society to organize major banquets, give out awards, celebrate their heritage and achievements, and "put an end to the subtle discrimination." He assembled a council of 1,000 Italian-American achievers to work with the NIAF's Board of Directors. Soon presidents, senators, governors, and heads of major business lobbying groups were vying to appear, speak, or just be seen at these massive gatherings. Twenty-five hundred people jammed the Washington Hilton in the nation's capital at the first gala dinner with Jack Valenti as master of ceremonies. Wide coverage on TV, radio, newspapers and magazines followed. He recalled: "It is one of the most exhilarating and successful sales of my life, and this peddler was damn proud!"

Jeno held the reins as chairman for seventeen years. He was showered with encomiums and printed many of them, along with a few denunciations (that's Jeno, so long as you spell his name right) over five pages at the beginning of his autobiography. They included senators and governors and presidents from both major parties—Governor Mario Cuomo and Governor Jeb Bush—as well as prime ministers, state attorneys general, lawyers, CEOs, former Vice President Fritz Mondale and, on the back of his book, a prominent message from former President George H. W. Bush:

> Barbara and I have the highest regard for Jeno Paulucci. Throughout his years in business, he has exhibited great leadership. When tackling a difficult problem, he always

comes up with the right answer. We Bushes salute Jeno as well for being a true Point of Light. His willingness to help others is not only well-known, but admired. JENO, YOU DA MAN!

All this while his son President George W. Bush was blowing up Iraq, slaughtering civilians, and miring our country in a quagmire of US casualties and zillions of wasted dollars. Did Jeno care about the "opposites" that regaled him, as long as they regaled him? In his writings he lathers his admiration for all presidents and politicians in power. Jeno had social justice positions; he helped people stomped on by the rich and powerful who included his endorsers. It wasn't so much just satisfying an overweening ego. It was more a quest for admirers who recognized his various works in life to go on the record. It was a way for him to open doors, such as those of Congress, to his various pursuits—from the commercial to his public activism. Lastly, it was his way of having fun and being able to tell people he can get any one of these powerful personages on the phone.

In 2004, during my presidential campaign, Jeno called. He said he liked my fighting for consumers, and he sent a maximum contribution of $2,000.

A few weeks later, he called again and said: "Why are you calling for all these regulations on businesses, getting into foreign policy and whatnot? You should stick to protecting consumers."

I hastened to reply that I was not a one-issue person, that in politics and power everything is connected to everything else and it comes down to fighting for the underdog, as he has. "Look at our website for my reasons, Jeno," I said.

No matter, he was upset and said he would no longer support me. He never really endorsed me; it was just one of his many whimsical decisions to help "a good fellow" who defended people from bad businesses. It didn't stop him from calling me or returning calls from me about his book, the Tort Museum proposal, and my attempt to get him portrayed before the millions of elderly people who could find his energy encouraging for themselves.

He never stopped. When his son and wife and brother-in-law bought some land near Sanford, Florida, where he had his winter home, someone proposed building a highway with the help of the powerful Minnesota Congressmen John Blatnik. Jeno got it done. But not before Jeno and his family bought an additional 5,000 acres. Then the suggestion was, why not build "a new town," sell condos, encourage development, and make lots of money. Done! Remember, Jeno is, first of all, a businessman. The planned community was called Heathrow, an upscale place where the American Automobile Association (AAA) decided to move its national headquarters from the Washington, D.C., Virginia suburbs. Getting AAA as the prestigious anchor corporation required some spectacular Paulucci persuasions, which included climbing a chain-link fence early one Virginia morning at age sixty-eight in a business suit with a clipboard to get to a short, but all-important meeting on time with AAA's president, Jim Creal.

It seemed at first strange that Jeno ended his autobiography with one hundred pages of interactions with seven presidents of the United States, from Lyndon Johnson to George W. Bush. He declared his opinions of them, narrated how he had advised them and donated to their campaigns, and how he had spent time on the road working with their campaign staff. Ask him and he would say he wanted to "become involved at the highest level . . . knowing that we are working to make a contribution to our fellow man." But despite being a close friend and supporter of fellow Minnesotan Hubert Humphrey, who ran for president in 1968, Jeno instead, four years later, became a working supporter of Richard Nixon (because, get this, he thought Nixon was "the lesser of two evils," the other being George McGovern) vying for the White House in 1972!

He told several stories about his time with these presidents, pushing one of his favorite ideas—creating regional "Business Responsibility Councils" where corporate members would contribute 5 percent of pretax profits to funds designed to produce needed jobs in infrastructure, housing, and other necessities. Although he garnered a host of major business executives and politicians to support the idea, it never happened. A promise by President Gerald Ford fizzled when Ford lost the election to Jimmy Carter.

Another anomaly, he pushed presidents to support a fair minimum wage, then turned around and worked on behalf of George W. Bush's 2004 campaign against John Kerry. Bush adamantly opposed a higher minimum wage, while Kerry favored such a raise. Jeno wrote that "it was my fondest hope to swing Minnesota into the Republican column in that election." He failed.

Some of Jeno's personal conversations should be useful to historians who might have scratched their heads looking for any consistent political agenda that Jeno carried with him. They are also of historical importance for other reasons. One, the narratives reflected very candid, private interactions under campaign pressure, trips abroad, or some other less routine encounters. That alone would make them valuable. Also, Jeno's book was privately published and probably not in the usual mix of the materials presidential historians consult. As an independent and being Jeno Paulucci, he felt he could always speak about what was on his mind.

At a small private dinner with President Ronald Reagan, questions were invited. Jeno launched his: "Mr. President, do you think it's right to cut taxes so much for all of us rich people, and then also cut benefits to poor people?" Jeno reports frigid silence settled on the room. "The President gave a cold stare as he and Nancy walked away to visit with some people."

Jeno praised George Herbert Walker Bush and his son, George W. Bush, supporting the former in 1988 and George Bush in 2004 against John Kerry. For some reason, he lost his lifelong sense of fairness by admitting to making "donations to the notorious Swift Boat Veterans, whose ads, critical of Kerry, made an impact in several states." He also related how he successfully pushed Ohio Republican Senator George V. Voinovich, a friend from Jeno's business presence in Ohio, to come out more forcefully and campaign in Ohio for Bush. Ohio, recall, was the swing state that put Bush over the top by barely 75,000 votes. Jeno, whose strong suit was not foreign/military policy, forgave Bush for all his war crimes, including Iraq, which Jeno, against all his instincts for the oppressed, called "a tough decision by a strong forceful leader."

Apparently, an unappreciative George W. declined to become a communicant with Jeno. So Jeno sent him ten "suggestions from the Peddler," which illustrate how Jeno could not be categorized. He called for an increase in the federal minimum wage, demanded that Bush's wars be paid for by a surtax of 1 or 2 percent on incomes over $100,000 and not "mortgage the future of our children and our children's children." But he wanted a sharp tax cut for the estate and gift taxes. He renewed his call for a plan, overhauling rail transport, and retaining the budgets for social and community programs. He insisted on cutting the cost of energy to consumers, workers, and the freight system without saying how, given he had agreed with Bush's huge early tax cuts for the rich. "You [George W. Bush] simply have to do something about double-digit unemployment, especially in depressed areas, where the poor are getting poorer and the rich are getting richer. That causes social and political unrest."

He advised: "Be sure your policies and appointments aren't skewed to the overly conservative side. You're a born-again Christian, and that's okay in your personal life. But not in the policies of this country. Be more of a populist president for *all* the people, not just the right of center or extreme right."

Bush, the Second, never bothered to reply to Jeno. He won his reelection contest in Ohio: he didn't need the peddler from the Iron Range or his candid and uncomfortable counsel. The ungraciousness of politicians did not daunt Jeno; he continued for six more years, selling and turning more of his properties and wealth over to his progeny. He passed away at age ninety-three in Duluth, on Thanksgiving Day, 2011, four days after his sweetheart, Lois, died at age eighty-nine.

In November 2004, he went to Palm Springs, California, to accept the inaugural "Ernst and Young's International Lifetime Achievement Award for Activism, Entrepreneurship and Leadership." In his acceptance speech, he told his fellow entrepreneurs that "We must become the public's advocate. We must take on projects that others wouldn't take on . . . so that we can have peace and prosperity throughout this world in our troubled times today."

Jeno was big on publicizing his awards, listing thirty-nine of them in his autobiography. For most people that would be a sure sign of an outsized ego, like that of Trump's. For Jeno, it *was* a sign of an outsized ego, as he would admit. But deeper, it was a way of affirming how he came out of his humble beginnings, made it big again and again, yet never forgot his roots or the impoverished people living there.

In 2003, Jeno said to a reporter that a personal net worth of half a billion dollars "was in the ballpark" for him. He and Lois established a myriad of trusts, some for his children, which after Jeno's death became the subject of bitter litigation with the trustees and between his grown children. By 2017, thirty-seven lawsuits had been filed in Minnesota and Florida and over $10 million in legal fees expended, according to the *Duluth News Tribune.*

The final settlement, the *Tribune* wrote, covered "the myriad of issues and side issues that permeate these disputes that has resulted in very expensive litigation which has drained the Paulucci family's wealth." Disputes extended to former and present trustees and the children and their heirs. There was a provision in the settlement that there will be no contact between one of their daughters, Gina, and her siblings, Mick and Cynthia. Imagine: all this happened within the ambit of an elaborate estate plan established by Jeno and Lois. One can only imagine how fast and fairly Jeno Paulucci would have settled these controversies. It was not the way he and Lois envisioned their material legacy would turn out.

Jeno had his faults. In his younger days, a fierce temper led to losses in control over his reactions to businessman he felt were cheating him. By his own admission, the combination of temper and alcohol came close to getting him in real trouble carrying long jail sentences. He sometimes went beyond puffery in his strenuous selling fervors. He seemed indifferent to the nutritional pluses and minuses of his packaged and canned food products, as long as they tasted and smelled good and were of good quality.

But his ability to learn from his mistakes, without hiding them, and his propensity to distill what he learned into Ben Franklin–like homilies suggest a formidable intellect driven by experience and judgment instead of academic reflection. The latter style is often given as the definition of an intellectual—philosophers ruminating while smoking their pipes. Jeno was the kind of intellectual who had to figure ways to surmount many serious setbacks and obstacles through quick thinking, who had a keen grasp of understanding human reactions under specific circumstances in order to get a desired outcome. The truth is that such mindful strategies require unusual intellects. Their applications require unusual mental and physical energies. So unusual that during Jeno's time I never saw their like among the civic initiators anywhere on such a scale in the United States. Citizen groups would swoon over such a cluster of self-driven talents as embodied by Jeno F. Paulucci.

6

SOL PRICE

Founder of FedMart,
Price Club, and PriceSmart

He never spoke of the past, neither about his business successes and adventures, nor his upbringing, family, or personal life. In nearly a dozen meetings and dinners I had with Sol Price, he always spoke and asked about the present and the future. The only exception was to recall his jokes. One of his favorites was delivered at a gathering of big box discount store executives, including Walmart founder Sam Walton and top managers from Costco, Kmart, Target, Home Depot, and Staples. Sol was praised as the father of this gigantic retail revolution. He replied: "I should have worn a condom."

A son of Jewish-Russian immigrants, Sol was born in a gritty, immigrant part of New York City in 1916. That location never left him. He lived up to its stereotypes, tough, gruff, no nonsense, hardworking, goal-oriented and, above all, ambitious—but not fast-talking or impulsive. The family's move to sunny California in the 1930s was preceded by his father, Sam, contracting tuberculosis. Often, when very successful people do not wish to speak of the past, it is because of their impatience over how much more they wish to accomplish in the future.

I believe that was true of the father of the warehouse club industry in the United States. Twice, on different occasions, he told me about the spectacular opportunities to revolutionize retail in the Soviet Union. He had visited the country with his wife, Helen, and quickly observed the many failures, the almost mind-boggling shortage of goods, and the indifferent treatment of Russian customers standing in their long queues. He related how shocked Russian retailers, mostly giant government-owned stores, were to learn that the spoilage rate of the Price clubs was only 1 percent, when the Russian losses were 10 percent or more— if they even bothered to keep track. Ultimately, he was never allowed into this vast potential market to realize such dreams for his ancestral country.

He graduated from San Diego High School in 1931, obtained his B.A. in philosophy in 1936 from the University of Southern California in between stays back in New York City, and earned a quick law degree in 1938 from USC with high honors. He essentially started his own law practice, renting part of a law library in a small firm, and doing much pro bono work to do good and perhaps get some paying clients.

His circles were heavily Jewish and his pro bono services were for nonprofit Jewish charities. These included the Jewish Welfare Society, the Hebrew Home for the Aged, and the Guardians, a Jewish fundraising organization. Sol and Helen's social life was within San Diego's growing tight-knit Jewish community of 3,000. By 1941, he had a modest, established law practice, enough for him and Helen to buy a house. Sol never denied his Jewish identity; he just refined it in ways that showed his independent streak of always figuring things out for himself. Which was remarkable, in a way, since most of his legal, business, and social friends were conservative observant Jews.

Chalk some of that contrarian spirit up to the fact that his parents were socialists, and his father was a major union organizer in New York City, who helped to start the International Ladies' Garment Workers' Union (ILGWU). Moreover, his parents were nonobservant, declining to attend synagogue because Sam had strong opposing opinions about organized religion in general. For some reason, young Sol attended the Passover Seders with his orthodox uncle. He even then was skeptical about why "God visited the plague on the first born and why the wine, which was poured symbolizing the plagues, was always given to the janitor."

Many years later, late in life, Sol did consent to an oral history, at the family's insistence, in which he elaborated his views on religion with customary honest acuity:

"I'm not a great student of the Bible. I can't rationalize giving God credit for mercy and all the good things that happen—who takes responsibility for the bad things? . . . It would be very easy for me to be an atheist except for two things: No. 1—I'm unable to understand or cope with infinity, and, No. 2—Over the years there have been many smart people—much smarter than I—who have wrestled with the concerns I have stated above, and who end up—in spite of that—believing. What am I missing?"

The lawyer turned businessman was not uncertain about his views on injustice. He was, viscerally and intellectually, a strong civil rights proponent all the way to his business decisions and with whom he would choose to contract. He long believed that the grand jury institution was irrevocably biased with its secrecy and completely one-sided power and control by prosecutors against those accused being indicted without having counsel. He wrote and talked about this unfair arm of the US criminal justice system throughout his life and once even placed an ad in the *Los Angeles Times* to express his views. Even if acquitted, he argued, the serious stigma, time, and expense could be ruinous to innocent people, apart from enabling prosecutorial abuses. He would show deep frustration with the civil rights leaders, committed to reform of the criminal justice system but not paying attention to arbitrary grand jury proceedings.

When Sol came to Washington for nonprofit board meetings or government advisory committee sessions, he would go to Congress to see if he could persuade its most progressive members to introduce his tax on wealth—about 1 percent per year. No progressive lawmaker would do so. More than most CEOs, Sol knew the masses had a breaking point, when passivity would not remain their routine; he thought the under-taxed super-wealthy and the large corporations were pushing their luck in that regard.

When once I mentioned Sol Price in a conversation with a corporate lawyer, he volunteered that "He is a thinker." I replied, "More than that, he is a *rethinker*." Which was key to his success— *rethinking* everything whether a business strategy, no matter how small or large, was or was not working. Sol's creative rethinking process allowed him to launch a powerful and successful sales idea, see that idea experience sudden buffeting or troubles, and then devise a solution that carried him over the hurdles that might force others to go out of business. He was always gracious in allowing for luck in his successes.

One of his major mistakes was his decision to sell a majority stake in his first large business—FedMart—to Wertkauf, a large retail chain in Germany. The deal broke up in December 1975, with the ouster of Sol Price and his team by CEO of Wertkauf Hugo Mann's majority-controlled board of directors. Price even had to sue to enforce his employment contract payments against the vitriolic Mann. Sol did receive a gratifying card of admiration and support by many FedMart employees whom he left behind. Typically, Sol promptly responded by saying he owes them his thanks and hoped they would "give your best so that FedMart continues to prosper."

Now came his famous resiliency. Within a week he secured an office with the new name "The Price Company" on the door. At age sixty, he started considering the next business model during long walks with his eldest son Robert—who had been a top executive at FedMart and left with his father. They carefully pondered what they had learned in building FedMart's many stores. They noted FedMart's no-frills warehouse overhead, its low-price merchandise, limited selection of brands, and wide category of different products.

What father and son also knew was that Sol Price—the strategist and teacher—was their main asset. One of Sol's most famous recruits was Jim Sinegal, who came to work for him at age eighteen in 1954 and eventually left to start Costco in Seattle. Jim once said, "If you're not spending 90% of your time teaching, you're not doing your job." He attributed learning everything that he knew from Sol Price. Another famous name in mass retailing—Sam Walton— who opened his first store in 1962 in Bentonville, Arkansas, had already visited FedMart. Years later he wrote in his 1992 autobiography, *Sam Walton: Made In America: My Story,* the following: "I learned a lot from Sol Price, a great operator who started FedMart out in Southern California in 1954. I guess I've stolen—I actually prefer the word 'borrowed'—as many ideas from Sol Price as from anybody else in the business. I really liked Sol's FedMart name, so I latched it right on to Wal-Mart."

However, there were notable lessons that Sam Walton chose not to learn from Sol Price. FedMart paid its workers above market wages and provided health insurance and retirement benefits. Price welcomed unions, being known to say, "I'm not pro union. I'm pro balance. Everything in economics and politics is about the struggle between capital and labor, over how big the pie will be and how to divide it." It would be hard to imagine Mr. Walton doing what Mr. Price did when he learned, in 1969, that FedMart's grape supplier was non-union and not providing good wages and working conditions to its employees. He told the FedMart produce buyer to switch to grapes picked by the United Farm Workers Union, headed by Cesar E. Chavez, even though the price for the grapes "was a little higher." That was not unusual. He prohibited FedMart purchasers from doing business with suppliers who treated their workers unfairly. Nor would the anti-union Walmart company ever consider what Sol wrote in a bulletin to FedMart employees:

> You must feel confident that you are working for a fine and honest company. Somehow, we must make this mean to each of you that you will be permitted, encouraged, and sometimes coerced into growing with the company to the limit of your ability. We believe that you should be paid the best wages in your community for the job you perform. We believe that you should be provided with an opportunity to invest in the company so that you can prosper as it prospers. We believe that you should be encouraged to express yourself freely and without fear of recrimination or retaliation. We believe that you should be happy with your work so that your occupation becomes a source of satisfaction as well as a means of livelihood.

Aside from this expression of what he called a "fiduciary duty" toward his employees, Sol believed, accurately, that employees treated well and respected are more productive and more loyal and honest, minimizing high labor turnover, a phenomenon which Walmart notoriously experiences. Basically, his labor policy made for greater profits.

Price's definition of a fiduciary relationship with his customers included a dislike of credit cards and their cost, a rejection of "loss leaders," superlatives, and other sales bait, and the idea that the company should get whatever price the market can bear.

In addition to working hard, Sol wanted his workers to think— he hated manuals for that reason. But he gave them a tool for thinking which he called "The Six Rights," as he told *Fortune Magazine*.

"I believed the business broke down into three categories—personal, product and facilities—and that the same six rules apply to them all. You've got to have the right kind, in the right place, at the right time, in the right quantity, in the right conditions, at the right price."

Elsewhere he declared, "If you recognize you're really a fiduciary for the customer, you shouldn't make too much money." That meant consistently high-quality merchandise and consistently low prices. It meant unconditionally guaranteed products with immediate cash refunds, "No questions asked."

Of course, such words as "high-quality merchandise" are relative when you sell cigarettes in bulk or liquor in volume or what had to be described as "junk food and junk drinks" in large package sizes. Sol was not about to deny his customers what they wanted to buy. If it was legal, he'd sell it, regardless of whether it is "good" for them or "bad" for them, or "good" for the environment or "bad" for the environment. He wouldn't knowingly buy an inferior product in a product category. But merchandising at the lowest possible margin, consistent with making a profit, did have its reasonable limits.

As Sol and his son, Robert, walked and talked, they knew they had both tangible and intangible assets. Robert himself was no dittohead to his father. In fact, Sol gave Robert and his two colleagues the main credit for the original conception of their next and most successful business—the Price Club. Shaping the Price Club model as a wholesale business selling merchandise to small, independent businesses to allow thousands of these firms to, in effect, pool their buying power by shopping at the Price warehouse, did carve out a unique market. After all, consider the context. At that time, a dozen giant big-box "discount" stores were expanding rapidly—Walmart, Target, Kmart, Home Depot, Office Depot, etc. The Prices were looking for a niche that could expand into a giant enterprise that stayed one or two giant steps ahead of any would-be imitators.

At the same time, Sol was expanding his philanthropic work, for which he had uncanny, but not always perfect, judgment. He took notice of a young professor of law, Robert Fellmeth, who was becoming one of the two most effective child advocates in the country. Sol and Helen Price endowed a chair in public interest law for Fellmeth at the University of San Diego School of Law. Sol would take long Sunday morning walks with Fellmeth, who soon asked him, in 1987, for funds to create a Children's Advocacy Institute (CAI) at the law school. Soon thereafter, The Price Charitable Fund provided a grant for the CAI, which became spectacularly productive and successful with groundbreaking reports, lawsuits, regulatory protections, and legislation advancing the health, safety, and economic rights of California's vulnerable children.

A few years later, I was meeting with Sol and Helen, where I told them that I had never seen such productivity and outcomes emanating from a small institute with a budget not exceeding $500,000 a year. Fellmeth, having been, from 1970 to 1971, one of our earliest and finest "Nader's Raiders" in Washington, authoring immense reports that resulted in books and actual changes, was a prodigious worker—the kind that the Prices must admire.

"Fellmeth is spreading himself too thin," groused Sol. "He should focus on fewer subjects." I joked that such a comment was ironic coming from the head of a business selling 3,000 different products. Then I added that Fellmeth was a systemic thinker and doer and knew that there were many parts to justice for children that were interconnected. He also knew that the whole was greater than the sum of its parts. Sol's adamant position on spreading oneself too thin had global consequences. For, at the time, he led and controlled the board of the Weingart Foundation—a result of a bequest from a former business colleague, Ben Weingart, who was a successful real-estate developer. Fellmeth proposed the establishment of children advocacy centers all over the Third World and had already made contacts in India, and other countries in Africa and South America. He would need around $21 million, a fraction of the Weingart Foundation's ample assets. In addition to not sharing Fellmeth's vision for expansion, Sol felt pressure to put a conservative businessman on the Foundation's board, such as Harry Volk, a former banker, John Gurash, a former insurance executive, and Robert Anderson, former CEO of Atlantic Richfield. He was outnumbered by board members who did not at all share his progressive policies.

The Foundation proceeded to focus largely on giving grants to local charities in San Diego and Los Angeles counties. The grants were in the range of $5 to $10 million a year in San Diego County alone. These charities were mainly traditional, needy ones, helping the poor and deprived. They were not out to take on or reshape powerful forces generating injustice through solid litigation and legislative initiatives, much less the production of enabling reports, all Fellmeth specialties. Price ended up losing control of the board. And Fellmeth lost his grand vision for the world's children fortified by his robust get-it-done expansive mind.

On February 13, 1976, the Price Company, the parent company

of what would eventually become 100 giant Price Clubs in less than two decades, was chartered in California. With only $2.5 million in equity and a $4 million loan from the Bank of America, Sol Price, Robert Price, and a tiny number of other experienced stalwarts got underway. The novel feature was the $25 club annual membership fee by the small business owners for wholesale cash-and-carry purchases. The first Price Club opened in July 1976, in a 102,000 square-foot former warehouse in the Rose Canyon area of San Diego.

In June 1976, Sol, well known in the community, sent a letter to most businesses in San Diego presenting the business model that would help small businesses compete with the large discount stores. He said that the Price Club would "substantially increase your business and profits at no risk and without any capital." He promised lower prices on the merchandise and supplies they sold without more capital. They would save time previously spent talking to salesmen, ordering, and waiting for goods to arrive. He pledged that whether you bought one or 100, the price would be the same—there would be no price increase because you didn't buy in quantity.

At the time, this was a singular merchandising concept, so singular that most of the responses were, "maybe, when you open, will come have a look and will see," an underwhelming response. By the end of the first week that July, sales, expected to be $200,000 per week, were only $30,000. What was going wrong? The "Six Rights" were all being violated—starting with the product selection; the Prices had assumed, for example, that hardware and variety stores would be major buyers when, in fact, there weren't many such stores in the city. Changes were made, step-by-step, and meetings were held with the new category of customer—the purchasing managers of government agencies. Then another barrier was broken with the decision to start selling to area credit union members. Monthly losses turned into break-even periods by November, and, by January, the first Price Club had nearly 13,000 full memberships. The group sales were outpacing the wholesale member sales. From then on it was an even higher arc of sales, profits, and more new stores.

His son, Robert, explained:

> Price Club was the product of Sol's brilliant business acumen and of everything that he had experienced and learned at FedMart. Whether selling automobile tires, institutional packs of toilet paper and detergent or office supplies, the Price Clubs limited the offerings to 3,000 items compared to 50,000 items in typical discount stores. The prices were overall far less than prices (an amazing 11.7% mark-up) available elsewhere, while treating their employees better than elsewhere. Price's brilliance delivered a 9% total operating expense and about $1,000 of sales per square foot—figures far better than was achieved at FedMart. It got better. By the end of the fiscal year in 1981, Price Club's accounts payable-to-inventory ratio has increased to over 120%. In short, Price Club's suppliers were financing the Price Club's company's business.

It was one innovation after another—for example, free lunch sampling was introduced to teach members about new products.

In 1982, The Price Company was listed on NASDAQ, and its stock shot up. The same year, the company missed an opportunity to quickly expand its stores around the country. A Seattle businessman called to ask whether he could enter into a franchise agreement. Harking back to the "problem franchisees" in the FedMart days, the Prices decided to say "no." They could go into the Seattle market themselves. So the businessman raised some capital and hired Jim Sinegal as CEO of the new Costco, which opened its first warehouse in 1982. Eleven years later, in 1993, the Price Clubs merged their US and Canada stores with the fast-growing Costco and the Prices concentrated on real estate deals and opening up warehouse stores in Mexico and the Caribbean. Those were the years that imitative competition came from Sam's Club (Walmart) and later Home Depot and Office Depot, whose founders—including Sam Walton—all visited a willing Sol to learn and apply his knowledge on their return. Sol realized the importance of competition for the consumer and the economy. How many big businessmen had that open air attitude? In the late 1990s, Sol told me he wasn't as much interested in making money as he used to be. He was clearly worried about the state of the country, the poverty, the seedy politics, and the lack of leadership everywhere. He saw the huge disparities between wealth and impoverishment everywhere, no less than in his own city of San Diego. I supposed also that his business experience became less of a challenge right down to how meticulously clever he was in demanding proper aisle width in his stores and maximum piling up of merchandise so customers can reach them. "Been there, done that," seemed to be what he was conveying.

Sol was always involved in supporting Democratic Party candidates—starting with Adlai E. Stevenson's two failed tries at the presidency against Dwight D. Eisenhower. He was active in the campaign of Edmund G. "Pat" Brown (Governor Jerry Brown's father) for the governorship of California, which Brown won. He was a John F. Kennedy supporter. His practical bent led him to refuse to consider third-party candidates closer to his views on the country's direction. It helps that he abhorred the Republican Party, then-California Senator Richard M. Nixon and his redbaiting, utter disregard for civil liberties and fair play against his opponents. So I was only mildly surprised when my friend, Sol Price, put a quarter-page ad in the *Los Angeles Times* against my presidential campaign in 2000, listing all the social safety-net programs that would be in jeopardy if, as he saw it, I took enough votes away from the Democrats to affect the race.

In an earlier conversation in Washington, I noted that Norman Thomas, the six-time Socialist Party candidate for the presidency, managed to push Franklin D. Roosevelt to adopt some of the Socialist Party's long-time agendas, such as Social Security, unemployment compensation, and stronger regulation of the banks. Yet Norman Thomas, a tall patrician-looking graduate of Princeton University, never got more than 1 or 2 percent of the vote. The problem with this Democratic Party, I observed, is that instead of being nudged by the Green Party, it started to seriously harass their candidates off the ballot in state after state and violate their civil rights. There was no moving Sol. For in his mind, it was all about his arithmetic—every vote for the Greens had to be a vote away from the Democrats. No nuances about the Electoral College, the ability of the Democrats to adopt some of the Green Party's "New Deal" type policies—such as a higher minimum wage or universal health insurance—to diminish what few votes the Greens were attracting and bringing out far more voters who were staying home. It was, to Sol, all about stopping the Republicans and not about pushing the Democrats—to my mind a least worst approach that has only made both parties worse every four years by Sol's own standard.

In that 2000 election, when Albert Gore won the national popular vote, the result was decided by the antidemocratic Electoral College and the multiple GOP shenanigans in Florida. This process was topped off by the GOP justices on the US Supreme Court.

Sol and Helen did not seek publicity for their political or charitable contributions. Politically, even though a very loyal Democrat, Sol was seen as a maverick, and outsider, especially on the "third rail" of Israel's domination of the Palestinian people and their shrunken lands. Although Sol always contributed to Jewish community charities in San Diego, he was not a financial supporter of Israel. Having struck up a friendship with Teddy Kollek, the mayor of Jerusalem, with whom he had exchanges of disagreement, Sol answered one of Kollek's pleas for funds this way in 1987:

> I am involved in trying to get a dialogue going between Palestinians and Israelis. In addition, I am trying to determine how best to give some economic aid to Palestinians so that they can develop some economic independence. More important, I am trying to make it respectable to discuss openly, in the Jewish and non-Jewish community, different approaches, including discussions with the PLO, without being tainted as anti-Semitic, anti-Israel or anti-American.

He continued these exchanges with Mayor Kollek in numerous unpublished letters.

In succeeding years, Sol did fund scholarships for five Arab Israelis to attend Tel Aviv University's law school, also a preschool program for Arab-Israeli teachers and parents at Al-Qasemi College and other assistance for Arab youth to receive training in occupational skills. Sol's impressive trait is that he was not partisan with his opposition to injustice; he could not abide by injustice from any perpetrator, including the Israelis. That took considerable moral courage given where his Zionist peers in the United States stood, and how they reacted both personally and in the business world.

Always out for the underdog—he experienced the dire conditions of so many millions of Americans in the Great Depression— he began to focus on the poor in San Diego.

In the early 1990s, after the heartrending death of his

fourteen-year-old grandson, Aaron, from brain cancer, the Price
Family Charitable Fund made a launching grant to San Diego
Hospice to provide financial pediatric assistance to families for
end-of-life hospice support. Later, another grant went to help
establish a new brain tumor research center at the University of
California, San Francisco, where Aaron was treated. So deep was
the Prices' grief over Aaron's loss that they established the ongoing,
living tribute called the "Aaron Price Fellows Program" for high
school students Aaron's age that would involve active experience in
exercising civic responsibility. The first year of the fellows program
drew fifty-four diverse students from ninth grades in San Diego.
Over the next three years, they were treated to a wide variety of experiences, including a rigorous five days at a campsite in the nearby
mountains and behind-the-scenes programs at hospitals and other
community organizations. After their junior year in high school,
the students were flown to Washington, D.C., for a week of intensive interactions with official and civic leaders. I was pleased to
be asked to spend time with the fellows at Sol's request. Sol made
sure the fellows program was well staffed and he stayed closely in
touch with it.

Always looking for philanthropy that "works and lasts and
builds on its achievements," Sol wanted to continue giving away
much of his wealth, citing Andrew Carnegie's dictum, "The man
who dies rich . . . dies disgraced." Like other enlightened affluent people, Sol believed it was a lot easier to make money than to
make the effective decisions in giving it away. Strange, how over
the years I have confronted just the reverse—that is, the paucity of
available monies for large numbers of recommended changes for
bettering society. As noted, Sol himself had two great proposals
that would have benefited by funding advocacy groups. He wanted
a wealth tax and to reform the grand jury. As a lawyer with a keen
sense of the need to work on power shifts to open the door for

considering and possibly adopting such reforms, Sol just chose not to start specialized civic groups. Instead, in 1993, at age seventy-seven, while overseeing Price Enterprises, the real estate business, and serving on the Weingart Foundation Board, he started his most ambitious transformation.

The poor City Heights section of San Diego, with over 70,000 residents, reflected intractability. He wanted to transform this inner-city neighborhood. Earlier in 1986, Sol had launched GatewayMarketplace, which was a retail complex in southeast San Diego. Working with an Economic Development Corporation, Sol conditioned his commitment by insisting on a "College of Retailing" on the second floor above the store. High school drop-outs could attend the College of Retailing, get retail work experience in the store below and prepare themselves to find jobs in the retail trade. The College of Retailing worked well. It was located on the same property as one of the Price Club locations. After the Costco/Price Club merger, the College of Retailing relocated and continued operations under the name Sol Price Scholars Program for many years. The educational component of the program was transferred to the San Diego Community College. Students continued to have work opportunities while they attended school. Gateway was converted to a Price Club. So, City Heights became the place where Sol's many entrepreneurial talents and experiences could engage in the sort of complex social innovation required for such a challenge. City Heights was a heavily immigrant neighborhood, with substandard housing, poor, deficient public services, high unemployment, and street crime. The level of detailed attention Sol brought to the task and his ability to mobilize resources and convene public officials and neighborhood leaders was beyond impressive. Here is one example: Sol wished to accelerate building a new police station that a city program, short of funds, would have taken four or five years to complete. As a condition for the loan, Sol asked for and got three changes made to the plans. First was for the city to build a gymnasium next to the station where police officers and community residents would meet and get to know each other in a recreational setting. Second, the city had to provide public meeting rooms for the community to use. Third, the police station had to have windows facing a major street running in front of the proposed police station.

The second agreement with the city involved a large, vacant parcel of land just across the street from the proposed police station. This redevelopment project became known as the Urban Village—to include a recreation center, a public library, a black box theater, a park, office space, and a Head Start preschool. The Urban Village was a $65 million investment from the city of San Diego, the Weingart Foundation, and the Price Family Charitable Fund. No one walked away from this plan. The Urban Village was completed in 1996 with Sol Price—the social innovator—enthusiastically present at the opening ceremonies.

Think of all the details, the meetings, the factions, and the personalities clashing and then resolving differences, and through it all the patience of Sol Price weaving this project into reality. What historic entrepreneur, the transformer of the retail revolution, widely imitated and regaled, affluent and in good health, would have plunged into this beleaguered community under siege to make it a "community that retains its current residents and attracts new ones." Sol developed "The Wheel," a circular pie chart listing the requisites for a healthy community such as good schools, health facilities, safety, high-quality, affordable housing, and public amenities. Parcel by parcel the area became a place for office buildings, county townhomes, and a multilevel 400-car garage, which attracted a children's clinic, an urgent care center and got San Diego State University to assume oversight responsibility for the three local schools. He also sponsored collaborative projects of experiential learning by the professors and the college students in those schools. The City Heights Initiative is still a work in progress and is visited by other city and community redevelopers, as was FedMart by its start-up emulators.

In his last years, Sol took care, at their home, of his wife Helen, who was suffering from debilitating ailments. They had been married for seventy years when she passed away in 2008.

He was quite firm about not writing his autobiography or even cooperating with willing biographers.

After Sol Price passed away in 2009, his son Robert summed up his business achievements this way:

> Sol's retail success was grounded in an absolute commitment to bringing the best value to his customers. Just as importantly, he insisted on paying high wages and good benefits, including healthcare, to his employees. He had a real conscience satisfied only by giving the best deal he could to just about everyone.

> As a retail revolutionary, Sol's creative brilliance changed the way we shop, first with FedMart in 1954, the retail format copies by Walmart, Kmart and Target in 1962 and then with the Price Club, the warehouse club format adopted by Costco and Sam's Club in 1983.

Then Robert alludes to the downside: "Consumers have seen their purchasing power grow, but perhaps they have lost something important—the personal connection with their neighborhood retailers."

These small stores are now being wiped out by Amazon and Walmart. Sol Price tried to resolve a bit of this benefit-cost of his innovations by enabling small retailers to buy cheaper supplies and merchandise at the Price Club. But he must've known that a sense of cohesive community was being lost, because he displayed such a concern in the way he devised a resurging community known as City Heights.

Looking back on this retail pioneer, this rethinker, I've often wondered how Sol Price, in his prime, would have responded to the rise of the Amazon Goliath. Price Club merged with Costco in 1993. Jeff Bezos started his little online bookstore in 1994. Twenty years later, the big box store companies, especially Walmart, are trying to figure out how to stop the Amazon juggernaut that not only meets them head-on but continually moves into other fields of commerce beyond them. Like Sears trying to head off fast-rising Walmart, it seems that their efforts are too little too late.

Costco so far seems to be thriving because the Price model and mode of merchandising still holds true. Some of the big chain stores have gone bankrupt or are on the brink. Others—getting fewer and larger—are adjusting, in the words of the *New York Times*, "to match the ease and instant gratification of e-commerce shopping." Price's fiduciary principles with his workers and consumers, together with his uncanny sense of combining low margin with convenience in the stores and over e-commerce, have made Costco one of the few companies that headed off low-wage Amazon before it gained such domination directly and with its increasingly conflicted platforms.

All those who worked with and admired Sol Price at all levels of his business must appreciate Sol's foresight. Jeff Bezos himself could also have been thinking how lucky he was to have started his emptying-Main-Street business after Sol Price retired.

7

ROBERT TOWNSEND

CEO of AVIS

The telephone rang one evening in the hall of my landlady's boarding house in Washington, D.C. I picked up the phone and heard
two gentlemen say they were from New York and wanted to speak
with me. "Go ahead," I said. Robert Townsend and Donald Petrie
were on the other line. It was in the tumultuous year—1968. They
described themselves as businessmen who had just read a feature article in *The Wall Street Journal* about my taking on General
Motors and other big businesses without even having a secretary.
Townsend specifically asked whether this "no secretary" was true.
I said, "Yes, I neither needed nor wanted one." They both chuckled
appreciatively and said they wanted to support my work, which
was receiving some national media and Congressional attention.
If they came down to D.C., would I have dinner? This was not a
usual happening, to say the least, but my incipient suspicion went
away as their jocular authenticity came through.

Over a fish dinner, they explained how much they liked my
"Lone Ranger" approach to overcoming bad corporate deeds.

Townsend had recently left after three years as a CEO, turning around Avis Rent-A-Car with the famous slogan, "We're Number Two, We Try Harder." His was an iconoclastic, no-nonsense, humane way of motivating company workers. Petrie was a lively investment banker at Lazard Frères & Co. and a longtime friend and collaborator with Townsend at Avis. Their discussions and views about the corporate world showed they were free thinkers. Then came the proposal. They would give me $100,000 to support my work, with two stipulations. That I not hire a secretary and that I never report back to them about what their donation was used for. In today's dollars, that was about $700,000. I agreed. They flew back to New York.

Townsend would call about other things on his mind, and one of them was his thinking about writing a book. Not any book, but a book of his pithy insights on breaking up a corporate bureaucracy and getting things done with enjoyment. That book came out in 1970 as *Up the Organization: How to Stop the Corporation from Stifling People and Strangling Profits*. It was a raging twenty-eight-week *New York Times* bestseller and continues to sell to this day as a manual on being a leader.

At Avis, he practiced what he later preached. As soon as he became CEO, he dropped the personal secretary, had no "assistants," answered his own telephone, made his own calls, and invited customers to call him directly if they had any complaints.

It's not clear when he became the open iconoclast, the unsettler of settled, smug ways of running an organization from the top down. He graduated from Princeton in 1940, served as an officer in the Navy during World War II, and attended the Columbia University Business School before working as a stockbroker. In 1949, he went to work for American Express, becoming Vice President of Investments and International Banking Operations of Hertz American Express until 1962, when Lazard Frères acquired Avis. Lazard's top boss, Andre Mayer, asked him to be the CEO of Avis in 1962 at a $50,000 annual salary. He insisted that he be paid $36,000 "because that's the top salary for a company that has never earned a nickel for its stockholders." He set the example quickly. He honed his irreverent sense while spending fourteen years at American Express. He described the company as "rich enough to do—and did—almost everything wrong. In that near-perfect learning environment, I formed a valuable habit of observing what action was taken, considering the *opposite* course, and then working back, when necessary, to what really made sense."

Some of his former colleagues didn't appreciate what they called his smart-aleck attitude there. "If we did so badly while he was here, why did we do so well when he left?" an exasperated senior official at American Express told a reporter. There is no record of a Townsend response, if any. But what he might have said, based on his writings, would be that he was talking about the larger corporate culture and more yardsticks of stifled potential than any increase in profits that may have been due to external economic conditions beneficial to this international company.

Townsend didn't get his back up when his blasts provoked outrage and rejoinders. To him, it was like bursting a boil—a necessary precondition for corporate bureaucrats looking at themselves in the mirror. What he could not stand was censorship, whether within the corporate institution or by the mass media. After appearing on Johnny Carson's *The Tonight Show* in the early 1980s, where he criticized NBC management, the network banned him. (NBC took years of criticism from the press before my getting on *The Tonight Show*.) It wasn't Johnny's decision; it was upstairs in executive suites or maybe even higher at the executive offices of NBC's owner, the giant General Electric Company. Townsend was always calm and unperturbed, except for his robust laugh. He followed up his ban by putting out a larger version of his book, titled *Further Up the Organization* that became a nine-week bestseller.

The corporate wavemaker never made gobs of money, but the ways he made his wealth seemed always casual, low-key, and seemingly effortless. In 1978, he became a top consultant to 20th Century Fox, where his very talented daughter, Claire, worked. His task was to make the company workplace both fun and profitable—the two go together in many ways, he taught. He was also variously on the board or an investor and advisor to Leadership Directories, Inc., Dun & Bradstreet, IGT, and Radica Games.

Robert was not into motivational speeches. He cautioned about any such stage presentations. "The way forward is to create an environment where people motivate themselves. That cannot happen," he asserts, "without the top persons in a company going to the bottom level where sellers and buyers interact." This was just one of the lessons that Bob Davids, co-founder and then CEO of Radica Games, took when he succeeded, after three tries, to get Townsend on his board of directors. "I didn't want to lose people around, and Townsend finally gave me the language for what I call egalitarian leadership. In essence, I learned that I needed to subordinate myself to those I led. Your job as a leader is to get to the lowest level and find out what your people need . . . to get the job done. When we were starting up in China, the employees were shocked when I got down into a ditch with them to help build a drain."

Abstract corporate bosses fifteen levels (GM had twenty-two levels in 1970) removed from the "shop floor" or the sales counter can factually starve these overseers into a reckless level of unfeeling ignorance. It could lead to bad outcomes when all the reports sent upstairs are monetized with charts and graphs. Large companies often get into deep trouble or go over the cliff when the corporate culture becomes overly bureaucratic, and CEOs lose touch with the nuts-and-bolts operations of their companies. It is an invitation for constructing a wall, called "deniability," when governmental inquests start looking for responsibility. Ask General Motors, VW, and Toyota how it happened to their bosses. General Motors CEO Mary Barra admitted that her company's delay in recalling cars with faulty ignition switches, linked to hundreds of deaths and injuries, was caused by a "pattern of incompetence and neglect." Abstract leadership has consequences.

One day years ago at a large luncheon gathering in Washington dealing with corporate ethics, I was sitting next to the CEO of Armco Steel. I started chatting about blue-collar workers. He volunteered that at a recent meeting of his board of directors, he took them way down one of the company's coal mines. They were wide-eyed with astonishment and didn't want to stay very long before returning to their comfortable boardroom. I asked him what their impressions were, once they had returned to open ground and looked up at the sky. He smiled and said, "Well, let's put it this way, they won't ever say again that coal miners are overpaid." That appreciation is what may be expected by going down where the workers generated the wealth.

In that period, just before the internet, I became dissatisfied with the long hold times that callers endured on airlines reservations lines. A recording would come on and say how important our business was to the airline and that they'd get right back to us after they take care of earlier callers. Wait, wait, wait while recorded music played. Sometimes half an hour. So I put in a call to the CEO of US Airways, who had gotten rich being the CEO of United Airlines. To his credit, he took the call, and I explained my problem, adding that at least I had my choice of music, at United Airlines classical music and at American Airlines New Age, but at US Airways all I got were promotional ads luring me to some Caribbean paradise. He laughed and said, not being close to the situation—his own reservations were made by staff from his office—he would get back to me. He wanted to make his own anonymous calls to confirm my experience. Less than a month later, we spoke, and he said each time he called he, too, was put on hold for an intolerable period of time. He was hiring 250 more telephone operators to fix the problem. That is what happens when CEOs go to the ground level, which they rarely do without provocations like Townsend's.

Some readers of "Townsendisms" could get the impression that his advice is part off the cuff and part reflective of his own business experience. This is not entirely correct. Townsend had lots of conversations with close business friends, like Donald Petrie and Jerry Hardy. He read books on management, trying to eke out some useful morsels from the self-assured verbiage. Then he came upon his favorite, *The Human Side of Enterprise* by Douglas McGregor, who required that his Ph.D. students work every summer for a blue-collar manufacturer. He developed a theory of organizations under two headings—Theory Y and Theory X. Townsend translated them this way:

Dubious Theory X had three assumptions: (1) People hate to work. (2) They have to be driven and threatened with punishment to get them toward organizational objectives. (3) They like security, aren't ambitious, want to be told what to do, dislike responsibility.

Interestingly, this is what a reflective slaveholder of a large cotton plantation in America's South might have attributed to his slaves. As labor becomes freer or at least had choices of workplaces, Theory Y kicks in accordingly, as described by Townsend:

People don't hate work. It's as natural as rest or play.

They don't have to be forced or threatened. If they commit themselves to mutual objectives, they'll drive themselves more effectively than you can drive them.

But they'll commit themselves only to the extent they can see ways of satisfying their ego and development needs.

More than a few of Townsend's advisories read like aphorisms, maxims, or adages. Brevity, however, was one of his insistences. He required that any problem within a company be stated on one page only. "If the writer couldn't do that, then he or she doesn't understand the problem," he declared. He despised policy or personnel manuals of any kind. They indicated failure of activity from leadership at the top that generates excellence all the way down to the selling floors. He once said, half factually: "If you have to have a policy manual, publish the Ten Commandments." (He might have been more precise if he simply said The Golden Rule). Adding this great insight: "One of the most important tasks of a manager is to eliminate his people's excuses for failure." Bureaucracies work, in just the opposite manner, to deflect blame on others either up or across the organizational charts. There should be no confusion. His writings are about the primary role of top management. As Professor James O'Toole observed: "It is often said that Peter Drucker invented management; if so, Robert Townsend invented leadership."

The recurring theme of his practice of leadership is to lead by example—visibly and tangibly and consistently. So, immediately, as CEO of Avis, he abolished reserved parking spaces, organizational charts, job descriptions, groveling to demanding, short-term Wall Street analysis, company planes, golf club memberships, long meetings or long conference calls, the P.R. Department, Personnel Department, and loads of vice presidents for this and that. You get the sense that he wanted people at the top with vision, honesty, and courage enough to want to get followers turning themselves into leaders. That pattern is called "de-management"—insinuating

self-reliant initiatives at all levels, implementing the virtue of putting consumers' trust at the top.

He had reasons for making or urging the structural "firings."
Here, for example, is his take on "The Personnel Department." "The
trouble with the personnel experts is that they use gimmicks borrowed from manufacturing inventories, replacement charts, recruiting, selecting, indoctrinating and training machinery, job rotation,
and appraisal programs . . . As McGregor points out, the sounder approach is <u>agricultural</u>. Provide the climate and proper nourishment
and let the people grow themselves. They'll amaze you." Whether
out of the forces put in motion from Townsend's declarations or
not, contemporary entrepreneurs, interviewed in large numbers by
former *New York Times* columnist Adam Bryant, revealed that they
considered the best use of their time to be *direct* interviewing of
needed people with questions that are anything but bureaucratic.

It is probable that some of the anger mixed with fascination
with Townsend by the entrenched corporatist stemmed from his
"upper class" pedigree. He should have stayed being one of them,
damn it, they must have fumed, as Townsend's talk show appearances for his book portrayed the absurdity of their pompous sine-
cure. After all, his family goes back to the American Revolution,
where ancestor Townsend was the "Intelligence" Advisor to George
Washington. He went to a private boarding school, Princeton
University (then mostly composed of preppies), and then onto Wall
Street and investment banking. It was said of the Townsends that
the Depression was when his family fired the gardener. The trust
funds for his five children were inherited originally from his immediate forebears. He came out of the Establishment, complete
with a large country house on Long Island. He strove to speak to
the business establishment whenever they wanted to retain him
as a lecturer at their conventions or annual meetings. (Soon we'll
review one such "professional" presentation at the prestigious

and powerful Conference Board, composed of presumably more thoughtful business executives.)

Any profile of Robert must not ignore his sense of fun and humor. He had to have fun working in all ways. He played hard at sailing, fishing, golf, and tennis. He had to laugh a lot at the absurdities of business life, and where the country is hurtling toward, and his own mirthful observations. He was a believer that "in humor there is truth." Here is one frequently quoted sample:

> Directors are usually the friends of the chief executive put there to keep him safely in office. Be sure to serve cocktails and a heavy lunch before the [board] meeting. At least one of the older directors will fall asleep (literally) at the meeting and the whole consequent embarrassment will make everyone eager to get the whole mess over as soon as possible . . . In the years that I've spent on various boards, I never heard a single suggestion from a director (made as a director at a board meeting) that produced any results at all.

Of course, as was his practice, he went on to provide details to make sure that his summary not be considered flippant. He could not stand rubber-stamp members of the board of directors, selected, wined and dined, and lucratively paid for their few hours a year flipping through their big briefing books and nodding their assent to the CEO and president's recommendations. Where was the heavy dissent on behalf of the shareholders, against self-dealing, and bad products and services that these corporate governors were supposed to be overseeing? He believed in "no outside directorships and trusteeships for the chief executive . . . You can't even run your own company, dummy." He ridiculed professional directors, who show up pro forma on twelve corporate boards and contribute to none of them.

From time to time, I would have dinner with Bob when he was in Washington, D.C., running, for no pay, the *Congressional Monitor* business and the *Leadership Directories*, which published directories of institutions, such as trade associations. He did have an equity interest in this business, which rolled over their profits every year to invest and expand the reach of this enterprise. He always spoke of serious topics, often satirically garnished, with a smiling visage. He wore his personality and its twinkling, patrician expression on his face. Patrician because it exuded a confident skepticism.

Now to the book that defined his legacy. He insisted to his illustrious publisher and editor, Robert A. Gottlieb of Alfred A. Knopf, Inc., that the title be *Up the Organization* unless Gottlieb could come up with a better one. Gottlieb couldn't and reluctantly went with the little title he did not think would work. But it sure did. The book sold 300,000 hardback copies in a few months. Reviewing it in the *New Yorker*, John Brooks called it a purported "manual for business bosses in the form of a sort of encyclopedia, its 97 chapters consisting of entries, under alphabetically arranged headings, which range in length from a couple of lines to 9 or 10 pages each. It adds up to a stimulating, irritating, entertaining, wildly uneven book that ought to be of interest to business watchers as well as participants."

It *was* uneven. He covered a lot of ground, often with more than one use of each letter in the alphabet. But he had to skip "Q" and "Z." Finding topics for letters in the alphabet makes for a strained exercise. By and large, however, he pulled it off and in a humorous, satiric way—it kept the reader's attention and anticipation.

Most of the articles about Townsend, during 1970, the year that *Up the Organization* was published, were pretty redundant and soon predictable. One that was distinctly different was a *Life*

Magazine feature written by William A. McWhirter, who had an eye for detail and nuance.

Here is his quick take on "The 'Up the Organization' Man":

> Townsend is at once a seriously involved and whimsically displaced figure. [He] now has gone to war against his former life and his fellow men at the top, against, of course, much of what he instinctively remains. He has become an entire generation gap onto himself . . . It may only be the spongy soles of the boots, but there is a goofy, high bounce to his walk that suggests a distracted, inner amusement. The face is not set in place, but rather runs on like a tanned waterfall of cascading pouches, lines and wrinkles. When he laughs, the upper lip curls as if struggling to swim upstream.

McWhirter described Townsend's book as a "breezy, A-to-Z business manual against the foibles of organization life . . . like a depth charge meant to blow the whole game up . . . When people ask Townsend if he's kidding in the book, he insists he's serious, and when they ask him why it's so funny, he says because things are so hopeless. 'The whole country,' he warns, 'looks like the sum of its original parts—sloppy, lethargic, fat, over the hill.'"

It is not surprising that as an admirer of Kurt Vonnegut Jr.'s mordant novels, Townsend sees the absurdity of the bureaucratic tiers at the top of large companies. He quit Avis after ITT, a vast conglomerate, bought it and brought its "soul-destroying" (a favorite word) corporate culture of charts and executive titles to this spirited, informal workplace. He couldn't stand all the titles—

VP for this, VP for that, assistant VP, deputy assistant,
special assistant to the senior director for that—blah, blah,
blah—top-heavy, swollen, pompous, self-regarding make-
work, very heavy network of monied men compulsorily
paid by their disappointed shareholders. Fraudulent, wasteful and, for those employees who do the actual work, the
climate lets them contribute only 20% of their capacity.

Townsend calls for a genuine corporate morality flowing from
"Judeo-Christian precepts and you grit your teeth when they seem
to go against your own interest. These moments will be more
than offset by your overall ability to be honest and moral about
your decision."

Adding a practical judgment, he notes that when a fair system
becomes more efficient, which includes paying people who do the
work fairly, the benefits cascade throughout the company and its
products. He admitted such homilies won't affect the bosses now
at the top, but he hopes to reach the "younger men who are highly
concerned about what these organizations are doing to their environment and their country . . . and not take the money and go
to sleep."

He thinks CEOs shouldn't stay more than six years, after
which they become "stale, bored, and utterly dependent on [their]
own clichés—though they may have been revolutionary when he
first brought them."

He told McWhirter what he would advise General Motors, the
technologically stagnant giant automaker selling millions of motor
vehicles for great profits. GM, one might say, had come a long way
profitably without Townsend's advice.

Rather than paraphrase, here is what he would have General
Motors say in a letter to its consumers:

We didn't realize until very recently what we were doing from the standpoint of air pollution and we're sorry we were so slow, but we're going to do better. For the next two years we are going to spend $450 million a year on this problem and we are going to develop a viable internal-combustion engine with no patents to anyone. We're in a crisis. This is our contribution. We're trying to save lives, our lives and your lives. We're sorry. And then I would tell our people they have only two years and that we weren't going to have any more style changes until this problem was licked. I would tell them to get out if they didn't believe in what we were to do or honestly give every bit of their talent to make sure we did it. Our stock might get clobbered, but I would buy the ass off it all the way down, because we were going to have the first comparable invention since 1874 and our stock would then go through the roof.

He infuriated business executives, including those who liked him personally. "Never mind the details, Bob," one exclaimed. Only two years later and $450 million a year to get this revolutionary transformation? Is he crazy? Environmentalists would say, wrong engine, that eternal, infernal, internal combustion engine. We need electric cars or something entirely new. Townsend transcends such commentary, saying at least he has them talking about such a momentous transition away from killer smog. As a jolter he would have started succeeding in shaking up the frozen complacency of a very harmful industry.

As usual, the perceptive Peter F. Drucker, the preeminent author and advisor on business management, caught just what Townsend is about. And he did it with brilliant, informed concision. He described Townsend:

as singularly innovative, singularly trenchant, completely straight and unafraid. He doesn't give a hoot for
management theory or good administration so much as
how to motivate people. He won't go down in history as
one of the great entrepreneurs, hell no; one of the great
managers, hell no; great administrators, hell no; he is an
incidental figure, but a very colorful one. He is not one
of the great generals, but a great guerilla leader, which
is harder.

"Completely straight," all right. He didn't have to tell McWhirter
about some of his five children's difficulties in their late teens and
twenties, concluding: "I ignored the hell out of my kids when
they were younger. I was a disaster as a father, and I take full
responsibility for everything they do."

Critics of Townsend pointed out that many of his wise nug-
gets could not be applied literally in daily business activity. Apart
from the ones dealing with honesty, integrity, candor, they might
have a point. Townsend's "sayings" are meant to *inform* judgment,
stimulate productive relationships, *lead* to accountability, not create these behaviors. He wanted to motivate people to want them
on their own terms and ambitions. That is probably the understanding that led the American Management Association and
the Wharton School for Leadership and Change Management to
put *Up the Organization* on the top list of "books every manager
must read."

MIT professor Warren Bennis put out a new edition of
Townsend's book in 2007 with some commentary by his publisher
and some younger business executives that were turned around by
his insights. In his introduction, Bennis offered some of his favorite Townsendisms.

– "Secrecy: A Child's Garden of Diseases."

– "Call yourself up. When you are on a business trip or a vacation, pretend you're a customer. Telephone some part of your organization and ask for help. You'll run into some real horror shows. Then try calling yourself up and see what indignities you built into your own defenses."

[I might add that this would be a very useful exercise for elected state and Congressional politicians, especially in an impersonal internet and voicemail age. R.N.]

– "True leadership must be for the benefit of the followers, not the enrichment of the leaders."

The latter illustrates aphoristic writing that can sound like obvious clichés to many from afar, but they are written for exactly the kind of lagging leaders Townsend had in mind.

Another caveat with such "shotgun strokes," is that they can be both true and false depending on the company. For example, Townsend writes: "Big successful institutions aren't successful because of the way they operate, but in spite of it. They didn't get to the top doing things the way they're doing them now." This certainly doesn't operate at Amazon, now in its twenty-ninth year of the same aggressive, take no prisoners, exploit one's workers, bully one's public officials on sales taxes way of selling. Jeff Bezos got to dominate the online selling business by doing what he's always done, then or now.

This is the way one can take apart maxims that have stood the test of centuries and still get repeated every generation, even when they are facially contradictory. Such as "Look before you leap," vs.

"He who hesitates is lost." All this does not capture the main point, which is that when pithy words and phrases that get you thinking and acting have served their less than cosmic mission—they've done their job. In Townsend's case, they cut through the fog of bureaucratic memos, delusionary charts and graphs, evasive rationalizations for self-dealing, self-perpetuation, and loss of human potential for the greater good.

Some of Townsend's chapters are so specific that they are now significantly dated. One is "Incentive Compensation and Profit-Sharing/Over-Time," which was written before executive compensation went through a dozen roofs (even adjusted for inflation), before executive stock option manipulations, before massive stock buybacks, and before clever gaming by the executives' outside compensation advisers. These differences also apply to workers who read his sequel, *Further Up the Organization.* He has much to say about union officials, the civil service, and professors. Unionism, say the most idealistic leaders, has deteriorated into a kind of industrial police force that also sells insurance. The labor movement is now a conservative bureaucracy that resists the creative change of the good manager.

Now that really is too sweeping. What would millions of non-unionized adjunct professors, barely making minimum wage from their colleges and universities, say about not needing a union? What about tens of millions of Walmart-type workers and their mistreatments? Later, Townsend concedes that a company can avoid a union by treating people well and if the company already has unions, "then deal with them openly and honestly." Importantly, he was an avid advocate of having workers become shareholders—"your people must be owners."

Townsend wrote in the best muckraking tradition about the big corporate "Sabotage of Free Enterprise." Hear him out:

It's not clear to me exactly when free enterprise became a joke. Was it after the Civil War, when big business, big government and the Supreme Court formed an unholy alliance to exploit the American farmer and laborer? Or was it later, when big labor got a partnership? Or when big military elbowed up to the trough? Or when big education cut itself in on the deal?

When the American system falls, it won't be Communists who bring it down. We aren't in any danger of being destroyed from the outside; we've perfected do-it-yourself methods.

A typical company agrees to indemnify its officers and directors. That is, if I'm sued and convicted as an officer of a drug company for knowingly letting a harmful drug murder or deform a few thousand people, my company will pay the $2,500 fine and legal expenses and deduct them from income (for tax purposes) as an ordinary business expense. (Judging by the Allison case, where a known defective airplane engine caused the death of 38 people, corporate manslaughter costs about $200 a head.)

So the government subsidizes murder.

He assailed "the double standard by which the law protects a corporate agent from the responsibilities normally weighed against a private citizen. If I shot my neighbor, chances are I'll be severely punished for my crime. But if, in my job, I am convicted of withholding information about a dangerous product that leads to the death of thousands of my neighbors, the most I'll get is a civil suit that amounts to a slap on the wrist."

Then he places a rarely focused responsibility on the corporate law firms who "have been working for years to preserve the myth (which their antecedents created) that criminal [law] doesn't apply to what I do as a corporate executive, that's covered by the civil code . . . This legal anomaly has led to all sorts of abhorrent corporate behavior . . . When the cops come, there is nobody home."

Continuing his rarely seen focus on the corporate lawyers, he adds: "It's no wonder you can't get senior partners of major law firms to work weekends. I simply sympathize with them. If I were doing to America what they are doing to it from 10 to 6, Monday through Friday, I'd have to get stoned on Saturday and Sunday, too."

In his later years, Townsend became, in his own way, more and more alarmed at the excesses of giant corporations and their top bosses. These embodiments of limitless greed and conflicts of interest between the top executive and their own corporate employees and powerless shareholders grew exponentially after Townsend passed away in 1998. CEO executive pay ranged from 350 to 500 more than the average employee wage in the twenty-first century's second decade. Until recently, Walmart's CEO made about $12,000 an hour, compared to his employees' wages of $10 an hour. But the avarice was showing itself with accelerating momentum even in 1984, which caused Townsend to recommend a rebalance.

Note his "No-No's" views on executive retirement security: "No pension plans for top people. Security is for people who don't have a chance to make it big. Above a certain level, you pick it, don't have pensions. Encourage your people to build their own security by building the company they own a piece of." It's not difficult to guess what he would say today to the huge double standard in pensions between the bosses and the workers, both in terms of gigantic payouts after retirement for executive suites and the looting and sometimes destruction of the workers defined benefit plans, as they are sometimes replaced by risky 401(k) plans.

To sugarcoat this greed and power come the image-makers whose task is to camouflage the ugly realities of loaded top management. Townsend lacerates this pompous vanity deception and expenditure. "The only image you should care about is the smile on the face of your customer as he enjoys your product or service. Or on the face of your stockholder as he scans the company profits."

One of Townsend's most celebrated speeches was before a conference of executives in the late seventies. He started off quite modestly: "I'm going to try to give all of you a Ph.D. in leadership." He would make a point—for example, "To hell with centralized strategic planning,"—and then provide an example or a personal story from his executive life. Another lesson from the "Leadership Kit" was "eliminating their excuses for doing lousy work." Or "fight the them-and-us lines that separate people in a company."

He gives an example that is shockingly quaint, compared to today's wild excesses of 350 to 500 ratios:

> One of the interesting lines in America is that the difference in salary between the CEO and the highest paid blue-collar worker is 36 to 1; in Japan it's 7 to 1. Now that's a them-us line that I think is hard to swallow, knowing what chief executives don't do for their companies.

Probably the most compelling advice to the assembled business executives was to go down to the counter or shop floor level and work there a bit as if you were a common laborer. He required the whole management at Avis to go through the rental agent school taught "by our finest rental agents, ladies in red uniforms, at O'Hare Airport." It was, he related, "an absolute condition of employment. We had to . . . spend two- or three-hours renting cars at the airport." The experience left them with far more sensitivity and respect for their workers.

Townsend was good at getting people's attention by saying who he would fire, as with his recommendation during that talk to "fire all your management consultants, all of them." Promise them a bonus if they will get off the premises by 5 p.m. and another if they won't submit a report. He then explained what he meant.

His technique: get their attention with a jolting conclusion, then back up to provide them with your rationale. It worked almost every time. Nearing the end of his presentation, he says,

"For the final part of your Ph.D., I'm going to tell you from my experience the *characteristics* of a leader . . . They come in all shapes and sizes and colors and sexes . . . You cannot recognize them physically. Charisma is not generally associated with a true leader, it is more associated with the opposite: the *corporate politician*, who is what is the matter with our country. There are too many of this type in our corner offices . . . Leaders have their *personal ambition under control*; they seem to get their kicks out of seeing their own people succeed and their own organization succeed. They are *visible* and *available* to their people and they are *good listeners* . . . He sees the best in his people, not the worst; he is not a scapegoat hunter. A good leader is simplistic, not complex. He makes things seem simple. He's persistent . . . He's fair and has a sense of humor and he has humility . . . I suppose the best way to tell a leader is, if you find a place where people are coming to work enthusiastically, and they are excited to come to work. Well, there's your Ph.D. in leadership. Good luck and God bless." [All emphasis in the original.]

In a memorandum to the reader on how to use *Up the Organization*, Townsend gets somber. People working in large organizations are trapped in the pigeonholes of organization charts, they have been slaves to the rules of private and public hierarchies that run mindlessly on and on because nobody can change them.

> So we've become a nation of office boys. Monster corporations like General Motors and monster agencies like the Defense Department have grown like a cancer until they take up nearly all of the living-working space. Like clergyman Anthony Trollope's day, we are but mortals trained to serve immortal institutions. This book is for those who have the courage, the humor, and the energy to make a non-monster company operate as if people were human. All you need is a talent for spotting the idiocies now built into the system.

People would always ask his friend, Donald Petrie, whether Townsend was serious. He would say resoundingly, "Yes." Townsend's editor, the former head of Alfred A. Knopf, Robert Gottlieb, explained:

> I believe the secret of the book's success was that everything Bob said and advised exactly reflected the way he behaved. His ideas were original, and they worked. His book is so provocative that it would be easy to label him a provocateur. In my view, however, he was a secular prophet—somebody who fervently preached exactly as he practiced. There is no room for hypocrisy in his writing or his life. Business fads come and go, but there will always be a need for such pure voices in the wilderness.

Although Townsend changed some ways in some companies and attracted some CEOs who practiced Townsend's approach to running their company, it must be recognized that what he warned about and reviled has, overall, gotten terribly worse in the marbled offices of giant corporations. It is as if these bosses—rich beyond the dreams of Croesus—have been delivering outrageous antonyms to his critiques and exhortations. Even he would not have predicted the demise of bureaucratically larded, smug General Motors into bankruptcy and subsequent extortion of a massive $50 billion government bailout on the basis that it was too big to fail. Just as were the large banks, brokerage firms, and other freeloaders engaging in criminal exploitation of "other people's money" during the collapse of Wall Street in 2007–2008 and the subsequent Washington bailout on the backs of the taxpayers.

Townsend never lived to endure the disgust of seeing the collapse of corporate capitalism's many pretenses and the supremacy of its prevarications. In 1991, he was diagnosed with heart disease that led to emergency triple bypass surgery. It slowed him down. In 1998, with his wife, Joan Tours, he chartered a boat in the Caribbean for a lengthy vacation. On the beautiful moonlit night of January 12 in Anguilla's harbor, sitting in a deck chair trading fishing stories with the captain, he slowly slipped away. That was probably the way he wanted to go—in a serene, natural environment, remote from all the corporate power plays, their hierarchies, crimes, waste, trivial and tragic intrigue, and denial of human possibilities for a better world. He was driven by how much better life on Earth could be, how much fun one could experience. Wake up "dummies," he often declared, with a half smile and twinkle in his eye.

In my conversations with him during his early seventies, I could sense a serious disappointment settling into his personality over corporate capitalism committing suicide because people did not matter first and foremost. His narration of best practices among some companies had fallen on deaf ears and minds.

Because he never asked, I did not tell him how I used the $100,000 that he and Petrie had donated. It started a nonprofit small foundation, without overhead, that has given over $2 million to a large variety of environmental, consumer, and other justice advocacy associations. It begat a new group called Essential Information that has done much good work. And by the way, I have not had a personal secretary since day one.

8

ANDY SHALLAL

CEO of Busboys and Poets

One Sunday, in the spring of 1987, on Washington, D.C.'s P Street, N. W., I spotted a change in the recovering neighborhood near a run-down, public outdoor basketball court. A sign on a nondescript three-story building that earlier was an old townhouse, spelled SKEWERS. A further look revealed a new Middle Eastern restaurant on the second floor. Its daily menu was posted at the sidewalk level near the outside stairs leading to a space with about ten tables, mostly empty. Little did I expect that from this humble beginning by Andy Shallal and his brother Tony—Iraqi immigrants as children—would expand to several bustling, D.C.-area restaurants. Each restaurant was of a different vintage, but all focused on also becoming community centers for artistic, civil, and political events, avoiding no controversial subjects and excluding no controversial participants.

After a number of adjustments and sales of his more conventional eateries, Shallal settled on a cluster of restaurants called "Busboys and Poets," taken from a poem by the Black Harlem

Renaissance poet, Langston Hughes. He chose what, in the 1960s, was considered the most dangerous street area of the nation's capital—14th Street and U Street, N.W.— known long ago as Washington's "black Broadway"; the area was gentrifying with white and black residents moving there.

Defying all conventions about what restaurants should be like, Andy Shallal (Tony by then had moved to other business fields) expanded on a similar model I suggested to him when he was running Skewers. Because of his vocal interest in public affairs and social tensions, I urged him to use the third floor to invite authors to discuss and sign their books. The famous professor and peace advocate Howard Zinn packed the place one evening.

At his first Busboys and Poets, Shallal created his now famously successful model—a tripartite arrangement comprising a dining area, a bookstore, and a room for civic events where people could also dine. All in one open architectural space with walls decorated with artist Andy's own murals and collages depicting the struggles for civil rights and other injustices.

The combination proved so irresistible to Washingtonians that Andy did not have to advertise from the first day of his opening nine restaurants in the D.C. area. This is how powerful word-of-mouth has been for this multiracial food-civic-artistic environment with higher-than-average pay and benefits for the cooking and serving corps who hail from multiracial backgrounds.

To the daily question—"Where is Andy?"—the answer had to be "Everywhere." He is an exceptional, all-functional talent. This tall, gregarious man moves, effortlessly, it seems, from designing his restaurants, to choosing suppliers of quality and frugality, to painting the walls with his artistic realisms, to bringing hostile groups together, to showcasing poetic talent from the black community, to feeding, for free, protesters for peace from out of town, to marching in front of the White House and Congress for various just causes, to risking arrest for nonviolent, open civil disobedience, to giving media interviews on "hot topics" of work fairness issues, to speaking out against the Bush/Cheney criminal invasion of Iraq—his ancestral land—to providing a venue for a presidential debate for Third Party presidential candidates, or the first debate ever on whether anti-Semitism against Jews is as prevalent as anti-Semitism against Arabs. (See: debatingtaboos.org)

He also managed to run for mayor of Washington, D.C., and later was named the chair of a city workforce council by the winner of that race, D.C. Mayor Muriel E. Bowser.

Those are just some of the groundbreaking roles assumed by Andy Shallal that caused me to give him the moniker "Democracy's Restaurateur." He has provided more voice and audiences to more excluded voices than any businessperson in the nation's capital by far. Shallal only knows the word "acceleration." He once told me that he is always looking to get out of his "comfort zones" and experience personal growth from new initiatives, new alliances, new ways to bring people together and have them experience new associations and awarenesses. Unlike most business entrepreneurs searching always for expansion and greater sales, Shallal is a Renaissance entrepreneur striving to erase sharp lines between business, community, and the wider world.

In one of his rare half-disingenuous moments, he even exclaimed: "I don't see myself as a businessman at all. I'm an activist and I happen to be in business." He hosted a weekly Monday morning show on WPFW (89.3 FM)—"the station for jazz and justice"—called *Business Matters,* on his work that explored "the intersection of business, passion and social responsibility." He invited guests who made a difference in their community, in the city and in the world by using business as a tool for social change. People who see the bottom line not just in dollar signs but in the impact they have on their society as a whole and on the environment.

With all his generosity and labor well-being, he always reminds those pressing for evermore "social" commitments that
he must make a profit, or he couldn't engage in all these other
collateral activities and services. Even when it pinches, he rarely
backs off, standing tall for the beliefs he and his staff champion.
Right after the inauguration of Donald Trump, immigrant workers planned a day-long strike, in mid-February 2017, across the
country. Some restaurants and schools went along with this demonstration against the new president's bigotry. It was called a "Day
Without Immigrants" boycott to show Mr. Trump the valuable
functions immigrants play every day in our country. Andy Shallal
closed all of his Busboys and Poets restaurants, taking a "huge
financial hit," to give his full-time and part-time employees paid
time off to participate in this proud public event.

It is not as if all his restaurant ventures have been unalloyed
successes. He sold off two restaurants in the DuPont Circle area
because they were not doing that well, and he wanted to transfer capital from the sales into his new locations. He replaced his
restaurant Eatonville, a southern cuisine eatery, with one called
Ancient Rivers, serving Arab cuisine. Eatonville did very well at
first but was slowing down toward the end of the lease period, and
Shallal wanted to try something new. High rent for this space
ultimately led to the closing of Ancient Rivers. But generally, giant condo developers in Washington, D.C., were offering him
ground floor space plus $500,000 to $3 million just to open in
their building and give their buildings added panache. Andy became wary of expanding his unique model too fast. He entertained
offers to build Busboys and Poets–type tripartite restaurants in
New York City's Harlem, near the Apollo Theatre, and in Denver's
former Rossonian Hotel, among other invitations. After prelimi-
nary temptations, he decided he couldn't spread himself that thin.

When I asked, "Well, why don't you franchise the model?" he replied that he didn't think anyone could replicate his model of multiple personal interfaces and controversy and still make a profit.

For a few years, Shallal engaged in international issues. After the Bush/Cheney invasion of Iraq in 2003, he created an event on Iraqi history and culture to educate the American people about an ancient land that Patti Smith chronicled in her song "Radio Baghdad"—"We gave you the zero and we mean *nothing* to you." He accepted a White House "good neighbor" trip to Cairo after the Arab Spring and was a constant participant in peace marches in the nation's capital. He worked for an end to the Iraq occupation by the United States and the occupation of Palestine by Israel— bringing partisans of these conflicts together for civil conversations in Washington, D.C.

These efforts produced few tangible policy results. Such demonstrations of conscience and knowledge are far removed from the power of decision-makers in government and elsewhere. It seems that in recent years, Shallal is directing his time and commitments to more hands-on local needs. With his restaurants and their almost daily civic events managed by his mostly minority managers, the ever-restless Iraqi American is focusing more on the racial divides, economic inequality, and the deep poverty that has long embarrassed the nation's capital with its plutocracy and oligarchy amassing ever more wealth and power and myopia. Gentrification is driving black residents from the District to the suburbs. Housing prices and rentals are out of sight. The public infrastructure—schools, roads, and water sewage mains—are always crumbling from deferred maintenance practices. While there is a black middle-class and some wealthy African Americans, Shallal knows that far too many African Americans are still locked out of all kinds of economic opportunities. He saw the shifting patterns of automation, shrinking public services, such as the Postal Service with its black personnel, and rising drug and other lethal addictions, taking a daily toll on the economic underclass.

Shallal has always known who he is, but he has always been puzzled and unsettled by the ways that some people, especially African Americans, view him. Back when he was in middle school in Virginia, students would ask, "Who are you?" Not black, not white, not southern, not northern, but of Middle Eastern background. It has caused him continuing frustrations, endless discussions, roundtables, fending off accusations that he uses black culture in his restaurants as a marketing tool for profits. Once at a small meeting he, I, and others had with the then D.C. Mayor, Vincent C. Gray, an African American, he held his arm next to Gray's and amusingly said, "Look, I'm more black than you."

It is a widespread irony in our country's civil rights struggles that minorities sometimes have a love/hate relationship with their most compassionate white activists. The complexity of such reactions did not escape Shallal. He has spent many years grappling with this paradox among his many black brothers and sisters, including fearful black-owned businesses about to be displaced by a Walmart or some other big box chain.

To illustrate the sensitivities, so unlike the more distant human relations grappled with by other CEOs in this book, consider this episode. On a busy weekday evening in February 2011, someone took away the life-size cutout of Langston Hughes in his busboy's uniform from the front of Andy's restaurant at 14th and V streets, N.W. A respected poet and photographer, Thomas Sayers Ellis, was apprehended as the taker. He explained he was protesting the low pay of $50 that featured poets, mostly African American, received for single readings at Busboys' events. It is not as if there were any other retailers of any kind regularly providing and touting a venue for such poets. Shallal's locations were singular. Nonetheless, Shallal got the heat again.

Black poet Fred Joiner signed a letter to Shallal with seventeen other poets declaring that Hughes once wrote of having been taken aback when he was called "a Negro busboy poet." As Joiner wrote online: "For many of us poets of conscience, poets of color, poets of compassion . . . seeing a Langston cutout from that era is not fun or a novelty to us, it is an insult." Once again, Shallal felt treated as an outsider, no matter how open and singular were his aims. One poet told the *Washington Post*, "I don't think Andy is insincere. I think in some realms he is uninformed."

Such experiences cause Andy's anguish—for being treated as an outsider—but his personality and his deeply rooted values keep him persevering instead of retreating or dropping out. He doubled the fee to $100 for the poets. He issued a new "tribal statement," mentioning race—namely, "Busboys and Poets is a community where racial and cultural connections are consciously uplifted." He gave public speeches on race at a high school graduation and a business gathering, and he encourages conversations about race among his restaurant employees. He doesn't sweep touchy topics under the table. His orientation for new employees has become famous for its directness. The new staff may be taken aback by such forthrightness but quickly get into the rhythm of wearing their hearts and minds on their sleeves before their new employer, who initiates and guides the discussion.

A hands-on illustrative exercise comes from the manner in which Shallal interviews new workers. Part of his success comes from his practice of interviewing almost all his staff hires (he has over 600 employees) at some length over a meal. On one occasion observed by Abha Bhattarai of the *Washington Post*, he was hosting a small group of eight new employee trainees.

192THE REBELLIOUS CEO

After they introduced themselves and sat down, Shallal jolted them with this question: "Which table would you rather serve, a party of four black women, or four white men in suits and ties?" After a few moments of looking down, in uncomfortable silence, an eighteen-year-old African American from Oklahoma says he would be more comfortable serving the black women, which prods a "yes" response from a white woman. But a student from Bangladesh in his early twenties disagrees: "When I see a group of people, all I see is money. The businessmen are going to spend more money." That's not a stereotype, but a fact he stresses.

"How do you know?" challenges Shallal. "They may not be successful, may be cheap or barely making it," he adds. The inhibitions start falling away in favor of a brightening discussion of race, gender, politics, and religion. He loves this part of his work, and not just because it is a crucial pragmatic part of getting a high-quality, motivated workforce. He loves the human touch of tolerance, of bringing the best, not their fears, out of people. He has a low-key passion for human justice, cannot stand bullies or the cold-blooded monetized minds of those who have no discernible boundaries or limits.

There are at Busboys and Poets no step-by-step training manuals or instructional videos. There are discussions, frank ones, and easy access between people. Tell us your stories from deep within you, Shallal seems to be saying to a gathering of twenty-two new employees. Typically, he had just spent the weekend at the Peoples' Climate March challenging Trump's repeated disbelief that there is any man-made climate disruption or even an approaching risk from more burning of fossil fuels. (Remember his mantra, "clean, beautiful coal"?)

Does Shallal need a broader context for himself in order to de-emphasize conflicts or stereotypes over race? Could he instead start the discussions with his would-be employees using subjects they are more likely to agree heartily with one another about? Matters affecting, for example, the treatment of children, consumers, medical patients, different kinds of workers, people being ripped off by big business, possible engagement with consumer cooperatives, labor unions efforts, or by discussing world peace and an end to the US Empire with its bloated military budgets that could be better spent repairing schools, public transit, roads, bridges, expanding libraries, community health clinics, securing safer parks and water/sewage systems? With such broader pertinent frames of reference (including the nutritious food they will be serving and eating), would the stories or expression about race and gender at the aforementioned table be different? Shallal may want to try such an approach instead of rubbing unvoiced wounds so much he makes them more painful. Could these civic exchanges about building economic and political democracy and health and safety paint a larger horizon that reduces the tensions over race and gender through such commonly held views and endeavors?

Shallal has thought about these frames of reference. At his first restaurants, Skewers and Cafe Luna, which were right in the middle of what some residents called a "demilitarized zone," he poured out bottles of French wines to protest the French government resuming nuclear bomb tests in the Pacific Ocean in 1995. He wondered out loud also "why aren't there more black people at war protests, or featured activists speaking out against other issues that impact people of color in a very dramatic way?" This has led Shallal back to "the foundational issue in this country which is race . . . in order to make progress anywhere we had to get into the root of the conversation. Race had to be front and center."

Cornel West, a friend of Shallal, might respond that for race to matter, class *must* also matter. Others may argue that class precedes being able to counter racial prejudices both personal and institutional.

Shallal grew up in a multiracial school in Arlington, Virginia, where he was viewed as neither white nor black. While a teenager, he worked at his father's restaurant, graduating from high school at fifteen, then receiving a degree in biology from Catholic University of America, and briefly attending medical school at Howard University. He went to work as a technical assistant to scientists at the National Institutes of Health, where he questioned some ethical lapses and left to start Skewers with his brother Tony.

As a student, he was something of a prodigy—not an ordinary restaurant owner-to-be. His intellectual insights and curiosity equipped him well in his ever-widening quest for a better society. Toward this objective he tried hard to break through the deeply ingrained habit of all cultures, in varying degrees, which is *self-censorship*. What people do not say about what they really believe or expect or observe!

At his sessions with new staff, he would ask, "Any atheists in the room? How many of you thought seriously about suicide?" When he receives the replies, he either joins the response or digs deeper into the person's response to uncover a second layer of self-censorship. No one is under any pressure whatsoever to answer if they believe their privacy is being invaded. One result: in Andy's restaurants the servers are pleasant, helpful, and competent. Surliness and indifference to patrons' needs, wants, and whims are rare occurrences there. People who come to eat, buy, and read books, attend poetry slams, and book readings, hear political speeches, and watch film screenings at the restaurant seem unusually comfortable, happy, and even exuberant. The food is nutritious, delicious, and fairly priced. Visitors discover long-forgotten tastes, flavors, and enticing recipes, such as the famous Moroccan Harira soup. Systems are in place, as Andy likes to put it, but the rhythms that give the sparks, the introduction of new subjects en route to new events and experiences still flow from Andy Shallal's electric energy, imagination, and refusal to be satisfied with his already achieved success. Should he decide to pursue a political or appointed career and leave the business, the systems he has put in place should be able to perpetuate these dining, thinking, and participating experiences. But without Andy's unique characteristics, the steak will have to be sold without as much sizzle—to use an out-of-date metaphor.

Andy is married to his accomplished wife, Marja, a low-key Iranian American social justice advocate of a different type. He has two grown sons from a previous marriage that started at age twenty, and two daughters from his present marriage.

His human resources chief, Marija Stojkovic, asked in a job interview: "Do you feel strongly about any social or political issues?" Staff are encouraged to speak out about them, including after work at civic engagements. She tells the *Washington Post*, "We believe we can teach people anything—they can learn the menu, the ingredients—but a culture of diversity and inclusion is the most important thing." Certainly all people regardless of their race, gender or religion feel welcomed at Busboys and Poets if only because they have seen people with diverse identities there regularly.

But Shallal is still not sure. Reflecting on a thousand of these interactive sessions, he tells the reporter, "Almost every time, someone will say, 'I feel like I'm colorblind so I'm a good person.'" He says, "Being colorblind is the absolute worst thing because we're not a colorblind society." Shallal says, "What we need is for people to realize, I'm not colorblind. I have prejudices, and I need to check myself in every encounter. That's the only way we move forward."

To what end, if there is never anyone who is colorblind? I know many people who are personally, socially, and economically quite colorblind. Are they supposed to admit to something they are not to have credibility with those struggling with such feelings?

He probably realizes that new approaches to counter structural racism, more nondiscriminatory incentives, and increased common cooperative experiences (such as responding to natural disasters such as fires, hurricanes, floods, and earthquakes) can change significantly ingrained prejudicial feelings. Professional and college sports based on merit have already done that in the wide arena of athletes and spectators. But he still thinks the change in bias comes first through personal interactions and shared introspections.

In the hierarchy of grassroots injustices, these connections with charity, the law, civic action, system reform, implementation, and more to avoid slippage or backlash, Andy feels he works best and most effectively at the intersections where people rub shoulders.

When I tried, in 2016, to persuade him to give remarks on US foreign policy and the Bush/Cheney/Obama Iraq situation at our eight-day "Breaking Through Power" convocations in historic Constitution Hall, he demurred. I persisted, saying that he was uniquely equipped by his background, historical knowledge and keen sense of how to communicate to both concerned citizens and those who have been inattentive on that disastrous Bush-launched mega-crime against the Iraqi people, adjoining nations, and the blowback on our country. He demurred again. It is not as if he hasn't candidly expressed his searing observations on the Iraqi sociocide. It just seems he doesn't feel comfortable operating on a more formal level of presentation with others laboring at that level of general advocacy.

What does the future hold for Andy Shallal, who is in his vigorous mid-sixties? After his loss in the multi-candidate race for D.C. Mayor in 2014, where he came in under 5 percent of the vote, he toyed with the prospect of running for Councilperson at Large in 2016 but dropped the idea shortly thereafter. He does not like to spend much of his money on political campaigns, including his own. He also was very busy with all his responsibilities and new projects. Unless the District of Columbia ceases being a colony and becomes the fifty-first State of Columbia—an unlikely prospect anytime soon—there are no new and important elective offices opening up.

Franchising his uniquely successful model of "democracy restaurants" around the nation is not his mission. He thinks, perhaps mistakenly, his success is too uniquely personal. That should not discourage other entrepreneurs from adopting this community invigorating model, in their own image and shape, for their locations. He certainly would share his knowledge; Shallal is anything but proprietary about his innovations and associated experiences.

What is more likely is that Andy continues innovating his community leadership and often direct sponsorship of bringing people together in different and exciting ways. For example, he started an alternative, progressive Presidential Inauguration Ball with enlightened celebrities and a large attendance. He is active and helpful in Washington, D.C.'s artistic and cultural scenes. He is committed to creating a good environment in D.C. for minority youth experiencing high unemployment or under-employment in the chronic poverty of many D.C. residents.

He gladly offers creative and ethical counterintuitive opinions, from a progressive business point of view, to the media that call him. No doubt his constant search for a life with meaning, and unconstrained by conventional boundaries and low expectations, can be very suitable for emulation by others around our country and the world. Speaking his mind and defending others who do so, regardless of whether he concurs or not with their positions, Andy Shallal reminds me of my father—also a restaurateur who spoke his mind behind the counter. Whenever he was admonished by his regular customers—"Mr. Nader, if you keep talking about what's on your mind, you're going to lose business, if you haven't already"—my dad would smile and reply, "When I sailed past the Statue of Liberty in 1912 to New York City, I took it seriously, do you?"

9

B. RAPOPORT

Founder of American Income
Life Insurance Company

I've lost count of the number of times B. Rapoport (he preferred to be called "B") called me from wherever to declare, "Ralph, when are you going to do more about Bigness?" The founder, president and CEO of the American Income Life Insurance Company of Waco, Texas, was not talking about big government. He was warning about Big Corporations and economic concentration of power. Knowing that he was a long-time supporter of progressive civic action and anti-corporate power groups, as well as the *Texas Observer* magazine, I would often respond: "When you fund an antitrust, anti-bigness action group, B!" He would jump over that suggestion and relate some example of why he was so concerned about Bigness. He had a memorable story. At a meeting with a top executive of the giant Bank of America in California, many years before the 2008 Wall Street collapse of our economy, he said: "You know, if your bank gets into trouble, it can cause great trouble for the economy; while if there were six or seven smaller banks, instead of yours, and one fails, the economic disruption would be small." More than that, he believed "as big business increases, it seems that loyalty becomes less important. Being nice to one another [especially the workers] also becomes less important." Moreover, as part of a huge conglomerate, "you make a business mistake and you're out. That has a chilling effect on innovation and risk taking." Bigness was really always on his mind, and it included the enormous influence giant corporations have on governments at all levels.

Who is this man, holding such opinions in Texas and running an insurance company, no less? B had never been shy about letting people know where he came from and what he stands for and with whom. To anyone who would listen, he said, "My father taught me Marxism and hard work. My mother taught me to love learning."

Born in 1917 in San Antonio to Riva Feldman and David Rapoport—Russian immigrants—he bore the mark of his parents' experiences. David Rapoport was sent to life in prison in northeastern Siberia for distributing anti-Tsarist pamphlets at age seventeen. He escaped and made his way to America and then to Texas where he became a peddler, often in the low-income sections of San Antonio. He never stopped talking about how the cruelties of capitalism contrasted with the ideals of socialism. Gathering at their home with like-minded immigrants from Russia, they would argue the politics of their day, with little Bernard listening and absorbing the fundamental message of fairness and justice to all people. To the end of his life, in 2012, he would convey again and again the same message to his legions of friends: "When the few have too much and the many have too little, how is this country going to survive?" He was always astonished at the limitless greed and parsimony of the super-wealthy, viewing these imperious traits as a threat to democracy.

B's father was a devoted supporter of Norman Thomas, one of the founders of the American Civil Liberties Union, who succeeded Eugene V. Debs as the leader of the Socialist Party. Like Debs did earlier, Thomas ran for president numerous times in the first half of the twentieth century. When young B asked his father whether he was sorry for not voting for Franklin Delano Roosevelt in 1932, after FDR had borrowed some of Thomas's proposed reforms, David Rapoport replied, "Son, if people like me hadn't voted and worked for Norman Thomas and put pressure on Mr. Roosevelt, he wouldn't be doing the things he's doing now."

That probably helps to explain why B, a fervent Democratic Party loyalist and funder, did not object to my third-party presidential candidacy. (Nor did he make a contribution, I might add.)

He grew up poor in a family with two children. Bernard worked several part-time jobs, such as selling *Liberty* magazine, but he always spent time reading, reading, and reading. His father built an in-home library of the classical writers, including the great Russian novelists Tolstoy, Turgenev, Dostoyevsky and Pushkin— all read by the time he was fourteen. Papa Rapoport always told him to maintain a sense of outrage at injustices and pay attention to the poor, while keeping a book in his hands at all times.

His dream fulfilled, B enrolled at the University of Texas in Austin, where in addition to working full-time at Zales jewelry store, he absorbed the teachings of several progressive, radical professors, who were always under attack by the corporate conservatives in the Texas legislature. This vicious attempt at censorship and attempted expulsion of these teachers entrenched B's everlasting commitment to academic freedom in an open society.

This led him to become the largest funder of the progressive monthly *Texas Observer* over the decades, even though sometimes its articles and editorials infuriated him. He found its humane voice for justice in Texas far more important. Ronnie Dugger, who started the *Observer* and set the standard for its unyielding integrity and independence, tells the story of visiting B in 1955 to discuss B placing ads in their monthly magazine. Typically forth-right, Dugger told B that life insurance is just an actuarial calcula-tion and "ought to be nationalized." B promptly agreed with him and just as promptly agreed to start decades of ad placements in the *Observer* as a way of keeping the publication afloat—and sell-ing some policies along the way.

As his business grew, his contributions to local, state, and in-ternational causes grew commensurately. *Fortune* magazine named him as one of America's forty most generous philanthropists, over-whelmingly for social justice and liberal political candidates. He was probably the least wealthy of the forty selected donors. What was amazing about B is that he seemed to be giving everywhere for everyone in liberal politics, education, and progressive civic groups like the Institute for Policy Studies and the Economic Policy Institute; he funded University of Texas scholarships and endowed chairs, and even gave $1 million to foster Jews marrying Jews after learning that Jews were increasingly marrying Gentiles, among many more groups and causes.

He really wasn't that rich, relatively speaking. At his death, his estate was well under $100 million. He carried a large personal debt to banks from 1951 to 1984. He had about 20 percent of his company stock but remained cash poor. Into his mid-sixties he remained in that state of rich in assets, poor in cash. That didn't stop him from writing thousands of checks to hundreds of liberal democratic candidates and other civic pursuits. In 1988, he sold his company, leaving him as CEO and president with about $25 mil-lion in cash. The *New York Times* reported in September 19, 1988 that "Mr. Rapoport, the company's 71-year-old chairman and chief executive, announced that he had decided to pursue a leveraged buyout of American Income, which is based in Waco, Tex., for about $18 a share, or $210 million. The board is scheduled to meet

today to consider the buyout, which comes after a strong performance during the first two quarters of this year."

At the age of 78, in 1994, B sold the company again, to the
Torchmark Corporation, leaving him with $150 million, from
which he put $43 million into the Bernard and Audre Rapoport
Foundation. Audre, his wife, was every bit involved with B's mode
of operation—sociable, progressive, independent with her philanthropy, and, like B, she recognized that she had that "personal
touch that is so important to everything you do in life, even in the
business world."

What was unique about B was how much he did with his ability to commandeer so much time out of a 24-hour day and how
much he gave, given his relatively modest fortune. Jovial, sociable,
a tornado when entering a room full of people—be they politicians,
local civic advocates or children in a poor school in Waco—he
seemed everywhere all the time.

Observing him over the years, here is how I think he did all
these things. He made zillions of phone calls and rarely spoke
more than five minutes per call. He leveraged his civic and political donations with others and made them count. He provided
everyone with contacts, advice, and strategies. Whenever he came
to Washington—which was often—his day was scheduled as tight
as a sardine can. But he never seemed tired; he just seemed to glide
from one get-together after another, one big hug, one big laugh,
before getting down to serious talk. Friendships always came before business, he would say. At least that's the way he made you
feel. He could size up people quickly, whether he was recruiting
them or being asked for a donation. Yet he never disclosed how
his intuition worked—that would seem too manipulative. He
said he rarely asked the political candidates he supported for anything or to do anything; he just wanted to help get them elected.

Obviously, he chose to support people like Senator Ted Kennedy, Senator Pat Leahy, Senator Frank Church, presidential candidate George McGovern, Jimmy Carter, Bill Clinton, Hillary Clinton, and Texas Governor Ann Richards because he knew they more or less stood for the issues that he espoused.

He probably could have been more demanding about the national Democrats paying more attention to Texas, which they abandoned in successive presidential campaigns. This neglect helped long-time Democratic Texas become a red Republican state all the way down to the municipal elections. Ben Barnes, a long-time Democratic Party leader in Texas, told me that, in addition to shredding the state Democratic candidacies down to elected dog-catchers, the abandoning of Texas and its forty electoral votes severely weakened the national Democratic Party and assured some Republican presidential victories.

Rapoport leveraged his influence nationally and at other state and Congressional elections by getting other donors, including his business associates, to give along with him. He made a major point of socializing with dozens of these candidates, knowing their families and always being ready to help in a crisis.

He almost never talked about insurance in my meetings with him. It was always the political agenda and philanthropy. As the years passed, that's where he appeared to spend most of his time. But appearances deceive. B knew that without a prosperous business, he couldn't do these other things. He paid close attention to his business, where he excelled such as in opening new markets, motivating salespeople and treating workers well. He found skilled people to do what he could not do or did not want to do.

Charles Terrell, an insurance executive, once said: "Rapaport is the greatest selling insurance executive I've ever known, and the greatest sales manager. Bernie developed his people, and he

developed the contacts that led him to business. He never put lay-
ers between himself and his salespeople."

Here is one illustration of what Terrell meant. *Every* Saturday
morning, starting at 6:45 until noon, he spoke on the telephone
with each of his fifty state general agents for about five minutes
each. Well organized, they focused on solving specific problems
every week, he said. He visited every agency once a year and had
an annual national convention so he could see everybody at one
time. He had a phenomenal memory for his people's names, in part
because he spoke to them so often.

Here is one approach to his operating business philosophy:

> I stressed to our people that I wanted them to operate like
> they were in a glass house speaking through megaphones.
> I told them that they had to act at all times as if the insur-
> ance commission was on their left shoulder, the SEC was
> on the right shoulder and Ralph Nader was watching from
> up above.

If they made their decision with that framework, he told them he
would defend them till the end.

He joked with them that they would make so much money
at American Income Life as a sales agent, they would give him a
"gold watch." It wasn't just the sales agents that he treated so well.
He treated all his employees "like human beings," *never had a layoff*
and from the beginning invited the unionization of his workers,
including himself! That was unheard of in the insurance business.
There was, moreover, a method behind his all-union company.
After he switched his company from selling hospitalization policies to life insurance, he broke open the large union market for
selling supplementary life insurance to union members. Here he

had little competition, so authentic a champion of the working classes and unions had he become, from his upbringing all the way to supporting pro-labor politicians. The doors opened to large numbers of customers. He attended more labor union conventions than all the rest of the gigantic insurance industry CEOs combined and then some. After all, he was a "brother," with a working-class background, starting poor, and then as a member himself of the American Income Life home office Labor Union in 1961.

What is there not to like? So there he was at the AFL-CIO, the United Auto Workers, the Teamsters, SEIU, the United Mine Workers conventions—both national and state. The labor union business made his company a sustainable success year after year. American Income Life had a virtual lock on the union business by default—its competitors couldn't even see the potential and didn't know how to talk with the union leaders who could open the door to their members. Things didn't slow things down when B hired some high-ranking, retired labor leaders to join his company to connect with labor union business. In October 1973, the AFL-CIO officially designated American Income Life and Union Labor Life Insurance Company of New York as Union Label companies, union owned and focused on large group policies.

With an advisory board of notable active union leaders, including heads of major unions and John J. Sweeney, when he led the AFL-CIO, no other company came close to challenging American Income Life. But B went even further. He waived premiums by union members when they were on an authorized strike. He allowed company staff to deduct automatically from their paychecks whatever they wanted to donate to the AFL-CIO's Committee on Political Education. American Income developed a college scholarship program for children of unionists. It contributed to the strike funds of unions engaged in lawful strikes. B would joke that he had so many retired labor leaders working with them that "it was difficult to distinguish between our company and the labor movement." He even produced the American Income *Labor Letter*, eagerly read and often re-printed by labor leaders from all over the world. He called the *Labor Letter* "the most effective public relations piece ever done with the labor movement outside the movement's own efforts." Except, I would add, for the huge circulation of Harry Kelber's pamphlets.

"The newsletter was all about access," admitted B, but his closer ties to unions and union leaders had three additional benefits.

First, it minimized the amount that American Income Life had to budget for advertising. There was no advertising in the American Income *Labor Letter* either. Second, B's advantage with labor unions over any of his would-be competitors was so overwhelming that they did not even try to compete. This avoided a struggle between companies for union business that may have induced corruption—bribes, paybacks for winning business. Knowing how union leaders often fell into such corruption during bids for these unions' pension business, among other scandals, B made sure there was no such temptation in his line of commerce since there were no such bidders.

Third, B used his union contacts to publicize the work of pro-labor politicians when they weren't running for office, including leading US senators, such as California's Alan Cranston and Indiana's Birch Bayh. This made the politicians happy and gave union leaders more access to them. What other life insurance company could even think of competing with B for the sales! B took great pains to assert that he never used his political connections to intervene and get his company business or for any personal gain or profit. That was a tightrope act that B maneuvered adroitly to avoid any whiff of corruption, though there was one close call as an ancillary witness, before a grand jury, which acquitted him.

B didn't spread his business values and business models of

behavior throughout his industry. He simply said he did not have time for developing much of a relationship with other insurance company executives. He probably also thought they were too rigid and set in their ways to be susceptible to the broader vision as presented by Rapoport. Notably, on a couple of occasions, B would call me up for a minute and say, "Business ethics, hah, that is a contradiction in terms, Ralph. There is no such thing as 'business ethics.'" End of call! For B, it was all about the personal, ingrained values of a business leader. It could neither be taught nor effectively enforced by law, he thought.

Publicly, B was expectedly silent about corruption among union leaders, though he knew what was going on in some large and small unions. Certainly, Congressional investigations, prosecutors, and media reports caught more than a few union leaders and their associates enriching themselves—as in the construction trade unions or the Teamsters union. It was not B's style to be a muckraking, wave-maker; he was not inclined to do anything beyond avoiding such entanglements and accentuating the positive. In his only book, *Being Rapoport: Capitalist with a Conscience* (2002), B described "an unusual opportunity through my business to contribute to causes that promote and benefit the labor movement. Despite all the ups and downs of the movement's history, I remain convinced that the American free enterprise system needs the labor movement to guarantee democracy on the job and fairness to workers. I am proud of the labor movement and I am proud of my relationship with it."

B had a skill at taking personal positions on controversial subjects and excusing others he had to deal with—friends, politicians, labor leaders, other business executives—from any criticism. For example, he, with great passion and facts, was "an anti-Vietnam War millionaire" in Texas—a hotbed of gung-hoism for that dreadfully brutal and boomeranging war. Were it not for the budget-draining burden of that terrible war and its shattering of his Congressional alliances, President Lyndon B. Johnson might have passed a full "Medicare For All" law in 1964, instead of the bill that provided healthcare coverage only to the elderly through Medicare and to the poor through the porous Medicaid program. Extrapolating from a later peer-reviewed Harvard Medical School report, at least a million Americans died in the US from 1965 to now because they could not afford health insurance to get diagnosed and treated in time—in addition there were larger numbers of people whose undiagnosed injuries and illnesses were not life-threatening but treatable but who could not afford those treatments.

B was, as noted, actively pressed for a labor union for his own employees. Yet he did not try to advocate for pro-union laws in Texas or in Congress.

He wrote that "labor unions' support for the war in Vietnam was a bitter disappointment to me. It was one of the few times in my life that I felt alienated from the movement." He made his distaste public without ambiguity. He gave money to anti-war groups and was active in the Business Executives Move for Vietnam Peace (BEM), which got underway in 1967. BEM brought together hitherto uncommitted business leaders and retired military leaders and helped jumpstart the presidential candidacy of Senator Eugene McCarthy. Suffice to say that B rarely kept his opinions to himself, writing hundreds of op-ed columns variously expressing his positions. He did not care about his opinions hurting American Income's business, remembering perhaps that when his father came to America, fleeing a country ruled by repressive Tsars, he took his freedom of speech seriously.

In his laudatory introduction to B's book, Bill Moyers writes: "The educated man is empowered to argue against his own privilege—and morally obligated to do so . . . lest he forget his roots, take his good fortune for granted and grow comfortable in the rarefied company of elites." B refused to draw the wagons of wealth into a circle around him . . . perhaps that's why he so loved the University of Texas, to which he gave millions of dollars and, in the 1990s, productively served as the chair of the Board of Regents.

But Moyers had one hesitation about B. "I may yet succeed in bringing him around to the one cause about which he remains ambivalent despite my years of hectoring—the radical reform of our campaign finance laws. In his heart he knows I'm right, but as a major player in the game, backing causes and candidates he believes in, he doesn't yet see the light." Moyers doesn't expect perfect. "After all," he exclaims, "here's a man who finances the liberal *Texas Observer* despite the habit of its editors to expose the predatory excesses of the industry that made him rich. Here's a man who supports political candidates who promise to increase his taxes."

There was one arena of B's life that very few of his friends, other than Maury Maverick, Jr., the great Texas journalist that B admired so much, chose to talk with him about. That was his commitment to the state and government of Israel, often without qualifications. This is the subject where B Rapoport had many subordinate doubts that did not rise to the level of risking any of his total loyalty to what he called early on "the Jewish homeland." It started, of course, with the Jewish Holocaust under Nazi Germany and his devout charitable work to raise money for that homeland. His father, a proud Marxist in the tradition of secular Jewish socialism, was absorbed with a world view of overturning capitalism by the superiority of a humane socialist movement for the world's workers. But it was B's mother and grandparents, embodying the spiritual religiosity of Judaism, who won B's heart.

He traveled with Audre to Israel many times, developed a friendship with Teddy Kollek, the energetic Mayor of Jerusalem, and donated millions of dollars to the Jerusalem Foundation, and other charities. While not willing to criticize or oppose the Israeli state's violent dispossession of and continual mistreatment of Palestinians or the establishment of unlawful Israeli colonies in the West Bank, he salvaged his compassion through acts of charity. As the *New York Times* wrote: "He gave to causes in Israel that sought accommodation with the Palestinians." What B meant was to support charitably "a wide variety of education and human welfare projects, not directly to support a two-state solution." Many of the Rapoport's charitable contributions were made through the Jerusalem Foundation and the United Jewish Appeal. They were major factors in the establishment of the Givat Gonen High School in a low-income Jewish section of Jerusalem, backed by the big Israeli Histadrut labor union. The school taught Israeli labor socialism for peaceful coexistence with the Arabs.

The school's curriculum reflected B's overall economic philosophy in his later life. In his words: "I think capitalism is the best economic system ever devised; socialism is the best social system. Capitalism acknowledges the greed instinct, socialism acknowledges the need for cooperation. It is when we integrate those two that we have a good system." Another way of paraphrasing what he came to believe is that capitalism produces the biggest wealth while socialism helps distribute it far more equitably to those who didn't get what they earned and to those in need.

B must have spent a lot of time on the Israeli projects. They were demanding of delicate negotiations that were time intensive. He had to convince US labor unions to co-fund a large park turned into a playground for Israeli children. He was deeply involved in a medical center, founded in 1982, to provide services "directly to the Arab population in Jerusalem and surrounding villages that handled 2,000 to 3,000 patients at a main facility and ten branch clinics." He and Audre also provided funds to equip an eye clinic for a medical center serving Arab patients. He believed "Jew and Arab have to live together, there is no other way." Yet he did not

pursue alternative ways to achieve his goal, beyond full, uncondi-
tional support for whomever was running the Israeli government
and military. He was the indefatigable promoter of the purchase
of Israeli bonds, successfully getting American unions and banks,
other companies and the state of Texas (the latter required a law to
be passed in Texas) to buy hundreds of millions of dollars' worth
of those bonds. In 1994, Israel gave him the Israel Peace Medal
in recognition of his work promoting Israeli bonds. Critics have
pointed out that the proceeds of such bonds went to West Bank
colonial development and the further repression of the Palestinian
people. But there was another side of Rapoport. Even after Senator
J. William Fulbright criticized the Israeli lobby working over
Congress for Likud, the right-wing Israeli Party that spoke of
Judea and Samaria being part of the greater Israel, he still supported Fulbright's last unsuccessful Senate re-election campaign
won by Dale L. Bumpers. He never forgot Fulbright's early, leading opposition to the Vietnam War and always regarded him as "a
civilized man" with many views B agreed with strongly. The first
time many people, aware of the Rapoports' many accomplishments,
learned of his views on the matter of Palestinian rights was in
his memoir in 2002—one year before Bush and Cheney, with the
enthusiastic backing of the Israeli government, commenced their
criminal invasion and sociocide of the country of Iraq. Here are
B's very candid positions:

> I am in favor of a Palestinian authority, and I support
> Israel's relinquishing of the West Bank and the Gaza Strip
> to the Palestinians. I have a reflexive response whenever
> questions arise about Israeli policy. My initial feeling is that
> Israel is always right, but I have always been opposed to the
> building of Jewish settlements on the West Bank. These
> settlements have a political rather than a social purpose,

they are unnecessary and they stir up resentment and ha-
tred. They are rooted in the old orthodox belief that God
meant for the Jews to inhabit all of the land. God never
shared that information with me, however. Although Israel
is small, the Israelis do have enough land . . . in the Negev
that can be developed . . . I try to be neutral in the matter
of Israeli politics. My strong sympathies have always been
with the Labor Party, but I have been scrupulous about
staying out of the politics of that country. We are all Jews,
and I have a sense of solidarity with all Israelis no matter
what their political affiliation. I have to admit, however,
that former Prime Minister Benjamin Netanyahu severely
tested my policy of strict neutrality. Netanyahu reminds
me of an Israeli Jesse Helms. He did great damage to the
effort to get peace established between Jews and Muslims
in the Middle East.

Omitted from B's candor is any mention of a two-state solution
or using the United States' large foreign military and economic
aid to Israel as leverage toward negotiations for such a peaceful
solution. He clearly was torn about going any further or in using
his considerable influence in Congress, or his many strategic and
personal friendships with key lawmakers toward the achievement
of these goals.

B was just far more comfortable in his element, playing and
hugging the children—both Arab and Jew—at the daycare centers and preschool programs. Ruth Cheshin of the Jerusalem
Foundation observed:

"Bernie had a wonderful time at the daycare center. These children sit in his lap and he holds their hands and gives them hugs
and there is much laughter and singing. It is an emotionally re-
warding thing to witness."

B's heart was always bigger than his bank account. So he often offered his heart in ways that cost him nothing, such as spending time with poor children in Waco. Once, while eating at his favorite restaurant in Waco, El Conquistador, he invited a young family and their eight-year-old son, Michael Aguilar, over to chat. Soon, he invited young Michael to his office to be interviewed for a Boy Scout project. He urged Michael to read five books a month and report back to him. But he passed away before that visit could be scheduled. Michael did show up at B's large memorial service in his Cub Scout uniform.

During his eighties, it seemed that B lost any expectation that much was going to come out of Washington on domestic policies. The George W. Bush regime and Republican ascendancy in Congress took away much of what he had hoped Democrats would enact. During the Clinton years, he was spending much time on the Board of Regents at the University of Texas—an experience of decision-making that made him more conservative. Let's say he was no longer what he had earlier called himself, when asked, which was, "I am an anomaly."

As part of the governing class at the university, his formerly very critical views on the regents mellowed as he got to know their successors better in a working relationship. For a lifetime, he had harbored such admiration for the faculty to whom he felt deeply indebted for making him "dig deep into myself to discover talents I didn't know I had." Before going on the regents board, he had already established two endowments in economics and three in the liberal arts. The regents, in his time on the board, had to make difficult decisions regarding tuition in a state with no income tax and a right-wing-dominated state legislature nearby. He had to defer to the big-time athletic lobby at the university and its rabid alumni, even though he personally didn't believe universities should have major athletic programs. He realized on the job that the Texas open meetings law was too strict. He opposed letting a student member come onto the board of regents. When this student asked why, given his liberal, democratic credentials, B replied that "if a kid gets exposed to all the problems we have to deal with as regents, that kid will become conservative much too young. I don't want that to happen."

Were these sentiments expressed before an auditorium of University of Texas students, they probably would have been received with groans, at best.

Back in the 1970s, we were organizing college students in numerous states, from California to Massachusetts, from Oregon to Florida, to form their own nonprofit civic advocacy organizations called Public Interest Research Groups, or PIRGs. Many did and they have done great work, sometimes earning them college credits, most times working with their older full-time staff (see: USPIRG.org).

Texas was a hard nut to crack given that the funding had to come from a student referendum establishing a small additional fee on their tuition bill (about five dollars a year per student), which then had to be approved by the regents. The very talented students leading this charge in the early seventies assembled huge student support and signed petitions and took that civic initiative to the regents, with such potential for training legions of UT students in forthcoming years in civic experiences and skills. The student leaders did their homework on every regent and met with them personally. At the formal meeting of the regents to approve the small addition to the tuition fee, they thought they had 5 to 7 votes. So did the crusty, reactionary lawyer, Frank C. Ervin, Jr. He asked for a recess and went to the men's room with another regent who was on the "yes" side. When they returned, Ervin came back with a victory margin of one vote and the stunned students lost 5 to 4. That was the last major attempt to start a Texas PIRG.

Conditions in Texas were not for the better over the years, having been deprived not only of a vigorous student advocacy group, but having fewer civic activists graduating from the university. Like most universities, UT did not have a civic practice curriculum or courses to educate, in theory and real life, how to practice democracy for a better society.

So when B became board chair of the regents, I was not the only one who was elated over the prospect of starting a Texas PIRG in Austin and the various UT branches around the state. Who better to argue for and lead the charge than Mr. Democracy, Mr. Free Speech, and Mr. Justice himself? Alas, it was not to be. B did not elaborate why, other than to note how immensely occupied he was with other university matters, not to mention the other duties with his business and political engagements. Being on the inside has changed many an outsider.

On this issue of the PIRGs, he was unusually aloof and cool. Too bad. Because B always would say that it took experience to learn the difference "between knowledge and wisdom." A Texas PIRG would have given many students wisdom from their civic experiences.

B had a dilemma from which he did extricate himself—namely, how far would he go to support serious justice reforms when it came to challenging corporate power and the system it entrenched. For example, he supported Ohio Senator Howard M. Metzenbaum, a self-made multimillionaire, despite thinking he was the Senate's most anti-business senator. That was incorrect. Senator Metzenbaum was against business crimes and against monopolistic industries and practices. He was for honest business. On the other hand, B was a good friend and supporter of Louisiana Senator Russell B. Long—a down-the-line conservative tribune of the oil and gas industry.

Overall, though, he had no illusions about the Democratic Party. Four months into the Obama Administration, B made one of his flash telephone calls to me: "Ralph, the Democrats aren't going to do anything. They won't even raise taxes on the wealthy. Whatever you think about businesses, Ralph, it's worse, believe me. We haven't made a dent."

On the other hand, in his congenial manner, B admitted his limits as a reformer and idealist, writing, "I feel about Ronnie Dugger [the incorruptible, hardline progressive editor of the *Texas Observer*] the way I feel about consumer advocate Ralph Nader. God help the world if we don't have them, but God help the world if they are ever in a position of power." Needless to elaborate, Mr. Rapoport did not explain such sentiments during any meeting we had over the decades.

In his later years, B and his wife Audre poured their wealth and time into the Rapoport Foundation with very specific instructions. This relatively small Foundation—donating about $3 million a year—would give 1/6 of its donations to Israeli "areas of education and childcare," 1/6 "must benefit the University of Texas" at Austin, 1/3 was to be "reserved for the community of Waco, Texas," and the remaining 1/3 was to be "allocated on a discretionary basis."

The grants were to go *directly* to benefit those they were to serve, bringing people together "without regard to race, religion, ethnic background, or finance." They wished to be involved in the effort "to eradicate poverty in Waco." B quotes Camus: "Poverty is imprisonment without a drawbridge." Education, to the Rapoports, was the drawbridge. We want to get people on their feet so they can take care of themselves.

They emphasized childhood education—"illiteracy and under-education are the key contributing causes of poverty in this country . . . Vouchers are not the answer for the education of American youth. Without a first-rate public education, there can be no de-mocracy," they added.

They were quite intent on providing details and examples back-ing up these beliefs. They were no armchair philosophers or ideo-logues. Their descriptions of what poverty is, what it means to the impoverished, what it leads to, reflected much thought, observa-tion, caring and engagement over the years with children. "Ours is a society," they wrote, "in which there is an increasing lack of community and a corresponding loss of dignity."

"Community and dignity are requisite for a sustainable society," declared B as he and Audre started the Waco 1,000 Program. That put 1,000 volunteers in Waco schools to individually tutor children in the elementary grades. One hour per volunteer a week, includ-ing B Rapoport. "It's a wonderful experience. Audre and I are hav-ing a good time. We can see, every time we come, how much love and attention these children need . . . They have become important because someone is coming every week just for them. That impor-tance translates into hope, self-esteem and self-worth." Profound!

B concluded his life at age ninety-four, in 2012, focusing on the basics, on the children, on being a farsighted ancestor for pos-terity's generation. His last spoken words were not reported. His last thoughts could have been predicted—"So much more to do."

10

YVON CHOUINARD

Founder of Patagonia

When Yvon Chouinard was a boy growing up in Lisbon, Maine, he vividly remembers seeing his tough French-Canadian immigrant father sitting in the kitchen next to the wood-burning stove drinking whiskey. Papa was not entertaining himself. With his electrician's pliers, he was pulling out some of his good and bad teeth. Because he needed dentures and was averse to the local dentist's charges, he decided to do that part of the job himself.

It could be that that jolting memory was the beginning of Yvon's interest in tools and their versatile uses, but, in his case, outdoors in the wilderness. More likely his takeaway was do-it-yourself—a propensity that grew to shape a free spirit of rock climbing, fly fishing, and surfing surrounded by a mind so disciplined, meticulous, and empirical that Yvon Chouinard and his wife Malinda created the billion-dollar company Patagonia, blazing new directions for what to some may seem to be an oxymoron—a responsible company!

Although Yvon has developed his company into a many-splendored quest to become a "responsible company," ahead of all the others, he is quick to realize that the quest will always be an imperfect but daring process of becoming, while still meeting far more than the conventional yardsticks of business success.

Even now, if you were to ask Yvon how he would want to be described by posterity, he would choose, out of a myriad of roles and skills, a blacksmith. Just as another historical figure, Benjamin Franklin—businessman, scientist, inventor, diplomat, plainspoken philosopher, citizen-builder of democratic institutions without peer—chose "printer." For it was from Yvon's desire to perfect tools for enhancing his climbing adventures that led him to discover similar consumer needs for functional outdoor clothing, and to the expansion of his company.

First the setting had to change. His mother, Yvonne, to alleviate his father's asthma, uprooted the family and moved to southern, sunny California when Yvon was nine years old.

Almost immediately, the intrepid youngster found a varied wilderness, where falcons nested. As a fourteen-year-old member of the Southern California Falconry Club, he learned how to train hawks and falcons for hunting. An adult leader, Don Prentice, taught Yvon and his boyhood chums how to rappel down the cliffs to the falcon aeries. Soon they learned how to climb the rocks at Tahquitz above Palm Springs and the sandstone cliffs of Stony Point. School? Classes? Not for this self-described loaner, geek, and D student. They were just staging grounds to get away at every chance as he went from lesser to bigger walls—and then to the giant challenge of the towering cliffs of Yosemite National Park. Although Yvon loved to bike, surf, fish, hunt for frogs, and dive for lobster and abalone in the Pacific Ocean off Malibu, the mountains were his Lorelei, his magnet, his lodestar.

At sixteen, he rebuilt an old Ford and drove to the wilds of the Wind River Range in Wyoming, where he solo climbed an untried route up Gannett Peak, the state's tallest mountain.

He started his own business climb by selling reusable pitons that he made from chrome steel for $1.50 each. Blacksmithing his way along the coast of California, Yosemite, Canada, and the European Alps in the mild seasons, Yvon traveled poor. He ate cat food, foraged in dumpsters, hunted small game, and slept in his army surplus sleeping bag. One time in Arizona, police arrested him and his buddy for vagrancy and jailed them for a couple of weeks. Something in his mind was being forged, some seeds were being planted that in later years he relied upon to create his sturdy character and personality and to withstand both temptations and easy ways to profit.

An Army year in South Korea introduced him to Korean mountaineers with whom he managed some of his first ascents. The geographic world became his stage from that time on. It was a world that demanded the best tools and materials Yvon and his friends could create to meet the most daring of nature's challenges. They were blessed with high expectations not remotely met in the existing marketplace, other than their own, exciting ones they stumbled into creating out of both pleasure and necessity.

When asked about Chouinard's constancy, his unwavering sense of purpose in the face of lures of immense wealth, longtime friends do not cite his tough living conditions in Maine. They cite his living long periods in nature—challenging it, adjusting to its obstacles, respecting its presence and never "conquering" it. He learned from the natural world lessons about not wasting, about focusing, and most of all about what commercial businesses did to nature. To this day, he and his company openly urge their customers not to buy Patagonia's clothes when they can repair what they have or can buy used clothing. That is one good definition of constancy of purpose: fifty years against conspicuous or excessive consumption.

In 2013, Patagonia produced a short film—"Worn Wear"—showing how people can maintain and recycle their clothing instead of simply throwing garments away. During the Black Friday shopping event that same year, Patagonia inaugurated the first "Worn Wear" parties, where consumers could go to select stores and repair or trade in their clothing or buy used from others trading in. Since 2017, Patagonia has made the Worn Wear program permanent, encouraging consumers to trade in their used Patagonia gear or to buy used from Patagonia. The company states that "the program provides significant resources for responsible care, repair, reuse and resale, and recycling at the end of a garment's life." This program is intended to cut down on waste—the company notes that 85 percent of clothing ends up incinerated or in a landfill. In 2019, Patagonia opened its first brick-and-mortar Worn Wear store. As of April 2023, Patagonia states that "Worn Wear is still up and running, including store stops and events all over the world. At this point, most stores can do Worn Wear events to teach people how to repair their gear as well. Worn Wear repair tours happen everywhere from Patagonia (the region) to the northern mountains of Japan."

From such a background, it is easier to strive for products that are the best in the world. Because if they are ones you use in the rugged outdoors, your own life can depend on the quality. Chouinard Equipment, the small company that proceeded Patagonia, claimed to have the best climbing tools in the world, tools that your life is dependent upon, in Yvon's words.

That quest for the best moved from one product to another. In their words:

Our clothes—from Baggies to flannel shirts, from underwear to outerwear—have to be the best of their kind.
Trying to make the best product also inspires us to create
the best childcare center and the best production department and to be the best at our jobs. Authentic, hard-core,
quality products made by the same people who use them—
a new generation of climbers, kayakers, fishermen and
surfers committed to wildness, both in the natural world
and in the sports they serve . . . and the willingness to take
strong stands on environmental issues.

You can imagine what the recruitment process must be to bring a
continual number of such steadfast people into Patagonia, people
who can maintain "a sense of urgency throughout the company"
without making excuses (and he categorizes these) as to why
something is impossible or "why a job didn't get done on time."
As many as four teams spend time interviewing and challenging
new recruits to make sure the newcomers understand at what level
they are expected to perform, mostly self-motivated. And some
still give themselves a long lunchtime to go surfing in the nearby
Pacific Ocean.

In Yvon's 2005 book, cleverly titled *Let My People Go Surfing,*
and candidly subtitled *The Education of a Reluctant Businessman,*
Chouinard starts with deadly seriousness:

Patagonia, Inc. is an experiment. It exists to put into action those recommendations that all the doomsday books
on the health of our whole planet say we must do immediately to avoid certain destruction of nature and the
collapse of our civilization. Despite near universal consensus among scientists that we are all on the brink of an
environmental collapse, our society lacks the will to take

action. We're collectively paralyzed by apathy, inertia, or lack of imagination . . . Patagonia and its thousand employees have the means, and they will prove to the rest of the business world that doing the right thing makes for good and profitable business.

Those sobering words were written almost twenty years ago!

I'm getting ahead of myself. The steps taken by Yvon and his friends are intriguing. How did this tiny group of people absorb John Muir, Henry David Thoreau, and Ralph Waldo Emerson to the core of their being?

Yvon himself often would recall a Zen Master teaching students to remain calm and focus on the work now that begat the next work stage. These were unassuming thinkers inspired further by their tinkering and their forays into the wilderness with their products. Who needed focus groups?

From 1965 to 1974, in partnership with Tom Frost, a climber and an aeronautical engineer, Chouinard redesigned and improved almost every climbing tool, making them simpler, lighter, and stronger. Their ideas came from their frequent trips to the mountains. By 1970, Chouinard Equipment was the largest supplier of climbing equipment in the United States yet remained a small business enterprise. Their main seller was pitons, which led to their first business crisis.

As usage of pitons grew, climbers hammered them into the same fragile cracks along the frequented mountains of Yosemite and other well-visited climbing sites. But repeated placement and removal damaged the rock along the ascent, and Chouinard and Frost were horrified during their ascent of the Nose Route on El Capitan that the path had degraded over just a few summers.

Maybe they had not read the economist Schumpeter's theory of "creative destruction of capitalism as stimulating economic renewal," but in 1972 they manifested it internally by scuttling their successful piton sales and replacing them with aluminum chocks that could be wedged by hand rather than hammered in and out of cracks.

This major and, to them, risky business decision was introduced in what has become a classic editorial by Sierra climber Doug Robinson on the environmental hazards of pitons. This practice of abstracting from the particular to the general, even to the philosophical, came to be the Patagonian way of learning from experience and banking it into the corporate culture.

Robinson's insights are worth more than a glance; here they are in full:

> There is a word for it, and the word is clean. Climbing with only nuts and runners for protection is clean climbing. Clean because the rock is left unaltered by the passing climber. Clean because nothing is hammered into the rock and then hammered back out, leaving the rock scarred and the next climber's experience less natural. Clean because the climber's protection leaves little trace of his ascension. Clean is climbing the rock without changing it; a step closer to organic climbing for the natural man.

A cynic would say they were switching from pitons to chocks to keep and expand their customers. Yvon and friends did this to protect the mountain from the ravages of human climbers on these celestial cliffs. If Yvon et al. had to choose between human climbers enjoying nature or the mountains staying solid and shimmering, the choice would be to protect nature's eternal majesty.

Fortunately, chocks started selling faster than could be fabricated and the piton business was heading for history. The production space expanded, and the multiple-drill jig replaced the drop hammer. Then came another Chouinard special. Shopping around, this time in Scotland during a winter climbing trip, he came across a regulation team rugby shirt and wore it rock climbing. Its adaptability to the task astonished him. It had a collar that would shield the hardware slings from cutting into the neck. It was blue, with two red and one yellow center strips across the chest. Voila. The functional and the aesthetic to replace the basic gray sweatshirts and pants, the tan cut-off chinos, and white dress shirts for Yosemite climbers. A minor fashion craze commenced and morphed into the main business with a newly named company Patagonia. Why Patagonia, where the Chouinard bunch journeyed to climb and swim? Patagonia's engrossing catalog explained: "because it brings to mind romantic visions of glaciers tumbling into fjords, jagged windswept peaks, gauchos and condors, and can be pronounced in every language."

From 1972, it was almost all about the perfecting of outdoor clothing and equipment—starting with polyurethane rain cagoules and bivouac sacks, boiled-wool gloves and mittens and hand-knit reversible hats. This perfected, in so many ways, so many discoveries forever, for many more benign impacts on families, communities, societies, environments, and the world. This defines a Chouinard perpetual motion machine in a setting of calmness and lots of time off for the workers. Sounds like fiction? No. Sounds like being empirical and visionary, respectful of the natural world and kind to humans and their fundamental needs, wants, and even whims. The team was driven, with apologies to Immanuel Kant, by a critique of pure reason regarding everything the company was touching, whether animate, inanimate, financial, or the surrounding competition.

Yvon once invited me to address the staff at Patagonia's Ventura, California, headquarters—part of an ongoing series of mutual stimulation. It was during the lunch break, and the nearby ocean visibly beckoned the surfers. My impression from that brief encounter was in meeting practical dreamers always on some cusp blending environmental righteousness with commercial success. Yvon calmly had lunch, calmly introduced me, calmly moderated, and calmly took leave. I returned to the airport. In his chronic calmness, I discerned a natural listener.

To my knowledge, the Chouinards—parents and two grown children, Fletcher and Claire—are not publicly introspective. They stick to their tasks, do their work, reflect on how to do it better, have fun, and avoid the celebrity or social circuit. The children were preparing themselves as successors to their parents by working inside Patagonia like everyone else there, with no nepotistic privileges. Yvon's tastes for being in nature or his distaste for other business executives don't interfere with his determination to share his innovations with any competitor and spark a larger transformation.

In his candid introduction to *Let My People Go Surfing*, he writes:

I've been a businessman for almost 50 years [now over 65 years]. I've never respected the profession. It is a business that has to take the majority of the blame for being the enemy of nature, for destroying native cultures, for taking from the poor and giving to the rich, and for poisoning the earth with the effluent from its factories . . . Yet business can produce food, cure disease, control population, employ people, and generally enrich our lives. And it can do these good things and make a profit without losing its soul. That's what this book is about.

He does not project himself as a brooding business perfectionist—though he is that—as in reaching out to help form loosely organized groups of companies pledging to give 1 percent of their profits, or better yet, their sales to environmental activist groups. Patagonia has been a strong backer of Planned Parenthood, a position that has provoked thousands of letters from customers saying they would never buy any more products from the company. What did the company do? It brought together all the similarly targeted companies for a unified response. When the Christian Action Council (CAC) started picketing Patagonia stores, Yvon told them that for every picketer, the company would donate $10 to Planned Parenthood in his or her name. Patagonia busted a similar boycott drive aimed at punishing the company for supporting forest protection organizations. Such steadfast commitments led to evermore loyal support from most of their customers who agree with those positions.

Patagonia has been involved in so many controversial causes, such as taking down dams and protecting designated wilderness areas and, more recently, suing the Trump Administration for shrinking the Bears Ears National Monument by more than 80 percent and the Grand Staircase-Escalante National Monument by half—totaling millions of acres—that opponents cease trying to intimidate this Ventura "Rock of Gibraltar." Patagonia doesn't mince words—leading the way with full page ads, signed by many outdoor businesses, such as one titled "The President Stole Your Land."

Appearing on the cable news channels, Chouinard stands for America's public lands, along with a huge majority of the American people, pointing out that Costa Rica had 10 percent of its land in national parks, compared with the United States' 4 percent. It doesn't harm his cause to have him note that "The $887-billion outdoor recreation economy employs over 7.6 million people in good sustainable jobs." He also plays hardball. Protesting Utah's policies regarding land protections, he was instrumental in shifting a business convention and exposition from Salt Lake City.

Always looking ahead, Patagonia periodically holds a "Tools for Grassroots Activists Conference," where young people are taught the "organizational, business, marketing skills small business groups need to survive in a competitive media environment."

Unlike Jeff Bezos's Amazon Corporation, which couldn't care less about the endangered *Amazon* tropical forest in South America, Yvon, fellow climber Doug Tompkins (former CEO of Esprit) and his wife, Kris McDivitt Tompkins (former CEO of Patagonia), in 2000 launched a land trust—Conservación Patagónica—for the "purpose of purchasing land in Argentina and Chile to create national parks and nature preserves." And did they ever; buying, preserving and turning over to these governments splendid, little exploited, regions of mountains, forests, beaches and seas. What is more, they have generated a remarkable, popular national park ethic and support in these societies that presages a solid base for posterity.

Here are some examples: The land trust bought 173,000 acres in the Valle Chacabuco in the Patagonia region of southern Chile. The area is the habitat of the few remaining species of huemul deer. Valley Chacabuco bordered on two existing nature reserves, creating a 645,000-acre area of protected terrain.

Another early purchase was the 155,000-acre Estancia Monte Leon, with its twenty-five miles of Atlantic coast line. The land is home to a large penguin rookery as well as sea lions, southern elephant seals, thousands of seabirds, pumas, guanacos, Darwin's rheas, and other plants and animals. On November 12, 2002, Monte Leon was officially made a national park in Argentina.

The preservation strategy is not unmindful of indigenous tribes who also are endangered by future development. For example, the timber companies planned to cut down Araucaria forests in Chile. The local indigenous peoples depend on pinon nuts for food. Doug Tompkins, Patagonia, and some associates formed the Labuan Foundation, bought and acquired title to the land in 1989 and placed it in permanent protection as the Cani sanctuary.

Their effort was just in time—with acreage being available for around $10 an acre—but not for very long, given the accelerating loss of wild or tribal lands to extractive industries, proposed dams and highways.

Yvon is a tested believer in small, dynamic groups he calls "civil democracy," responsible historically for the great advances in justice. "We need the river keepers, the bay keepers, the forest guardians and the protesters who chain themselves to the front doors," he declared. Like nature, civil democracy hates monoculture and centralization. That's why his company donates small grants (around $5,000 each) to thousands of small groups with passion, focus, integrity, and very little bureaucracy.

One long-time observer says that Yvon does all these things, including changing courses, as with the different transition from chemically grown cotton to organic cotton, because unlike most other CEOs, he is always directly observing, experiencing, and thinking. This immersion—between long interludes of fly fishing, ice-climbing, or just living in the wilderness—makes it look easy. Making something look easy lowers the frantic atmosphere in the workplace. Eruptive emotions over deadlines, quotas, and other markers disrupt focus and interpersonal work practices. Such markers are the opposite of an efficient use of time in spotting opportunities that are not on your desk. (The Chouinard's have no offices at the company headquarters where they work.)

Take the marvelous story that started with a protest against the possible destruction of their surf break, in the early 1970s. The city of Ventura was planning to channel and develop the mouth

of the Ventura River—"one of the best surf points in the area" and
some five-hundred yards from Patagonia's office. The river was a
man-made mess—much of its water is diverted by two dams, with
water at the river mouth coming from the sewage treatment plant.
The steelheads had almost disappeared. Experts at the hearing declared the river was "dead," so the proposed channeling wouldn't
have any effect on either what was left of the wildlife or on the
surf break.

At that time, a lone activist, Mark Capelli, a young twenty-
five-year-old graduate student, intent on rescuing the river, gave
an eye-opening slideshow of photos taken along the river. The
company gave him office space, a mailbox, and small donations
to save and get the river restored. He started the "Friends of
Ventura River" and victory after victory resulted in restoration
of the habitat for fish and other species and restored river flow.
This encouraged Patagonia to support other small groups working to restore habitats, committing in 1986 to donate 10 percent
of its profits.

Two years later, Patagonia plunged into support of an alternative master plan to de-urbanize the Yosemite Valley. Having
worked in beyond-beautiful Yosemite the summer out of college,
I could sympathize with that quest. I worked at a small supermarket serving visiting urban dwellers, who left thousands of
cars some miles away at a parking lot to savor the outdoors. But
they insisted on the amenities of the indoors. Shocking to many,
Yosemite Valley in 1955 was experiencing air pollution! Thirty-
three years later, the wear and tear of these visitors spawned alarm
even beyond the concern of some conservationists. Writers provided articles that were printed in Patagonia's catalog (imagine L.
L. Bean doing something like this). Messages were displayed in
the company stores. The intrepid firm catapulted itself into serious
controversies. As Yvon wrote:

As we became more and more involved, we waged campaigns on behalf of salmon and river restoration, against
GATT and "free trade" agreements and genetically modified organisms (GMOs), for the Wildlands Project and, in
Europe, against heavy truck traffic through the Alps.

One of the most famous advocacy advertisements was a full-
page newspaper ad with the headline: "What Does an Outdoor
Clothing Company Know About Genetically Engineered Food?
Not Enough, and Neither Do You."

As you might expect, all this activity pushed Yvon and his associates to look inward and begin systematically examining their
own corporate role as a polluter. The initial response in 1984 was
to use recycled paper waste for their catalog—first in the United
States. The result was "disastrous"—the still experimental paper
didn't hold the ink very well, and the photos were blurry. But the
company added up major savings in electricity, millions of gallons
of water, many saved trees and thousands of pounds of pollutants
out of the air. The next year, the quality of paper greatly improved.
Many other executives would not have waited until next year; they
would've returned to their regular paper. This recycling ethic was
just the beginning. From recycled paper, Patagonia moved to recycle and reuse materials in their construction and remodeling endeavors. Working with Wellman in Malden Mills, they developed
recycled polyester for use in their Synchilla fleece.

In the late 1980s, Patagonia expanded so fast that it struggled
to keep up with the demand for office space and the capabilities of
their suppliers, bankers, internal information systems, and managers. Yvon doesn't use computers and has no interest in any digital
distractions, but the company had to keep getting larger and larger
computers, one of which, the IBM System 38, he mistook for an
air conditioner.

By 1989, the company was selling "technical shells for mountaineering, skiing, paddling, fishing and sailing, as well as insulation and underwear for all outdoor activities."

Expansion internationally brought all kinds of sleepless nights, problems with licenses, distributors, and managers. That was when Yvon decided to open retail stores in France and Tokyo to learn more about the requirements there and in the United States for success. In his book, Yvon went through all the mistakes they were making, noting that the company was "restructured five times in five years; no plan worked better than the last one." That open self-criticism has proved to nourish Patagonia's remarkable resiliency and longevity. But not without major financial bumps and nagging doubts about why the Patagonians, stateside, were in business at all.

During a rare retention of a no-nonsense consultant, Dr. Michael J. Kami, who, some believe, had turned Harley-Davidson around, Yvon answered his first question: "Why are you in business?" with words about making a profit and then giving it away to civic groups grappling with the omnicidal direction of the world. To which Dr. Kami responded, "I think that's bullshit." Elaborating, he said, "that if they were really serious about giving money away, they could sell the company and put the proceeds into a foundation, invest the principal and give away the interest every year." Yvon replied that he was worried about what would happen to the company and its environmental/worker/consumer ethic under the new buyer. Dr. Kami's quick riposte: "So maybe you're kidding yourself about why you're in business." Yvon recalled his personal reaction. "It was as if the Zen Master had hit us over the head with a stick, but instead of finding enlightenment, we walked away more confused than ever."

Then suddenly in 1991, after years of 30 to 50 percent compound annual growth and trying to have it all, as he put it, Patagonia hit the wall—the national recession disrupted the company's overextended equilibrium. Executives were let go. Layoffs were ordered for the first time—20 percent of the workforce. Yvon took a dozen of his top managers to the "wind swept mountains of the real Patagonia" in Argentina for "a walkabout." (Can you imagine Jeff Bezos taking his managers to the real Amazon in Brazil to discuss what kind of company they wanted to become?) On their return, during a new board of directors meeting, one of them, Jerry Mander, a deep thinker about corporate entities, skipped lunch to compose a mission statement.

It's too long to reference more than its essence here: All life on Earth is jeopardized; all decisions of the company must be made in the context of the environmental crisis; maximum attention to product quality defined as durability, renewability, multifunctionalism, and non-obsolescence. Tithing for community activism is required. Patagonia must encourage the board, management, and staff to engage in proactive stances that reflect our values to influence "the larger corporate community to also adjust its values and behavior; and that top management of Patagonia operates with maximum transparency . . . while we simultaneously seek dynamism and innovation."

The multiple roots of the Patagonia company tree were planted after that mission statement. Yvon took busloads of staff to Yosemite or the Marin Headlands above San Francisco to camp out and talk about the company's business and environmental ethics and values. He wrote that high-risk sports had taught him never to exceed one's limits—translated into "know your strengths and limitations and live within your means."

There was an additional lesson from Zen philosophy that Yvon studied for many years, drawn to by his proficiency in archery.

In Zen archery, you forget about the goal of hitting the bull's-eye and instead focus on all the individual movements involved in shooting an arrow. You practice your stance, reaching back and smoothly pulling an arrow out of the quiver, notching it on the string, controlling your breathing and letting the arrow release itself. If you've perfected all the elements, you can't help but hit the center of the target.

He then tells people that the "perfect place" he found to apply "this Zen philosophy is in the business world."

To get out of the mess the company was in at the time, Yvon didn't look to other corporate turnaround case studies. No way. He looked to the Iroquois and their seven-generation planning. All decisions henceforth for Patagonia had to be made as if the company would be in business for 100 years.

The turnaround was very quick for a much more focused and purpose-driven organization. With a controlled growth rate of 5 percent, Patagonia received all kinds of awards for their treatment of workers, especially working mothers. Its catalog received twenty Gold or Silver Awards from *Catalog Age Magazine*. By 1994, Patagonia commenced their first environmental assessment report with the lifecycle analysis that led them to move from industrially grown cotton to 100 percent organically grown. Recycled plastic soda pop bottles were turned into Patagonia's Synchilla jackets. Recycling, preventing waste in their own production process, and imposing tougher sustainability requirements on their suppliers made Patagonia a model for other companies. Ninety-five percent of the materials for their warehouses and their three-story office building in Ventura came from recycles. At the same time, Patagonia stepped up its support for grassroots conservation activists.

Here are Chouinard's global yardsticks: "We measure our success on the . . . old growth forests that were not clear-cut, mines that were never dug in pristine areas, toxic pesticides that were not

sprayed . . . damaging dams dismantled, rivers restored and listed
as wild and scenic, the parks and wilderness areas created." Not
claiming sole credit for these victories, Patagonia "provided seed
money or was a major funder for many of these initiatives."

Turning company philosophies into adaptive guidelines shaped
"the design, production, distribution, image, human resources, finance, management, and the environment," guiding the company
through the process of designing, manufacturing, and selling
clothing for the mountains to the oceans.

Let's say you are a new hire at Patagonia in Ventura (often a
friend of an employee). You've gone through a rigorous recruitment process and have digested the values, philosophies, history,
and purposes of the Patagonian ecosystem. Yvon invites you and
several other new hires to surf during the lunch hour followed by
snacks and drinks around an outdoor table. What do you think he's
going to talk about? Let's guess. First, he may tell you he can't wait
to get out of town and fly to his little home in Moose, Wyoming.
He doesn't recommend that you spend months, as he does himself,
in your favorite place—fishing, climbing, contemplating, thinking.
He does tell you to take it easy, take time off (flextime), but you are
trusted to get your job done and then imagine getting it done better in all ways. He may startle you by informing you of his MBA
style of management (Management By Absence) as a sign of his
trust in you.

Do you get the sign? Sure, and you feel good. He reminds you
that there are no VIP parking spaces, and that the best spaces
are reserved for the most fuel-efficient cars, no matter who owns
them. The cafeteria, serving healthy organic food, is open all day
as an informal meeting place. Decisions made through *consensus*
are superior to decisions made from *compromise*. He recalls the
time Patagonia had organizational psychologists who concluded
that the company's employees were "so independent that [they]

would be unemployable in a typical company." You laugh, somewhat nervously, wondering what's coming next. Yvon reminds you that he and Malinda own the company; it is a private company, not a publicly traded one. You, he says, looking straight at your eyes, are free to say what you think about any product, process, condition, or dream. You can come at it as a consumer wearing or using Patagonia's wares. You are free to be civically active and take on the powers destroying Earth's habitat. Don't worry about how management may react to you on Monday morning. Because the owner and management of Patagonia don't have to worry about big shareholders pushing for mergers or stock buybacks, or about Wall Street analysts on the telephone every quarter demanding you do nonsense things to jack up the stock price and violate the values of the company.

With that, Yvon takes a warm leave, and everybody goes back to work in spaces devoid of offices, walls, or closed doors. When the COVID pandemic struck in March 2020, Patagonia shut down all operations to protect its workers and paid them fully throughout the closing period. The company showed more of its heart during those hard times.

Yvon has a knack at hitting my nerve as a consumer advocate long fed up with a little observed trick by manufacturers. They sell us products that are only as good as "every link" and make sure there are "links" that wear out much faster than the rest of the item. This sabotages durability and prompts discarding the item. Collars on shirts start fraying early. Erasers on pencils get hard while the pencil stays usable. Zippers fail and should be easily replaceable. Too early expiration dates for a "best use" on food packages.

Well, read Yvon, writing from the view of a consumer:

Because the overall durability of a product is only as good as its weakest element, the ultimate goal should be a product whose parts wear out at roughly the same time and only after a long life. You may notice that a great product like Levi's jeans will get a hole in the knee at about the same time you notice a hole in the rear or in the pocket. Conversely, the worst examples for wear range from electronic equipment, which have become virtually disposable when one element fails, to a pair of pricey swim shorts whose elastic waistband loses it stretch, from the chlorine in pools, while the rest of the garment still looks new. Technically, those shorts, as well as the electronics equipment, can be repaired, but because the cost of repair is too high relative to the original purchase price, the product usually gets junked.

To get all the components of a Patagonia product to be roughly equal in durability, we test continually in both the lab and the field. We test until something fails, strengthen that part, then see what fails next, strengthen that, etc., until we're confident that the product is durable as a whole.

This is part of what Patagonia means when they say they treat customers with respect. That includes direct contact as well. The company rejects the terrible customer phone service with its "transaction quotas, intentionally long-hold times and managerial indifference that farms out phone calls to a service bureau in Delhi."

Yvon has a book inside of him that could mark or satirize with a searing impact the conventional world of business—its trivialities, its deceptions, its greed at the top and its destructiveness on workers, consumers, and the world at large. Here is a glimmer of what I mean: "When I die and go to hell," writes the great surfer, "the devil is going to make me the marketing director for a cola company. I will be in charge of trying to sell a product that no one needs, is identical to its competition, and can't be sold on its merits. I'd be competing head on in the cola wars on price, distribution, advertising and promotion, which would indeed be hell for me."

Think of his satirical approach to the clothing and fashion companies: "The most responsible way for a consumer and a good citizen to buy clothes is to buy used clothing. Beyond that, avoid buying clothes you have to dry clean or iron. Wash in cold water. Line dry when possible. Wear your shirt more than one day before you wash it." He once placed a full-page ad with the headline "Don't Buy Our Jacket." He refers to a study by Dr. Thomas M. Power of the University of Montana that says only 10 to 15 percent of the money Americans spend on goods and services is necessary for survival. What they pay far more for is wants beyond mere survival, lured by the sizzle to get them to the steak.

No account, however brief, of Chouinard's life is complete without going into his collaboration and friendship with the late super-stalwart Doug Tompkins. Tompkins was the climber, surfer, innovator, great land preservationist, successful businessman, co-starting CEO of Esprit, and practical idealist for products and visions. They questioned, probed, challenged, and discovered together during their trips into the rugged wilderness and the turbulent seas. After seeing Doug wearing a brushed wool Fila pullover, Yvon spawned the idea of polyester bunting, Synchilla, and many other micro-fleeces. From their discussions came a resolve to dramatically shorten the wasteful supply chain, which had coursed through four countries and three continents before landing in the catalog or company store. With Doug in the lead, first going to Chile and buying up huge inexpensive tracts of unspoiled wilderness for nature preserves and national parks, Yvon was a constant advisor and traveler to selected regions in Chile and Argentina. These preserves were turned over in perpetuity to the Forest or National Park departments of the two countries who receive them with great futuristic enthusiasm, promising to add vast additional acreage. In Chile and Argentina, Doug and Kris Tompkins turned over an area of 2.2 million acres, almost two-thirds the size of Connecticut.

When Doug Tompkins was working on his first preserve in Chile, vested interest adversaries poured vitriol on him and his motivations and jeopardized his safety. He was a courageous, determined humanitarian. At the peak of his successful additions to the list of national parks—having sparked public excitement there for many more parks—Doug remained the daredevil, showing Yvon the way for dozens of first ascents and descents of mountains in Chile and Patagonia.

Then came December 2015, when Doug, Yvon, and two comrades were on a five-day paddling trip at a remote lake in southern Chile. A sudden gale came up. Chouinard and Jib Ellison managed to get their kayak to an island. But Doug and Rick Ridgeway capsized and spent nearly an hour trying to get to safety. Finally towed to shore, they were helicoptered to a hospital where Doug expired from hypothermia. Ridgeway survived. The difference: Casual Doug wore only a T-shirt and light clothing. Ridgeway wore more formidable clothing and the difference in minutes took the life of a great visionary, determined doer, and naturalist transcending cultures and languages in pursuit of his public land preservation dreams for posterity.

Kris Tompkins, his wife, told a writer: "We thought we'd die together. We were obsessed with one another for twenty-five years. It's the Great Amputation . . . Yvon and Doug . . . calculated risk better than most." Surviving scores of imposed and self-imposed perils in his business and adventuring life, Doug lost his final outdoor adventure for a lack of an adequate Patagonia-like set of clothes.

Yvon is not one to weep, though he will never get over the narrow margin between life and death that took Doug's life.

He is a "carrying on" type of personality—always observing data or vistas that spark action by his company. At one time, he learned that the post-sale of clothing products produced four times the amount of harm as the entire manufacturing process. Patagonia's constant research and testing and experimenting led to that finding, and then to insistent advice to the consumer to buy used clothing where possible.

Traveling through potato farmland in Idaho, he saw beyond the fields. He learned about the toxicity, the pesticides, the contaminated well-water used by farm families. This led to "Patagonia Provisions," a new food initiative to find and sell sustainable food.

Many people perceive Patagonia as a hell-bent, risk-taking company. Chouinard says that is partly accurate, but "what they don't realize is that we do our homework." This swashbuckling firm, busting through conventional norms, is very much a hands-on systems-creating operation. When so many variables, so many links in a chain are involved, there must be systems to be followed. My US Army sergeant once told our platoon: "The Army is a system devised by geniuses so that it can be run by idiots, like you! You better believe that!"

In addition to do-yourselves systems, Yvon believes, of all things, in lists. He breaks down the "most complex and far reaching of Patagonia's philosophies, its environmental philosophy" in five ways:

Lead an examined life.

Clean up our own act.

Do our penance.

Support civil democracy.

Influence other companies.

These are not just motivational or extraordinary phrases. He spells them out in greater detail as a continuing work in progress, more than I've ever seen in any corporate social responsibility document. Its most recent addition is the book *The Responsible Company: What We've Learned from Patagonia's First 40 Years* by Yvon Chouinard and Vincent Stanley (2012). His paean to the historical and peerless roll of civil democracy is profound, as he refers to our better history. That's why most of the company's philanthropy goes to grass-roots activists with specific objectives—such as shutting down a harmful dam.

He truly has influenced other companies, and not just through the coalition pledging to give 1 percent of the company's profits or sales to environmental causes. He has influenced Walmart through his direct contact with S. Robson Walton and the latter's eye-opening visit to Ventura. Patagonia was instrumental in launching the Sustainable Apparel Coalition, a consortium of large retailers to start grading their products for consumers.

He doesn't do what Ray C. Anderson—the late great CEO of Interface, Inc.—did. An admirer and collaborator with Yvon, Anderson would make up to 200 speeches a year around the country, proselytizing business audiences or executives. Yvon, if asked, would respond; if he spotted an opening, he would tap into it and nudge.

There is one side of Yvon few people know. He is quite conventional and stands in line when it comes to presidential electoral politics. During two of my campaigns for the presidency as a Green and as an Independent, I called him for assistance and input. He quickly and politely turned me down, with no interest in further discussion. He is a least-worster, reluctantly favoring the moribund, corporate Democratic Party over the more dreaded, commercialistic Republican Party. He simply told me he was supporting John Kerry and later Barack Obama and declined to hear me out, either strategically or tactically. A bit knee-jerk, I thought, hanging up the phone, and certainly unlike his usual methodical way of analyzing multiple choices before him. Because so many enlightened people took his path and supported the Democratic machine, without any conditions or nudging demands, the smug, fat-cat funded Democratic Party lost election after election at the state and national level. This emboldened the cruel and corrupt Republican Party into declaring that they received the mandate of the people for entrenching their brutal corporate state over our deteriorating, fragile, self-styled democracy—in the legislative, judicial and executive branches.

However, Yvon has no hesitation at being smartly strategic as a corporate citizen, teaming up with ardent right-wingers who happen to share his opposition or support for important protections of the environment. Recently, he co-authored an opinion-piece with Land Tawney in *The Denver Post*, early in the Trump era, titled "Hunters, Hikers Unite to Protect Beloved Public Lands, Waters." Land Tawney is well named—a fifth generation Montanan, he leads the Backcountry Hunters & Anglers, North America's fast-growing organizations of sportsmen and sportswomen. You can guess where he comes from politically—the opposite pole from Yvon. Yet they unite in opposing the privatizing or commercial pillaging of the public lands and waters. The joint article—a left/right alliance—listed three examples for direct action. First, opposing Interior Secretary Ryan K. Zinke's overruling of the US Forest Service to allow industrial sulfide-ore copper mining near the Boundary Water Wilderness in Minnesota—the most visited wilderness destination in the nation. Supporting 4,500 jobs, they hasten to add. Second, Congress and the Department of Interior appeared ready to allow the Land and Water Conservation Fund to expire. Established in 1965, it helped protect 5,000,000 acres and generated $4 in economic value for every $1 invested. The fund, write the authors, comes from a tiny percentage of revenues from offshore drilling.

Third, stop the assault on the public lands by President Trump.

The article ended with a flourish, typical of Yvon; "Now is the time for everyone who loves the outdoors to speak up, whether you feel more comfortable in camouflage or Capilene. The threats are dire and the stakes are high."

Yvon and Land have struck a neglected vein of political gold, that of an unstoppable left/right alliance, once it gets focused on the Congress and the executive branch. As the two unlikely authors say, "If hunters and treehuggers can come together, maybe Washington will too, and once again make conservation a bipartisan priority. If we do, the forces that divide us won't stand a chance."

There are other pithy ways to try to understand Yvon Chouinard, such as from his brief observations made to *The New Yorker*'s Nick Paumgarten in 2016, to wit:

—It's impossible to be a public company and be responsible.

—We have a rule here. Whatever you touch first in the freezer, you eat. It's mostly game. I touched a goose. Watch your teeth.

—I had a 401(k), but I took that money out of the market and put it in trees. Second growth timberland in the Pacific Northwest in part to protect salmon and steelhead watersheds.

—Fly-fishing has become so esoteric. People have decided to learn more and more about less and less.

—Fishing was the way to get them to care about the water.

And, in his writings, Chouinard says:

—We would rather earn credibility than buy it. The best resources for us are the word-of-mouth recommendations from a friend or a favorable comment in the press. We advertise only as a last resort.

—Since we don't mind taking a stand or risk giving offense, there is all the more reason to get the facts right.

During our project to legalize the growing of industrial hemp in the United States, I once wrote Chouinard asking if his company would use more industrial hemp in its clothing products were that 5,000-year-old plant, grown by Thomas Jefferson and George Washington, allowed to grow in the United States? He wrote back saying of course he would.

Yvon knew plenty about industrial hemp and how it was grown in remote, rural areas of China by proven, though difficult, ancient methods.

He was eager to "wear-test" such clothing as he had done with other clothing and equipment in the most extreme conditions of the Himalayas and South America.

How many active owners of a company, growing too fast and overextended, would have chosen an unproven general manager—in this case Kris McDivitt, who for thirteen years, starting in 1979, learned as she managed to levels the Chouinards characterized as spectacular and amazingly intuitive. Her secret was to admit she did not know about this and that and ask experienced people, including bank presidents, to help her.

"If you just admit that you don't know something, they will fall all over themselves trying to help," she said.

By now, dear reader, you may be asking the question that has occurred so many times. How could such a successful company as Patagonia and its meticulous yet laid-back management be a teachable model? Why doesn't such a model diffuse rapidly? How could another budding company in one field or another replicate its shaping philosophy, values, and operational practices, its intangible recruiting practices? Is anything about Patagonia replicable? Not in any comprehensive way and not if a company remains a private company. But perhaps the essences of this collaborative are replicable but in different expressions that stress comparable intangibles on route to tangible, material outcomes. Some of these firms belong to the Social Venture Network. Yvon would be the first to insist there is no formula, no set of rules, only insightful guidelines enhancing inventiveness, innovation, respect, and the self-critical traits that spell corrections and adjustments along the perilous way to business and environmental unknowns. Increasingly, Patagonia's uniqueness is in its longevity that improves multiple performances over time. Under it all are the character and personality of its founders, who use their company's products in the risky treks through the nature they earnestly work to preserve.

Other partially comparable companies such as Ben & Jerry's or Seventh Generation or The Body Shop did not last very long before they were sold to larger conventional corporations. Chouinard himself wants Patagonia to last 100 years—probably because he doesn't think the "home planet," as he puts it, will be livable past then. Will the people and institutions acting to save the Earth become numerous or powerful enough to challenge and reverse the destructive, omnicidal global corporations deploying runaway technologies while controlling governments?

In recent years and months, Chouinard and his team have been taking Patagonia to a higher, more urgent level, drawing on their successes and scaling them up in both quantity and quality. The magnitude of this newly arrived at billion-dollars-in-annual-sales private company is really prompting a move toward a reinvention of the company.

For one thing, Patagonia is moving to influence the outcomes of congressional and presidential elections. Chouinard was encouraged to go bigger in 2020, because the company's help in electing senators from Nevada and Montana in 2018 seemed to impress the candidates as being a tipping of the scales. He is measuring which candidates Patagonia supports or opposes, not surprisingly, by whether the candidates are "climate deniers," or champions of making confronting climate disruption a supreme priority.

From a multifaceted ecologist running an ecologically de-termined corporation, Chouinard stepped up to call himself "an avowed socialist." His definitions are nowhere near the textbook definition of "government ownership of the means of production." As he told Jeff Beer in *Fast Company* magazine (November 2019), he meant "socialistic countries like those in Scandinavia." In short, comprehensive social-democratic societies.

This political assertiveness marks an elevated recognition that setting a corporate example, as nearly no other company does, is not enough for systemic change. That to make systemic transitions from fossil fuels, for example, requires a committed new Congress and a new president.

Let's say that Patagonia's CEO has evolved from the time I asked him to support my 2000 and 2004 Presidential campaigns on the Green Party and Independent line, respectively. As noted, the phone conversation was short. He informed me that he was voting for Al Gore and John Kerry. But he wasn't helping to fund them big time. Later he told people he intended to step it up for the 2020 presidential election when he promised "we're going to be very, very active."

Early in 2019, Chouinard wrote a new mission statement for the company: "Patagonia is in business to save our home planet." Not an indirect goal, but *the* goal. It included a "commitment to be fossil-fuel free by 2025." It included a big plunge into an endlessly discoverable "regenerative agriculture," that is beyond just growing organic cotton; it includes, for example, using a minimum of tilling, a maximum amount of compost, and planting revenue-producing "cover-crops," such as chickpeas and turmeric, which are in big demand. These crops help protect the soil's nutrients and help to control pests. Patagonia has 600 small farmers growing cotton this way in India, who have almost doubled their income with the bonus money and the sales of their cover-crops.

Patagonia and Chouinard are in an excellent position to relaunch the remarkable advocacy espoused in a discussion between Thomas Alva Edison and Henry Ford in the late 1920s. They presented our country with a choice. We could either go with the emerging chemical and oil companies and develop an intensely hydrocarbon-based economy or we could go the way Edison and Ford believed was a preferable way—developing an expanding carbohydrate-based economy. They knew that anything made by hydrocarbons can be made from carbohydrates more self-reliantly, much better for our farm economy, the land, and the health and safety of the people. They also knew it was the path toward a more locally based, renewable economy of deconcentrated power, rather than the heavily capitalized chemical and fossil fuel companies already dominated by the DuPonts and the Standard Oils of their day.

There are still many people who view a "sustainable economy" or a Green New Deal as revolutionary. Instead, their objectives could be viewed as a restoration of past ways, updated with facilitative technology. After all, as Edison and Ford well knew, the carbohydrate path proceeded hydrocarbon materials by many centuries. Hydrocarbons, like coal, oil, and gas, have been in significant use less than three centuries.

Unlike Paul Hawken, whose attitude was steady, always upbeat, Yvon harbors a philosophical pessimism that he uses to drive himself into action. He told Mr. Beer that "we're in a triage situation. Things are so grim, it is World War III. I lived through World War II, and I remember what the country had to do to mobilize."

Personally, he is working toward a new state park at the tip of South America—perhaps taking a cue from his close friend, the late Doug Tompkins. As Yvon described it to *Fast Company*, "There are about 800,000 acres of peat bogs and swamps and 200,000 acres of sea, that sequester more carbon then almost anywhere in the world."

Also, as part of the reinvention, Patagonia is going into short, exciting, motivating film-making—one of which he says has already had a distinct effect in Western Europe. One is called *Artifishal*, and warns against offshore fish farms, as for growing salmon. These fish farms must use chemicals to keep diseases and lice at bay due to the close proximity of the fish to each other, emitting feces.

The other film came out in 2014 and is called *DamNation* (learning from the great David Brower) regarding the damage dams do. He claims that it led the Obama Administration to no longer view dams as green energy.

For a hard-nosed rationalist and operating empiricist, Chouinard, now in his eighties, believes that people make decisions on emotion (does he have the Trump voters in mind?).

Therefore, "the best way to elicit emotion is through film . . . not through books or catalogs or speeches." Patagonia is going big here, producing ten films at a time. I assume he means informed emotion—the kind that propels people to realize injustice and the need for action to correct it.

Yvon Chouinard clearly is becoming more confident than ever about exponentially expanding the reach of his past pioneering breakthroughs. He is getting his colleagues to press harder on the firm's suppliers to emulate what has worked for Patagonia—such as going solar, going organic, conserving energy and materials. In addition, he is far more extroverted in trying to persuade large companies to get on board. When Beer asked him what he would tell the CEOs of JPMorgan Chase & Co. or Apple (who talk a good game), he replied: "If I had enough time, I would just give them example after example of how doing the right thing ended up making us more money."

Notice he said "us." I think that would make CEOs Jamie Dimon and Tim Cook privately regard the modestly paid Chouinard as naïve, since they are first interested in how much the companies they rule can make for each of them—with stock options, bonuses, etc.—and they then shape the companies' operation and time skills accordingly.

Far less naive is Yvon's late-day plunge into electoral contests at the federal level. If he can bring others in his circle of companies along to focus on successfully getting-out-the-vote big time and getting the planet-preserving positions to be held seriously, as mandates, by the candidates they support, that is when the possibility of exponential action can become real.

It took four years for Yvon Chouinard to put into pioneering practice Patagonia's new mission statement, "We're in business to save our home planet." On September 14, 2022, in the courtyard of the company's national office in Ventura, California, staff and alums were called together to receive an announcement that made worldwide news garnished with editorial astonishment. Chouinard, his wife, Malinda, and two children, Claire and Fletcher, were giving away this privately held company and the entire voting stock (just two percent of total shares) to a new creation called Patagonia Purpose Trust, instructed to perform according to well-defined Chouinard civic, environmental, and economic values.

The remaining 98 percent of the shares are placed in another new entity called the Holdfast Collective, designated as a nonprofit 501(c)(4) that would receive dividends (amounting to about $100 million for 2022) to donate to effective, smallish ecology groups devoted to planet Earth protective action. The Collective is also able to pursue civic and political advocacy in the US and around the world.

Patagonia remains a for-profit firm reinvesting its products and processes toward further heights of planetary protection while offloading its profits to the Holdfast Collective.

At a spry eighty-five, and still the happy outdoorsman, Chouinard is not sailing into the sunset. He and his family will keep a mortal eye on their two institutions, structured for perpetuity, and encourage other entrepreneurs to consider establishing similar dynamic legacies.

Notwithstanding that these governing and receiving nonprofits are chartered for perpetuity, the Chouinards know that they will operate only as well as the trustees running them. Toward this reality, the Chouinards have devoted much time, in their meticulous way, to making their choice of stalwarts. As is said, time will tell.

11

GORDON B. SHERMAN

CEO of Midas International Corp.

It was during the turbulent year of 1968 when I accepted Gordon Sherman's telephone invitation to visit him in Chicago and discuss his interest in providing our young Center for Study of Responsive Law with a grant from the Midas Foundation. It was a visit so unusually offered by a foundation chief that it has never been replicated in my years of experience. I flew out from Washington and had dinner and stayed overnight at his spacious home, where his wife Kate and four children lived. They shared the house with a large, attached aviary full of domestic and some exotic birds, striving to satisfy Mr. Sherman's insatiable curiosity; the aviary was just one of his passionate hobbies. He was one dedicated and knowledgeable field birder. At dinner, we neither had to come to any agreements nor learn more about each other. He had followed the initiatives of Nader's Raiders and my expanding challenges to the foibles, failures, and fatuousness of Big Business with expressive relish. Those were the days when our efforts were regularly covered by the major newspapers and network television.

For my part, friends in Chicago had been advising me about this business executive, who was rapidly expanding Midas Muffler Shops' franchises while applying his student background in the "Great Books Curriculum" of the University of Chicago, then headed by the iconoclastic football-abolishing Robert Maynard Hutchins. They called Sherman a "no BS" scholar running a counterintuitive business with a keen sense of history's injustices and their cover-ups by managing autocrats.

Gordon Sherman was not just a backstage funder of progressive causes in Chicago. He lived to make waves by strategically advancing provocative ideas. The next morning, we had breakfast and spoke some more until it was time for lunch at a magisterial, prime business club of Chicago's plutocrats. Never one to be muffled or to muffle, the Midas boss escorted me ever so slowly through the fully occupied tables so that the corporate executives would have ample opportunity to arch their eyebrows and flare their nostrils at the sight of the uppity Sherman and the most publicized adversary of their domain of alleged free enterprise and capitalism. Making eye contact as I brushed by them, I could see that Sherman had succeeded by the time we reached our small table for two. For a couple of minutes, he sat quietly, reveling in the dark looks and the accompanying murmurs over his audacity to exploit his own recent admission to the membership with such a direct affront to the long-treasured dignity and decorum of the Club's atmosphere.

I wouldn't have been so surprised by his bravura—after all, he had business dealings with some of the diners—had I done more homework and read *The New Yorker*'s "Talk of the Town" interview with him in its September 15, 1962 issue. It wasn't long—they never are in that front section—but it was downright funny for the impact that he had on the reporter.

In those times, "Talk of the Town" notes were usually much

comment and observation by the writer, sprinkled with quotes from the interviewees. So verbally scintillating was Sherman that, after introducing his subject while having dinner at Trader Vic's, the enthralled writer simply provided one quotation after another, strung together with short elisions.

The Chicagoan entrepreneur was in New York City to look over the twenty-five Midas Muffler Shops, then known for unheard-of speedy service—muffler installations while you wait. The writer discovered that Sherman talked with a biographical directness so loved by reporters, to wit:

What I have tried to do is remove the diaphanous membrane that separates humanism from business. I started out by advertising in such learned journals as the *American Psychologist* and the *Bulletin of the American Association of University Professors* for field counselors—gentlemen, eight in number, whom I proposed to pay handsomely and whose task it would be both to arrange franchises for prospective dealers and to maintain a liaison with those already franchised, the result being kind of a gigantic pulmonary effect. I was particularly interested in teachers of psychology and allied subjects. No mystery about that. I simply wanted men who understood the potential of communication, the application of cause-and-effect, who knew that the history of *life* consists of finding out what it's all about—men who could, furthermore, look at *themselves* with a cold, acid gaze, as though formaldehyde. A hybridization, one might say. The aggressive intellectual.

By this time, the reporter had discovered a transcendentalist in business garb. No one could possibly have memorized these words and delivered a prepared act. Besides, Sherman wanted more to elevate the discourse and shred the stereotype of the businessman than merely to display his personality at the dinner table.

He continued: "I deny the whole concept that there is such a thing as a *businessman*. Business orientation is a response to a condition of casualty. In other words, it boils down to this: We want shops, and we want people to come to them. I'll have the subgum chicken chow mein, waiter."

There you have him. The cerebral jolt, the humor, the sudden descent down the abstraction ladder to the menu, the drama, delivered in a melodious baritone, all of it delighted the speaker and probably the listener.

After a brief fatherly exchange with his nine-year-old son, Skipper, Sherman reminisced to the reporter: "When I was nine, I made my own bagpipes. You can get wonderful effects with pipe music. All that ornamentation, in the Bach sense." "He's a brilliant classical pianist, too," interjected Milton Shamitz, a regional Midas manager. "Ah, the piano," said Sherman.

> The joy there is in the idea of a man pitted against himself! At Chicago, I won some modest honors as a member of the gymnastic team. Haven't touched a parallel bar for years, though. My chief extracurricular interest these days, aside from piano and bagpipes, are horticulture—I have my own greenhouse—and the study of Hebrew. My approach is not so much to study language as stereotypical linguistics. I am also deliriously married and have three other children at home.

Sensing that the reporter wanted to take away something about the innovative Midas business, the Renaissance man got down to business:

What we offer—besides gold paint—that some of the retailers in mufflerdom may not, is honesty, a certain specificity and half-hour-while-you-wait-service in a bright, pleasant shop that says something. It says, "isn't it great to be alive and in the muffler business!"

"Most people think aesthetics is a rarefied art," said Sherman, "but we get into applied aesthetics. We are always hammering away at the amalgam of effects." At this point, Sherman became prideful: "And when it comes to ideas, we take them from any of our employees. There is a complete abnegation of status in our organization."

The New Yorker ended the interview with Sherman describing his store psychologist turned expanders of Midas franchises who continued to pursue their "intellectual life," referring to Jung and other masters of their profession. "We have transcended communication," he trumpeted, "like the Zen archer."

It isn't known whether the reporter thought Sherman's performance was an act or, if it was, it didn't matter because, exhibiting Sherman's distinct imprint, his business was booming. What is known is that Sherman was a man of steady flamboyant authenticity with a deep public philosophy tinctured with a mournful sensitivity to the tormented world into which he was born. His scholarly, colorful language on important subjects should have attracted mass media attention and made him a nationally known business pioneer and leader. But for all his assumed controversial positions—controversial, that is, to the established power which he spurned—Sherman remained largely a Chicago media phenomenon. But a quietly seething one. His daily absorption of the struggles by the deprived and dispossessed for equality, safety, respect, and opportunity connected with his continuing immersion in the humanities. He spoke out, irritating the one man he could not impress, no matter the vast expansion of the auto parts business that Nate H. Sherman, an immigrant, started in 1932.

The stern father did not welcome the son's public positions, fearing it would produce a backlash from the Midas dealers and the banks. Then a single event shook Gordon to his moral core. The Democratic National Convention, in 1968, turned Chicago into a riot zone, later called by the National Commission on the Causes and Prevention of Violence a "police riot" against the thousands of protesters opposed to the Vietnam War and other atrocities surrounding the International Amphitheatre.

Sherman junior, moving more of Midas profits into the charitable Midas Foundation, started upping the ante with his grants. Numerous meetings with the legendary community organizer Saul Alinsky (author of the classic organizing manual, *Rules for Radicals*) led to foundation grants that funded a training institute for community organizers. One such graduate was Cesar E. Chavez, who went on to make history organizing a union of migrant farmworkers in California and elsewhere. Alinsky's Industrial Areas Foundation was chosen because, in Sherman's words, "It channels the passions of neglected people toward a free and open society."

In rapid succession, Sherman funded other civic groups, often with seed money, including our center. His most prominent legacy was launching the Chicago-based Business and Professional People for the Public Interest (BPI). Its fair and tough-minded litigation and advocacy continues to this day. BPI's focus is on justice reform, police accountability, public education, housing and community development, and holding politicians accountable to the law and open government. Its operating values, featured on its website, are "integrity, independence, effectiveness, tenacity and innovation." Its visions are that "all people will live in a just society with a quality of life that includes equal access to opportunity, healthy learning and living environments and a voice in decisions that affect their lives."

What so pleased Gordon Sherman was the sheer fearlessness of the BPI lawyers and staff. In 1969, they were crucial in blocking the absurd city plan to create a new Chicago airport in Lake Michigan. In 1971, BPI sued and later blocked construction of a nuclear power plant in the Indiana Dunes. They won landmark court cases, notably *Gautreaux v. CHA* in the US Supreme Court, a case that improved the rights of thousands of public housing families. BPI changed conditions on the ground for powerless people. Their proud founder modestly commented: "BPI is a little bit of redemption, a humanizing contribution where horrors abound."

Gordon's moral and historical education really shaped this remarkable renaissance man. It turned his abhorrence of war, mega-weapons, and violence into action. He once said, "it was Vietnam that turned me on. Something began to rise in me. Before this I'd been a typical hawk by default. But I became serious, I read." He became chairman of the local chapter of the effective Business Executives Move for Vietnam Peace (BEM), started by Henry E. Niles, board chairman of the Baltimore Life Insurance Company, and Harold Willens, Californian president of the Factory Equipment Supply Company of Los Angeles. BEM pressed for a stop to this quagmire war in Asia. Gordon became active in the national campaign demanding a freeze on nuclear weapons between the United States and the Soviet Union. Marches and mobilizations pushed our government to negotiate nuclear arms control treaties with the USSR.

"Horrors," as we shall note, was more than a word for Gordon. It encapsulated the impact on his kaleidoscopic conscience of the unjust, brutish conditions afflicting so many of the world's people, including those in his own country. Most business executives automatically screen out such awareness and restrict their blotter to what affects their company or economic sector from which they have developed knee-jerk plausible retorts. Not so for the Midas Muffler man. He took in the horrors, realized how little he could do about most of them, and saved his soul through music, bird-watching, nature photography, and other sane hobbies. That didn't mean that he escaped what he viewed as his responsibility to accelerate the "arc of the moral universe."

Flush with his success flowing from well-considered grants by the growing Midas Foundation, he had plans upon plans for escalating the pursuit of justice. He told me excitedly of his determination to pour far more profits from the Midas Company into its foundation. The company was doing well, based on systems he and his associates developed and placed under the management of expansion-minded managers. He expected to spend less time with corporate matters and more time and imagination on foundation matters. He sought to impact, through his own example, other foundations, both family ones and large ones.

Then a double tragedy struck, a patriarch's backlash and a cancer diagnosis. Gordon and his family were not the only ones affected. Many nameless persons lost their chance for a just life as a consequence. Nate Sherman was fuming over his son's radicalism and presumed alienation of dealers and customers. Midas's expansion and profits did not quell his anger. Any company stumble, and Chairman of the Board, Nate Sherman, pounced and blamed Gordon. There were private arguments, leading to the resignation of his prodigal son. The strong-willed father took over the company and fended off a subsequent proxy fight initiated by Gordon in 1971 to regain control of the company. It was over. The Sherman family uprooted themselves and moved to Mill Valley, California.

Gordon lived with terminal cancer for years; when asked how he was, he told friends that "dying is a great way to live."

He meant it. He stayed active in the San Francisco Bay Area environmental and nuclear arms control causes, taught music at the Dominican College of San Rafael, at the San Francisco Conservatory of Music, and at the Lighthouse for the Blind. His music appreciation course had the Shermanesque title of "The Rapture of Music: A Gentle Introduction." He wrote articles and kept an eye on the meanderings of the corporate world as only a perceptive former insider is able to do. Many of these reflections he kept to himself and friends until asked by my sister, the anthropology professor Laura Nader, to deliver a lecture at her Berkeley class on "controlling processes." It was early 1987, a few weeks before he died on May 8 of that year. The recorded transcript of his remarks was vintage Sherman. Paraphrasing serves the reader poorly. Thus, his own excerpted words:

In his last famous short story, *The Heart of Darkness*, Joseph Conrad describes the death of his hero/villain Kurtz. The man has coursed up the Congo River, deep into the heart of Africa, which stands as a metaphor for the heart of darkness in man, in society, as well at that time in the mid-nineteenth century—dark continent. He has gone in quest of ivory. He has plundered, corrupted, exploited the natives and now he lies dying from her hideous festering disease, and Conrad records his last words as "the horror, the horror." In gasping out this exclamation, Kurtz seems to be, at his last moment of consciousness, contemplating his own past—as a capitalist archetype, as a pre-corporate figure in astonishment and disgust at what he has done and what it signifies.

This phrase—"the horror, the horror"—has run in my head for decades. I have read the story many times and pondered its significance as the world—far, far more compounded on its perilous course toward self-extinction, since Conrad wrote—proceeds unchecked. And I have wondered what it is, "the corporate process"? What permits or encourages us as a society to tolerate that? To allow it to happen? What influences of control tempts us to succumb, and, not only tolerate, but to be part of this horrible, calculated, extermination and destruction of the globe?

The students were more than usually intent—computers and cell phones were not the existential distraction that they were to become some years later. Sherman continued:

I am a full-fledged corporate type. In my corporate time, I was steeped in all of the devices and techniques in the theory of corporate management. I came to know and understand with fascination the machinations of boards of directors, who put their seal-of-approval to so much that corporations do, even though . . . without much interest in its consequences and any deep understanding of its affairs . . . I created the Midas franchise system—and I was able to draw from that all kinds of corporate conclusions because the franchise system—no matter whose it is, or how it is run—is essentially a modern adaptation of feudalism.

The students probably had no idea of what a startling admission that was, to be describing millions of small businesses franchised by the likes of McDonald's, Krispy Kreme, and others scattered in every nook and cranny of the country in this way. The Midas franchises were given an above-average fine-print agreement, but Sherman was not making any self-serving exceptions.

After pointing out his regular interactions with the Federal Trade Commission, the Securities and Exchange Commission, and the Justice Department, he dove into his corporate philanthropy, which went well beyond "the conventional receptacles of uncontested corporate philanthropy" [such as the Boy Scouts and the symphony orchestras].

> I know what it's like to fund the outcasts, the people on the very cutting edge of social, legal and corporate change. I once very conspicuously funded a celebrated figure who has had, certainly up to that point, been known almost exclusively for his determination to ride herd on the automotive industry in which I made my own living. And that got a certain amount of commotion in the press for a while because the idea of anyone giving anything to the reduction of his field of exploitation was apostasy in the corporate world.

That was me he was referring to—earlier as Midas President, he publicly drove his father, Nate, up the proverbial wall, when he declared: "I told Nader it was okay if he put us out of the muffler and exhaust business so long as he put all our competitors out of business too."

He then distinguished the Judeo-Christian ethic—which is, again to summarize simplistically, "compassion toward the human condition," [whereas] "the corporate ethics of counter distinction is opportunistic. It simply says, and I try to offer this dispassionately, 'we will do whatever we can to carry it off. Whatever the opportunity provides, we will undertake.' Now that's the raw ethic."

Coursing through trenchant observations about the scientific method and the legal system, Sherman must have felt he was confusing or frazzling his young audience, so he homed in on the "free enterprise system . . ."

> it's in the name of this dreadful threat [socialism and communism, that] the free enterprise, the practitioners of American free enterprise capital, close ranks and insist on laissez-faire, on being left alone, on being dealt with as if their system is sacrosanct, for fear that if the slightest trade-off, the slightest surrender is made, that all kinds of dreadful systems of government ownership, and the redistribution of property will take place . . .

> I am a darling of free enterprise. I have prospered. I have known its rules; I've played its tricks. I may say, in a time when self-vindication is highly received [Ronald Reagan was president], that I behaved honorably and legally. But I say this about the free-enterprise system, that although it is the greatest system yet developed for progress as we narrowly define it, there is no system like it on Earth for the systematic destruction of practically everything. It is the most efficient way to lay waste to our environment ever developed. And that's simply a product of its virtues. It is so efficacious, so powerful, that it sweeps everything in its path. It is a juggernaut. And if unstopped it will, I submit, be self-devouring.

Contrary to the "great apologists of free enterprise's" admiration of Adam Smith, Sherman correctly pointed out that Smith was writing about small businesses, "a certain modesty of scale," not the corporate capitalism that was coming into being then. Smith was not writing about, Sherman observed,

> corporations that would grow immense, their power would be immense, their capacity to manipulate and finesse and side-step laws [and], legitimately, perhaps, loopholes, would rise exponentially and that the capacity to accrue power to itself would grow at a pace in a way that completely transcends the more modest configuration of his economic theory.

He got Adam Smith right—a deep-thinking philosopher and self-taught economist whose book *The Theory of Moral Sentiments* expressed an aversion to business *uber alles* and a preference for public works, public education, and healthcare.

Warming up—though keep in mind he was in the last painful stages of his erosive illness—Sherman dug deeper for the students: "What we fear from corporations is irresponsibility; and that is a natural fear because the corporation is soulless. When I say soulless, I don't mean a judgment. It is *defined* as soulless and immortal. The stock company, which is one of the great inventions of the Western mind, has as its principle feature limited-liability." He related that the corporation could use up all its monies, strand its lenders and creditors, become bankrupt and "I, the stockholder, am untouchable" beyond my investment in the company:

> They can't come and take my possessions, but that gives me a certain detachment, verging on irresponsibility as to the conduct of the corporation. And because it has immortality, it can go on and on—as corporations now have for well over a century and longer. It has a life of its

own and yet the irony is still that it is soulless. It has no
central, essential, continuous being that is answerable to
us or to itself.

The defect of corporations is that inherently they have no
sense of consequence, no sense of legacy, no sense of future.
Their future lies two or three years out. They live in a swim,
they drift in a sea of expediency, 'expediency' meaning the
most practical, profitable, ploy that will serve the near
present. And they're kind of strapped in that condition.

It wasn't apparent that Sherman's general characterizations—bereft
of proper name examples of corporate behavior, or corporate horror,
to be more concrete—were going very much into the students'
retentive memory. That changed when he described how the
"corporate process" controls society by making it "submissive and
abject in its acceptance of much of the mischief of the corporations":

The phrase is this: universal complicity. That's where we
miss the point if as liberals we point to the corporations
as something separate from ourselves that are evil. There
isn't one of us that hasn't participated from the time we
brushed our teeth to this moment here today in some act
of complicity in participating in this whole sweep that the
corporate world has made possible. In driving here, using
the lights, anything that has to do with the environment,
even before you get to the wasteful practices. So, the corporate juggernaut is part and parcel of our way of life, we're
swept in it, we're all on it . . . we're all aboard. We're impli-
cated in the whole corporate cycle, in our name as consumers, employees, stockholders—they are all really different
manifestations of one general thing.

Though he remarked that technology and its amenities swept up everyone, even he could not have foreseen the dispensing pits of complicity on steroids exhibited by the worlds of Facebook, Google, Apple, and Amazon.

Now the student audience of over 200 was starting to connect because he had taken it to their daily life of tenants, credit cards and loans, fast food consumption, pollution, healthcare, and Berkeley's big corporate-style bureaucracy. The concrete imagination had kicked in.

He then cited some known controlling processes. They included corporate political action committees, the revolving door, "the so-called Iron Triangle" of the Pentagon and its defense contractors, the regulatory agencies, such as the Federal Communications Commission—a "staging ground" for lucrative positions in the communications industry.

He explained how corporations use "jobs" as the way to co-opt the labor unions, chain the desperate non-union workers, to advance their privileged demands upon the lawmakers, including demands for subsidies, bailouts, tax escapes, and protection from regulatory enforcement actions.

As the insider he was, Sherman unfurled "something far more sinister" that "perverts objectivity of judgment and promotes conflict of interest." He called it "camaraderie, the locker room. These are buddies!" Going from business into government and then back into business. "They live that way, and they embrace each other as a kind of quiet but elegant self-preening aristocracy. And it's this warmth of human attachment, of friendship, of personal loyalty that is among one of the most dangerous and invisible aspects of corporate political identity. They are intertwined, inextricable."

He called the military-industrial complex that President Dwight D. Eisenhower warned against as "too simplistic." We see them as separate entities and we are constantly coaxed into that view. And they are at a superficial level. But just a little bit below—when they fly each other to their hunting lodges and goodness knows what other places, when they accommodate each other in such a way—"we're seeing the inextricable intertwine of these two aspects, these two sectors of society that should be held carefully separate and distinct."

He then raised another kind of corporate control:

> how they control through the lack of opposition. They have a certain solemnity of purpose. I don't know how sensitive you are to it. I have been very sensitive to it, both from within and without. There's a kind of sniffish hauteur, as if everything they are doing is sacrosanct and incontestable under the rubric of free enterprise . . . whether it's some general complaint or some particular assault or some effort to salvage an area from development or whatever . . . It's a façade. It's something to break through. It's a surface tension, but it's there and it's very significant. It is as if today, as a stern offended parent, 'How dare you?'

"Then there is public indifference and exhaustion." Corporations are relentless with endless resources to oppose "tiny groups" with "exhausted volunteers" and very little means, facing "dreadful odds."

The "amusing, pathetic" irony of it all, mused Sherman, is the "money that we have to raise to fight corporations must unavoidably come from corporations. We go to the foundations, who are nothing but interlocking directorates with corporations, or worse yet, corporate types . . . we have come to them, hat-in-hand, to derive the means with which to strive against them."

He concludes the weakness of the opposition by noting the "legal massiveness of corporations . . . their wall of legal swagger [meaning their law firms and wars of attrition]." He illustrates by saying what it takes for environmentalists to preserve some land from development—"All victories are temporary. All losses are permanent."

If challenges to corporate control from without encounter such barricades and erosions, what about from within? "How does a corporation control its people from within?" Here Sherman becomes specific and talks about one of the great whistleblowers of recent vintage—A. Ernest Fitzgerald, the internal Pentagon auditor who went public over the huge cost overruns and defects of the giant Lockheed C-5A cargo plane.

"How can these decent people in the Pentagon countenance this?" Sherman asks of Fitzgerald when they met. Fitzgerald replied, "religious truth." It's the team sense, translated Sherman, who referred the students to Desmond Morris's book *The Naked Ape*. Morris told us what many do not want to hear at all. He said that many of the most vicious practices of the human race come from "the kindest virtues—loyalty, patriotism." Hubert Humphrey's loyalty to Lyndon Johnson during the former's presidential run against Nixon caused him not to break with Johnson on the war in Vietnam. This probably cost Humphrey that close election of 1968. "Patriotism," added Sherman, "is the rubric under which we murder our opposite number in other nations. And so the idea of shared aspirations and shared enemies is an empowering religious truth."

Sherman then asked, "How does the corporation control the manager within?" He called it the "corporate predicament . . . [that] The manager . . . is held hostage to his own success." To keep the stock market analysts happy, the managers must keep exceeding their own successes at an accelerating rate, related Sherman, who told the students he was speaking from his own "personal experience."

> If he [the manager] gets the record this year, all he's done
> is raise the threshold of his performance for next year . . .
> The stock market deals largely with illusion and expecta-
> tions, so a steady increment in yearly net profits is not
> enough . . . The increment has to be incremental at an
> incremental rate.

That's what he meant by becoming "a hostage to his own success."
"See what that does to the viscera and the soul and the submission
of the corporate manager."

Sherman paused and then said he would now "become editorial." His words were chilling, all the more so with the passage
of subsequent decades. The students probably had not heard their
future portrayed with such grim, unsparing belief:

> I've watched this from within and without, with horror.
> I think that what's going wrong in this world, certainly
> ecologically, demographically, and choose whatever field
> you wish, is only capable of understatement. The words 'the
> horror, the horror,' is an understatement. We cannot know,
> the mind cannot encompass the ravage and pillaging that
> we are all collectively, systematically, largely through the
> corporate thrust, visiting upon this world. We are leav-
> ing nothing but blight and debt and danger to succeeding
> generations . . . If I am wrong, I am only wrong in terms
> of pace because one thing is unmistakable—it's all headed
> one way.

He sketched a few illustrations of the worsening trends—
deforestation, as in the rainforest of Brazil, the ozone layer, the
nuclear weapons threat. Most humans, to get through the day or to
justify their commercial impacts, simply screen out the bad news,

remember the sparse good news, and sugarcoat what they see every day in their own work. Sherman is just the opposite—he welcomes examples of good things done but doesn't turn away from the bad news about decay or deprivation.

Certainly, since his passing in 1987, debt levels of students, consumers, and government have risen exponentially, the land and the oceans are worse off in many ways, most wages have been frozen, savings are very low, automation is on the verge of exponentially displacing human jobs, even those that pay well. Silicon Valley has enveloped swarming modes of control over their users, from privacy invasions to controlling attention spans. The growing opioid epidemic didn't exist in 1987, many more nonviolent people are in prison and more prisons are corporate owned, home ownership has stopped growing, public facilities are crumbling even more, the military budget is off the charts, there are quagmire wars in the Middle East, Ukraine, and elsewhere draining public budgets. Corporations continue to burn trillions of profit dollars in wasted stock buybacks to skyrocket further executives' compensation packages, epidemic diseases have emerged or expanded, and traditional private pensions are disappearing or being looted by corporate management, Wall Street speculation with other peoples' money keeps testing higher levels of derivatives risk fifteen years after crushing the economy in 2008 and requiring the taxpayer to bail it out. Corporate welfare or crony capitalism is more brazen and runaway than ever. Then there is the gigantic risk—man-made climate disruption or climate violence hardly dented by the rising market of solar and other renewables. Meanwhile, new technologies like biotechnology, nanotechnology, and artificial intelligence accelerate their controlling corporate ways without any ethical and legal frameworks, while violations of the law by the rich and powerful become far more normal than the deviation. Since 1987, access to justice by wrongly injured or defrauded people has diminished due to corporate indentured legislators, and fine-print consumer contracts have all but destroyed one of the pillars of our democracy—freedom of contract. Union membership is sharply down and, increasingly, millions of workers are part-time (the gig and Walmart sub-economies) and set adrift as coerced "independent contractors." Sherman might have alluded to the vast projected growth of adjunct teachers in colleges and universities. And for the first time, the average life expectancy in the US is declining.

Time was running out that day in Berkeley in early 1987. Professor Nader wanted time for student questions. Sherman wrapped up precipitously.

> The only hope is opposition. There is still that sense of Judeo-Christian ethic that suggests that outrage, scandal, abomination is still distasteful enough to this nation among others, that its exposure is motivational and correctional. And so does the irony, the paradox is that those of us who strive to check corporate license are ourselves the most devout believers in free enterprise and freedom.

His latter point must have brought the students back from the brink of youthful fatalism. Many hands went up.

Question: (paraphrased) "Where is there room for people with Judeo Christian ethics in a corporate America?"

Sherman: "It's not enough to protect your sanctimony by turning your back, you have to speak out and be willing to take the consequences. Most of us in this society spend our lives avoiding encounters with danger and we worship physical courage. Physical courage is chemical, it's hormonal, it's anybody's guess. Moral courage is more difficult, more challenging because it's cooler and slower and you have to parcel it out at night when you're lying awake and the world sleeps; it's that kind of moral courage that must be brought to bear."

Question: "Have you been ostracized by your former colleagues from the corporate community?"

Sherman: "No . . . I was a pariah, but I worked at that, in part so I have a view of the perverse in me. It's as if I wanted to distance myself by simply being a little different even while succeeding within the corporation within its own proper terms . . . I cannot begin to describe the cowardliness of corporations, which derives from this sort of original sin of corporations—limited liability."

Question: "What tools does one use to check corporations?" (A vast question with limited seconds for reply.)

Sherman: "Exposure . . . So mockery, humiliation, humor—exposure. The courts . . . as a last resort . . . Boycotts . . . Learning of the successful experiences is very empowering. Corporate leaders want to be respectable. And if their malfeasances are alleged or exposed, then you have them suddenly in a very vulnerable position."

Question: "I was wondering how they live with that contradiction, then?"

Sherman: (paraphrasing). "There is an extraordinary capacity of the human mind to accommodate self-serving hypocrisy . . . And what is amusing to me, to the point of revulsion, is to hear any apologist in the corporate life try to explicate his personal ethic, his personal behavior and to reconcile it with the public good. It is an exercise in rhetoric that is always amusing. One forgets the fundamental mendacity, one puts aside the fact given that the guy is lying through his teeth and just simply sits back and try to enjoy the rather polished performance."

Question: "I was wondering if in the involvement of your company, if you experienced any internal moral dilemmas?"

Sherman: (paraphrasing) "Let me make a quite relevant point. For all their malfeasance, corporations are engaged in constructive endeavors. I hope I haven't shifted too much my emphasis; they get into mischief when they start getting repetitive." (Sherman meant by endless expansion without any perceived limits, corporate damage or malfeasance increases.)

Question: (Paraphrasing) "Does this corporate locker room camaraderie find its expression among environmental political groups?"

Sherman: "It's not the same, I don't believe. For one thing, it's a difference in scale. For another thing it's usually out in the open. The poor Sierra Club will take some benevolent congressperson to lunch or something."

Question: (Paraphrasing). "To what extent do you think the corporation's own solemnity of purpose and the spread of that viewpoint makes the corporate action seem repulsive to its stakeholders, to its stockholders?"

Sherman: "I don't think it does at all . . . Large, small, active, stockholders are pablum feeders, they just want the check. And it's on that residual, on that substratum, that broad base of that kind of formalized indifference that the corporations then gain their primordicy, their preeminence to proceed as they do." (He earlier qualified these remarks by saying the company had to be succeeding.)

A student asked Sherman if there was "one event that happened at Midas that might exemplify the corporate world as you describe it?" It provoked Sherman's most stunning revelatory response. The context for the answer: In 1971 Sherman was in a knockdown, drag-out, life-and-death proxy fight for regaining control of Midas International Corporation from his father, Nate Sherman. It was coming to a climax and if the son, Gordon, lost, as he said, he'd "be out on my arse." By astonishing coincidence, Sherman's creation, the aforementioned BPI, the public interest law firm, was about to publicly expose the banks of Chicago that had "punitively," as it turned out, cheated on their city taxes; or, at least gotten undeserved covert privileges.

"This was happening exactly on the day that I was appealing to one of those banks who held a large block of [Midas] stock, of stock in trust, which was a swing vote. At that moment it seemed under the pressure of the moment it would either make me or break me. I was meeting at their office in solemn sessions on a Monday. On Friday night the lawyers of the BPI called me and said, 'Gordon, we know what you're going through. We have to tell you that we have a story . . . it should break Monday morning; we're willing to let it break on Tuesday.' And I smiled, because most of us while we avoid the challenge of moral courage, yearn for the opportunity. And I said 'No,' not for a day, let it go. And it did and it hit the headlines, and we had our meeting. I sat at the head of the table and the bank's vice-president . . . was next to me and he cleared his throat . . . saying, 'I must excuse myself in a few minutes, the television cameras are gathered in the chamber beyond.' I lost the proxy fight, but I gained my soul . . . as it turned out in the perspective of the years, I thank God for it, as I do for your questions."

It is doubtful whether the students had ever received more insights about power and the powerful and more opening of windows to exercise their curiosity and analytic skills and ponder their own future roles and significance than during that casual hour they spent with the creator of six hundred Midas muffler shops. He was nourished at their age by Robert Hutchins's "Great Books Curriculum" at the University of Chicago. Nobody knows how indelible that hour was on the students or whether for many it was viewed primarily as a spectacle, as a one-off display by a corporate maverick long gone from the fray. Many of them did take notes, and Laura Nader's "controlling processes" provided a before-and-after context conducive to more than ordinary student retention.

I still meet Laura's former students—there have been thousands of them who took this very popular course—around the country years later. Invariably, they see the class as a turning point in their awareness of how power is exercised and what it takes to pull that controlling power out of the shadows and examine its pervasiveness, resiliency, and vulnerability. I wonder often why our better media, our better academics did not search out Gordon

Sherman to visit with him and share his special viewpoints and characterizations with a larger audience. He should have been a natural choice, at least for NPR and PBS, *The New York Times* and *The Washington Post*, if not suitable for more rancidly commercial, cowardly, and stupefying mainstream media and press. It was not to be. His life has not been lost to history. But history has not been nourished nearly as much by this gentle gentleman-scholar-businessman-philosopher-musician-naturalist as it could have been and still can be. In a self-conscious society, Sherman would have been depicted as a "Renaissance man" for a nation and culture acutely in need of a renaissance.

As the students gathered around him to ask more questions, Gordon Sherman knew that this was his finale, his impromptu valedictory. A few weeks earlier, he was heard to exclaim in his family's presence, "1987 is the year I'm going to die." After he left Chicago for California at age forty-four, he was diagnosed with advanced cancer, which he fought for over fifteen years. He had hoped not to have to leave Midas. His fondest dreams he spoke about out loud. He wanted to run Midas, expand its profits and pour 5 percent (then the limit of tax deductibility for a charitable contribution) each year into the daring Midas Foundation. As he told the Berkeley students, "I wanted to fuel the Foundation and run with it in strange and unconventional ways."

It is permissible to speculate what he would have done with that expanding foundation. First, give grants that start or enlarge civic advocacy organizations striving for structural justice. He knew the difference between justice and charity, between prevention and necessary palliatives. Second, he would have looked for the most pioneering but marginalized leaders to wrap his grants around. Without such people, nothing could change. This is how he supported Saul Alinsky's inner-city creations. Third, he would've collared to join his kind of efforts with other small foundations, directed by entrepreneurs such as himself. Imagine him at large in Silicon Valley! Fourth, he would've challenged and shamed, in his inimitable erudite manner, large foundation directors around their executive tables. Fifth, he would never have stopped learning, experiencing, sensing how to best bring out the better angels of corporate people, find the ones already congenial to his pursuits, and show how choosing well the valorous in the civic community precluded any micromanagement.

Who knows what roles his perceptive, progressive wife and four sturdy sons might have assumed? Alas, such glory speculation remained just that in the face of what the nation and the world lost due to the tragedies of Sherman's corporate miscalculation, family divisions, and the whims of bankers and other institutional investors that sealed the fate of Sherman's business and civic leadership.

12

PAUL HAWKEN

Co-founder of Smith & Hawken
and Founder of OneSun

In 1965, anyone knowledgeable about the activities of young Paul Hawken at the core of the civil rights movement would not have been surprised to know that he would become the foremost operational connector of people with knowledge to protect global and local environments in the world. They, however, might not have expected him to become a successful early entrepreneur promoting environmentally benign products.

For in that year, Hawken was the press coordinator for Martin Luther King, Jr., in Selma, Alabama—one of the historic non-violent, civil disobedience battlegrounds of that turbulent period. There was nineteen-year-old Paul issuing press credentials, keeping the press and radio and television reporters informed, and becoming acting marshal for the final march. Earlier that year he worked as a field photographer for the Congress of Racial Equality and participated in voter registration drives in Bogalusa, Louisiana, and the Florida Panhandle. These were frightening hot spots, but nothing like what he experienced in Meridian, Mississippi, where his photographic work after the three young civil rights advocates were tortured and slain attracted Ku Klux Klan members who assaulted and briefly captured him. The slippery teenager escaped when the FBI started to intervene in that locality.

His energy to apply what he learned didn't provide time for a college degree. For decades he has been everywhere in the world because the world is what he so deeply wants to preserve and nurture. Whenever I think of Paul, I think of these aphorisms— "Those who are supposed to know but do not act simply do not yet know," by fifteenth century Chinese philosopher Wang Yangming; and "Freedom is participation in power," by the ancient Roman lawyer Marcus Cicero. Paul Hawken realized the importance of public education and awareness for protecting the natural world, so largely neglected by formal educational institutions. That led him to an unavoidable focus on the importance of changing the business community regardless of how it was structured.

In every society, the role of business is dominant and must be variously addressed from the inside and outside. Paul has lost count of how many business audiences he has addressed. This tempo increased following the publication in 1993 of his most famous book, *The Ecology of Commerce*. At one of these conventions of business executives was, as we have seen earlier, Ray Anderson, the engineer-CEO of the Atlanta-based large carpet-tile manufacturer, Interface, Inc. As if struck by a thunderbolt, Anderson returned to his office, assembled his top staff, and announced a twenty-five-year drive to transform the company into a 100 percent recycling and zero pollution company. Leading sustainable thinkers and doers would visit Anderson or meet with him at his many proselytizing addresses to business groups around the world to learn about his cutting-edge firm and methodical progress toward his goals. He was on schedule until cancer claimed this practical philosopher visionary in 2011.

Paul Hawken has had that kind of acknowledged impact. He shapes his big picture appeals and challenges accordingly tailored to his audiences. If it is at a commencement address where the graduating classes are impatient and joyous over the immediate celebrations, he speaks crisply and searingly. If it is at a business school—where his book *The Ecology of Commerce* is widely used—he talks about what students will have to confront both occupationally and personally inside their chosen corporate workplace. Before government agencies, he speaks of taking one's conscience to their bureaucracies and building the coalitions inside these institutions to change settled cultures. Hawken is not a denunciator as he etches the catastrophic trends afflicting mankind and the planet. He doesn't chase corporate criminals, governmental ogres, or other members of the repressive classes. He has his own non-adversarial style but doesn't dilute his message. In his impersonal-adversarial approach he doesn't mince words about what vested interests and vested ignorance have unleashed onto our living world.

He is an early pioneer in the school of sustainable thought and deed (Amory and Hunter Lovins among his collaborators) because this approach is good for the planet and the corporate bottom line. The additional force that Hawken brings to his arguments comes from successful companies he has started. He began in the 1970s with the Erewhon Trading Company selling food produced from 30,000 acres of showcasing sustainable land. In 1979, he co-founded Smith & Hawken, with several dozen retail stores and catalog sales of garden supplies. As CEO of Smith & Hawken, he gained easy entry into the councils of business previously inaccessible to this learned advocate. In 2009, he started OneSun, an energy company using low-cost solar based "on green chemistry and biomimicry." You get the business strategy by now. He ploughs new territory, makes his practical success, and then moves on to the next frontier.

As a youngster, Paul had a lucky choice of parents who paid attention to what it takes to develop a mixture of curiosity, imagination, and relentless energy in pursuit of major betterments of society. His father was a librarian at the University of California, Berkeley, where Paul went to school but did not complete his degree. His family environment was such that, in his words "we could deconstruct anything." Hawken's constantly searching mind narrated his teaching, writing, doing, coalition-building, and business. There is the Hawken who co-authored the head-jerking book *Natural Capitalism* (1999) with Amory and Hunter Lovins that gave readers the message that natural resources, such as minerals, water and soils, can be used and reused ten to one hundred times more efficiently than they are presently wastefully being used to make products.

In 2005, following his criticism of socially responsible investment funds (SRIs) as having too lenient standards for admitting companies into their portfolio, Hawken partnered with Baldwin Brothers, a Massachusetts-based investment firm, to start the Highwater Global Fund with stricter standards for investing in companies "that have a clear sense of current global trends and future societal needs." He has become wary about the too-loose evocation by companies of the words "sustainable" and "socially responsible," giving examples of corporations that do just that. On the other pragmatic hand, Hawken has worked with Walmart and Ford Motor Company on projects to take these giants into new environmentally sound frontiers.

Hawken says:

Many of these (SRI) funds employ the term sustainability. This is a catchall term that . . . has come to mean less than it could and more than it should. At Highwater, we also use the word, but we believe that sustainability is a scientific concept, not a feel-good term. It is rooted in biology and physics and describes the limits within which society can grow and prosper over time.

Hawken excluded Whole Foods from the Highwater Global Fund, in part, because it was selling, under the Whole Foods 365 brand, a vegetable assortment called the California Medley that actually came from China. Out also were big money-center banks "because of liar loans, teaser rates and usurious interest rates on rampant consumer credit." It's what a company does, not what it says it does.

He refers to Kellogg's in 2010 as a company heading down a road that doesn't serve society into the future, no matter how it says it is getting there. The lofty goals of Kellogg's values statement, Hawken finds, are repudiated by Kellogg's lack of mention of children or health.

He adds: "There is a children's health crisis in the US due to obesity and type 2 diabetes.

Advertising and promoting Cookie Crunch, Frosted Flakes, and Star Trek cereals, all of which contain more than one-third simple sugars, during Saturday morning cartoons, belies Kellogg's value statement."

However, to illustrate how slippery big companies can be over a few years, in 2010 Google, Ford, and Honda passed Highwater's performance test. So did Amazon "for the trees being saved because of the Kindle." As its power grew and grew, Google began to violate its founding motto—"Do No Evil."

Hawken becomes more effective over time because he has the consummate civic personality and a passion for a just, safe world; he's chronically eager to give others credit, stays up to date with science, technology, and geopolitical currents. He is a top practitioner of the power of aggregation. He understands that too often a scattering of smaller efforts by business leaders or civic advocates doesn't attract significant attention or support. A compelling big-picture vision can, however, unify and motivate people to take on important issues and challenge political and corporate adversaries. Not surprisingly, in 2008 Hawken delivered a book about aggregation titled *Blessed Unrest*, reflecting his pleasing, upbeat but laser-beam personality. The subtitle tells the contents: *How the Largest Social Movement in History is Restoring Grace, Justice, and Beauty to the World*. For years, Hawken has spent some of his time research-ing organizations working to restore and solidify the internal cul-ture of these groups to ensure that social justice is at their heart. They include large nonprofits to stalwart individuals, influential in their localities, including assertive indigenous peoples, making change from grit, smarts, and tiny resources.

Donna Seaman, writing in *Booklist*, describes what Hawken discerned in his world travels:

> Rather than an ideological or centralized movement, this coalescence is a spontaneous and organic response to the recognition that environmental problems are social-justice problems. Writing with zest, clarity, and a touch of wonder, Hawken compares the gathering of forces to the human immune system. Just as antibodies rally when the body is under threat, people are joining together to defend life on Earth . . . Hawken presents an unprecedented map to this new 'social landscape' that includes a classification system defining astonishingly diverse concerns, ranging from child welfare, ocean preservation, and beyond.

Such "Blessed Unrest" has not gone unnoticed by the corporate establishment. Gone are the days when companies would promote postcards about Pittsburgh showing dark pollutants billowing from factory smokestacks to declare the city's economic prosperity.

Today no company wants to be caught any distance from its environmental boasts. Skeptics accurately call out such marketing as "greenwashing," Which is particularly prominent on Earth Day every year. Lip service is the first sign of change; it leads to a little more boldness by conscientious people inside the company, which leads to a more open realization climbing up the corporate ladder that ecological means more efficiency, better recruitment of young applicants, less liability and litigation, and more enhanced public relations. Hawken makes many more precise arguments in these and other regards; yet he is under no illusions when speaking or consulting with corporate executives. He can point to the giant BP corporation, which earlier led the way in talking up renewable energy, even spelling out BP into the moniker "Beyond Petroleum" in tons of advertisements.

Then erupted the gigantic BP oil spill in the Gulf of Mexico in April 2010. Disclosures, month after month, of BP's institutional negligence, corner-cutting, and neglected visible warning signs, exposed quite a different corporate culture. BP paid out billions of dollars in fines and damages to those who lost their businesses, had their property poisoned, and their health harmed. BP executives failed to internalize their external recklessness, which resulted in the deaths of eleven workers on BP's Deepwater Horizon drilling rig. The Department of Justice charged BP with eleven counts of felony manslaughter, one count of felony obstruction of Congress, and violations of the Clean Water and Migratory Bird Treaty Acts.

"Blessed Unrest" received widely favorable reviews around the world, but it was not seen as a "muscle" book creating waves among those rich, powerful, and political. Nobody knew this better than Paul Hawken. Consequently, he went to the next stage. In 2014, he created Project Drawdown, a nonprofit aggregating known and already utilized ways to reverse not mitigate global warming. This newest fruit of ecology's Johnny Appleseed, in his words, "maps and models the scaling of one hundred substantive technological, social, and ecological solutions to reverse climate disruption and climate-driven violence among humans and diminishing natural species."

Paul Hawken is almost the opposite of David Brower, the fiery, savvy, relentless environmentalist, who built up groups like the Sierra Club, then clashed with the organization's Board of Directors who were too willing to compromise. Hawken has been described by friends as "too nice a guy."

Environmental groups delight in having him on their Boards of Directors because he is "too nice a guy." Bureaucracies like Conservation International and the National Audubon Society had him as a Board Member, a star in their crown that they can shine and not allow to show what he truly wanted them to become.

His varied experiences with business, civic, and educational organizations have undoubtedly informed his eight major books, including his bestsellers: *The Next Economy, Growing a Business, The Ecology of Commerce, Blessed Unrest,* and *Drawdown.* It was *The Ecology of Commerce* that struck home with some business leaders who were trying to make sense of this "ecology thing." This book called for increased mandatory standards by government agencies and called out the mythical corporate allegiance first and foremost to the shareholders, whom CEOs have stripped of power, voice, and internal information. The book was also adopted by sixty-seven business schools as the number one book used in environmentally oriented courses and has been translated into many foreign languages.

These executives knew the difference between short-termism and long-termism and how the former can devastate the survival deeds of the latter. Short-term corner-cutting while downloading the costs to nature, the powerless, and poor is what has denuded massive forests, depleted oceans, poisoned the waterways and lakes, and created massive soil erosion and loss of trillions of tons of crucial topsoil. Long-termism means spending for transition costs to technologies and processes that in the long run will be far more efficient and placid for corporate P & L statements. Hawken shows that ignoring the inevitable tipping points for short-term profits is devastating. Production processes must begin with life-cycle costing, incentives to foresee and forestall calamities, large and small, local and global, and must be built into the company's daily cost calculations. Ideally this leads to the adoption or discovery of more immediate cost savings, as, for example, Interface, Inc. has been discovering annually—truly sustainable practices cut costs and increase profits. In thousands of pages, Hawken provides illustrations of this central point for listening businesses using their own pragmatic language.

Both the strength and the limitations of Hawken's approach are seen in the remarkable one hundred science-based proposed solutions to avoid climate catastrophe. These rock-solid proposals are meticulously outlined in *Drawdown*, but received a fraction of the attention they deserve.

Hawken's *Blessed Unrest* is a vast collection of organizations working to further environmental and social justice initiatives. When interviewed about this book, Hawken said:

Our democracy is corrupt from the top down and I think this movement is forming from the bottom up to correct the lack of process and governing principles that inform democratic movements. Although most of the media thinks this unnamed movement is about protest, my guess is that more than 98 percent of it is about solutions, and these are usually about solutions to problems in regions or communities. To achieve this requires the creation of what I call handmade democracies, processes that are not win-lose, and it requires a quality of interaction, respect, and listening that is now lost in US politics.

The media hasn't paid adequate attention to Hawken's work, but he is still hopeful that seeds he and others have planted will foster a more just and sustainable society. All this is not to say that Hawken has struck out with the media. His book *Growing a Business* was the basis for a seventeen-part PBS series that he produced and hosted, exploring the challenges of starting and running socially responsive companies. This series was shown on television in 115 countries reaching over 100 million people. The growing level of urgency in recent years regarding climate disruption would argue for more such PBS-type series. Unfortunately, this issue is not given the attention it deserves by PBS or other broadcast networks.

Drawdown represents the highest point of Hawken's sense of time running out for the planet. *Drawdown* is defined as "that point in time when the concentration of greenhouse gases in the atmosphere begins to decline on a year-to-year basis." Increasingly, close observers are wondering whether it is too late already, no matter what humans do to reverse the trauma to Mother Earth. Hawken, with a stiff upper lip, lists the one hundred most substantive, existing solutions, parts of which are in place, that can roll back global warming within thirty years. They include rooftop solar panels, educating young people about the environmental impact of population growth, and afforestation (creating forests where there were none). There is a type of seaweed that when fed to cows reduces their deadly methane emissions by 70 percent, while growing that seaweed reverses some of the acidification in ocean dead zones. One critic of Hawken was troubled by the relative lack of ocean-related solutions to allow more creation of oxygen and carbon sequestration. In his defense, his selection of one hundred is meant to be a convenient and elegant number to reach; Hawken certainly has more ideas in mind and vigorously invites people to add more.

Yet there is something tragic about a book of lists. Our ocean awareness project, Blue Frontier, published a unique book titled *Fifty Ways to Save the Ocean*, by David Helvarg. Most of the suggestions dealt with changing our cumulative destructive behavior near and far in the ocean. Recommendations were given. Media attention was minimal and, most importantly, there was little actual utilization, including by schools and colleges. Hawken surely knows that saving the Earth needs a greater series of command performances by governments and other controlling institutions. As the leading action-oriented academic ecologist, the late Barry Commoner wrote, prevention is far superior to amelioration or gradual regulation. He gave a total government ban on vinyl chloride in factories and the prohibition of lead in paint and gasoline as illustrations of his point. Gradual regulation to diminish use often leaks badly and can slide backward. Ask the people of the EPA. At any rate, it is too late for gradualism, which is necessary but nowhere near sufficient.

In 1993, President Bill Clinton and Vice President Al Gore released an official government report ominously warning in detail about the fast-approaching calamity of global warming. It was well-written, graphic, and visual. It went nowhere. In fact, both men announced that they were not going to further regulate auto fuel efficiency, choosing instead a voluntary partnership of domestic auto giants that blew out one billion taxpayer dollars with no accomplishments. What the program did do was displace regulation and antitrust enforcement against collusion between the auto companies. Indeed, GM, Ford, and Chrysler did nothing under the auspices of a White House surrendering to false promises littering a stagnant path backward.

It is instructive to compare Hawken with another leader of the battle to reverse the planet's greenhouse effect—Bill McKibben. He teaches at Middlebury College and responded to his impatient students to create the now worldwide group 350.org. McKibben has written, like Hawken, for leading publications, and believes in direct, nonviolent disobedience. He organized a protest in front of Obama's White House that led to 1,500 arrests—a historic record in the annals of protests there. He and his allies pressured Obama to eventually stop construction of the Keystone XL pipeline so defiantly opposed by first native American tribes. He raises alarms regularly in publications such as *The New Yorker*, marshaling facts with senses of morality and civic duty for posterity, along with describing the rising menaces that he has observed firsthand in his travels. He can make you cringe with personal foreboding when he describes, for example, the accelerating effects from the melting of the permafrost in Greenland.

Hawken and McKibben work toward comparable goals but in different fields and styles. They have different experiences in life and different temperaments. Hawken has taken up the challenge to connect his work to persuade industry to change faster, using the rising civic, consumer, and some labor pressure, and demanding fundamental investments and conversions in technology and usage.

Hawken is inspirational, but he lays out an empirical base for achievement through structural frameworks for action. Very often with young people—those who don't act on the ramparts—idealism is the entry-level to any subsequent action.

In his foreword to *Dream of a Nation* (2011)—a beautifully edited anthology about what sustainable societies could be, Hawken recounts an exchange with a *Fortune* magazine journalist who, after concluding his interview, told him he was dreaming, and that reality was different. For Hawken, that was the equivalent to a fastball down the middle. He replied:

> Of course I am dreaming . . . someone has to dream in America because dreams of a livable future are not coming from politicians, bankers, and the media. It is our right to dream, and it is something we owe our children's children: it is a gift to the future and the future is begging. The dreams we should have carried forward by our ancestors have been buried by fear, numbing polemics, pervasive greed and a culture of erosive individualism.

Then came the vintage Hawken, following a powerful narrative of multiple crises our country faces:

> The way to restore the vitality and health of an ecosystem or immune system is to connect more of a system to itself. The way to restore society is to restore the lost and severed connections between people and place, between livelihood and production, between food and farmer, to re-knit the commonwealth. A society is far too complex for any one person to understand or dictate. It needs the same interventions that healing a disease requires, which is to create the conditions wherein the organism can heal itself. This book underlines the idea that rather than being adrift in America, our potential and capacity to adapt, grow and prosper in a fair and just way is alive and in desperate need of forward momentum . . . Inspiration is not garnered from the litanies of what may befall us; it resides in humanity's willingness to restore, redress, reform, rebuild, recover, reimagine and reconsider.

Finely chosen words, each of which give us pause to ponder. But what of the powers-that-be that obstruct, undermine, co-opt, and sometimes destroy these incipient efforts? What of the corporate supremacists building an ever-deeper corporate state, often finding common interests with deep dictatorships? They control ever more of our governments, our academies, our mass media, and even our indoctrinated educational systems all the way to graduate schools. Hawken starts to come closer to the *real politique* of the rule of the few over the many by quoting the poet Denise Levertov's words: "We have only begun to know the power that is in us if we would join our solitudes in the communion of struggle." For everyday impact, the Hawkens of our times must elaborate the daily impacts on the daily lives by the named giant global corporations, with their absentee control over the ebb and flow of our political economy, including dominating the vast wealth of the *commons*—the public lands, the public airwaves, the giant shareholding pension and mutual funds, and the vast taxpayer-funded government research and development monies *owned* by the people but *controlled* for both profit and concentrating power by big business. These are seized critical assets to be freed for a popular democratic resurgence and recapture.

Hawken understands that trying to work in both worlds is very difficult and certainly his work as an activist could threaten to close some corporate doors that he believes he can open to enlightenment stage by stage. Whereas McKibben takes apart Exxon's "shocking" behavior of suppressing their own scientists, who early on measured the effects of burning fossil fuels on the biosphere, it is hard to imagine the deliberate Paul Hawken doing so.

The argument can be made tactically and strategically that both approaches are cumulative, and that Hawken will be listened to more and more from inside corporate and government councils as he and we build up the pressure from the outside by the movers and shakers who understand the importance of shifting power. Indeed, most social justice movements have succeeded in those ways—certainly that was the case with the labor and consumer movements, in addition to the post–World War II awakening of environmental protection dynamism.

Since selling his companies, Hawken has become an educator and negotiator-connector. It is an open question whether he will become more forceful, more of a slammer against the companies and their political toadies who, with exceptions, tolerated Trump's disastrous policies of withdrawal from international climate accords and his freezing or repealing of government regulatory standards and other efforts to reduce the current accelerating environmental violence. Is Hawken's eloquence, rooted in evidence, being extended by the citizenry and press? Are they instead being calmed by the too-little-too-late concessions here and there by large companies? When I hear people regaling speakers for their inspiration, I remind them that inspiration without perspiration dissipates quickly.

Hawken has given many commencement addresses before students and their families impatient with the formalities of graduation exercises and wanting to get on with the celebrations. It is not easy to hold their attention. Their restlessness does not come subdued—one can feel and hear it from the stage. Few respond better than Hawken. In 2009, he gave what has been called the "best environmental commencement speech ever" at the University of Portland. He titled it "You are Brilliant and the Earth is Hiring." Not a long speech, recomposed, he told me, the night before, but long enough to require some verbatim excerpting and reflecting.

Here are his words:

> You are going to have to figure out what it means to be a
> human being on earth at a time when every living system

is declining, and the rate of decline is accelerating. Kind of a mind-boggling situation . . . Basically, civilization needs a new operating system, you are the programmers, and we need it within a few decades.

This planet came with a set of instructions, but we seem to have misplaced them. Important rules like don't poison the water, soil, or air, and don't let the earth get overcrowded, and don't touch the thermostat, have been broken. Buckminster Fuller said that spaceship earth was so ingeniously designed that no one has a clue that we are on one, flying through the universe at a million miles per hour, with no need for seatbelts, lots of room in coach, and really good food—but all that is changing.

There is invisible writing on the back of the diploma you will receive, and in case you didn't bring lemon juice to decode it, I can tell you what it says: You are Brilliant, and the Earth is Hiring. The Earth couldn't afford to send recruiters or limos to your school. It sent you rain, sunsets, ripe cherries, night blooming jasmine, and that unbelievably cute person you are dating. Take the hint. And here's the deal: Forget that this task of planet saving is not possible in the time required. Don't be put off by people who know what is not possible. Do what needs to be done, and check to see if it was impossible only after you are done.

When asked if I am pessimistic or optimistic about the future, my answer is always the same: If you look at the science about what is happening on earth and aren't pessimistic, you don't understand the data. But if you meet the people who are working to restore this earth and the lives of the poor, and you aren't optimistic, you haven't got a pulse. What I see everywhere in the world are ordinary people willing to confront despair, power, and incalculable odds in order to restore some semblance of grace, justice, and beauty to this world . . . Humanity is coalescing. It is reconstituting the world, and the action is taking place in schoolrooms, farms, jungles, villages, campuses, companies, refugee camps, deserts, fisheries, and slums.

You join a multitude of caring people. No one knows how many groups and organizations are working on the most salient issues of our day: climate change, poverty, deforestation, peace, water, hunger, conservation, human rights, and more. This is the largest movement the world has ever seen. Rather than control, it seeks connection. Rather than dominance, it strives to disperse concentrations of power . . .

It is made up of teachers, children, peasants, businesspeople, rappers, organic farmers, nuns, artists, government workers, fisherfolk, engineers, students, incorrigible writers, weeping Muslims, concerned mothers, poets, doctors without borders, grieving Christians, street musicians, the President of the United States of America, and as the writer David James Duncan would say, the Creator, the One who loves us all in such a huge way.

Inspiration is not garnered from the litanies of what may befall us; it resides in humanity's willingness to restore, redress, reform, rebuild, recover, reimagine, and reconsider . . .

Millions of people are working on behalf of strangers, even if the evening news is usually about the death of strangers.

This kindness of strangers has religious, even mythic origins, and very specific eighteenth-century roots. Abolitionists were the first people to create a national and global movement to defend the rights of those they did not know . . .

Three out of four people in the world were enslaved. Enslaving each other was what human beings had done for ages. And the abolitionist movement was greeted with incredulity. Conservative spokesmen ridiculed the abolitionists as liberals, progressives, do-gooders, meddlers, and activists. They were told they would ruin the economy and drive England into poverty . . . a group of people organized themselves to help people they would never know, from whom they would never receive direct or indirect benefit. And today tens of millions of people do this every day. It is called the world of nonprofits, civil society, schools, social entrepreneurship, non-governmental organizations, and companies who place social and environmental justice at the top of their strategic goals. The scope and scale of this effort is unparalleled in history. [Generates the feeling that help and restoration is all around us.]

At present we are stealing the future, selling it in the present, and calling it gross domestic product. We can just as easily have an economy that is based on healing the future instead of stealing it. We can either create assets for the future or take the assets of the future. One is called restoration and the other exploitation. And whenever we exploit the earth we exploit people and cause untold suffering. [By this point, close listeners may be asking, why aren't we doing this obvious thing; who is standing in our way when Hawken uses the word "we"?]

You are graduating to the most amazing, stupefying challenge ever bequested to any generation. The generations before you failed . . . Nature beckons you to be on her side. You couldn't ask for a better boss. The most unrealistic person in the world is the cynic, not the dreamer. Hope only makes sense when it doesn't make sense to be hopeful. This is your century. Take it and run as if your life depends on it.

There was robust applause; some stood, others looked at each other approvingly.

It would be instructive were there to be a study following up nearly a decade later to see whether any students changed their routines, avowed to change their career trajectory, resolved to consume or work in a more sustainable manner, or joined an active environmental initiative—as a result of Hawken's stirring, image-ridden words. In my experience, some graduates who years later recall these concrete commencement address exhortations or calls to action attribute to them a prod to connect with civic groups whose missions were already in line with the graduates' public stances or beliefs. Once in a while, one hears the words of exquisite gratification—"your speech changed my life and took me away from a business career to full time work for a just world."

Regrettably, militaristic orations have moved young men to committing themselves to war more than to a similar impulse to wage peace and justice.

When someone does more than 99.999 percent of all the people do, it is tempting to build upon such great achievements and insist on more from that person or persons. Mea culpa with Paul Hawken—a gentle soul with tireless vision embracing varieties of continually renewable determinations.

That is why when the editors of *Time* magazine invited me

in 2009 to select one of TIME's 100 most influential people in the world, I unhesitatingly chose Hawken, with these much-abbreviated words:

> Paul Hawken is a relentless networking advocate for sustainable business worldwide. His books (for example, *The Ecology of Commerce*) and companies have persuaded businesses to see the efficiency and productivity of environmentally harmonious practices.

CONCLUSION

I am not highlighting these CEOs because their efforts were one-of-a-kind. I'm highlighting them because the planet is running out of time and there are huge recovery opportunities for the CEOs of the future. Each of these CEOs realized the marketplace isn't perfect by any means. Not only in the sense of economic perfection, but also in the sense that the marketplace is flawed in a variety of other ways.

Anita Roddick and Ray C. Anderson perceived one of the most significant flaws: the marketplace by itself does nothing to recognize environmental damage caused by corporations. Nor does the marketplace inherently give consumers the information they need to mitigate the damages through their purchases. So Anita and Ray set out to do this themselves—and inform consumers of their impact.

But little by little, we see greater evidence of this becoming something that both consumers and government regulators perceive—and are willing to address. The SEC now wants corporations to disclose their impact on climate change. More and more investment funds are measuring companies' social responsibility before investing in them, small starts that portend next steps.

All the CEOs profiled revealed senses of humor and irony—to varying degrees, of course.

The easygoing nature of these CEOs might explain why they were remarkably open and willing to share what other corporate CEOs would consider to be competitive secrets. They all were open, especially Sol Price, even with competitors wanting to know his strategies. Sol Price had many big-time visitors to his FedMarts and then Price Clubs, both original business forms that became templates for imitators. He fully answered his competitors' penetrating inquiries about how he solved problems in running his retail stores. He freely shared what they would have had to pay a ton of money for, were any consulting firm to possess the same know-how.

Such generous spirits flow from their desire to have *all* customers and *all* workers treated in other businesses the way they were treated by their enterprises. Sounds corny, but I believe it to be true.

Most came from humble backgrounds. Perhaps they grew up among hardscrabble blue-collar workers, such as Jeno's father, who labored in the iron mine region of Minnesota, and Bernard's father, who started as an immigrant peddler. A few had middle-class parents, such as Paul's librarian father. Only Robert Townsend was born with a silver spoon. Bogle was born to the purple, but the Depression pulled the family harshly down to earth, so that manual labor was the early lot for John and his twin brother.

These CEOs practiced open self-criticism and listened, with discrimination, to others' critiques.

It was as if they sometimes wanted the goad of the public lash to turn their admitted mistakes into good teachers. They also turned their ears to listen hard to what their employees had to say. They generated a company culture that valued self-criticism from all in their ranks. Some did it very analytically, like Yvon Chouinard who rethought things when alone in the wilderness or in discussions with his team, leading to the refined climbing tools they sold or to making the decision to convert from using industrially farmed cotton to making all their products with *organic* cotton. It could be in the dogged, arduous step-by-step conversion that Ray Anderson led his company through as it moved toward zero pollution and total recycling. Others made decisive, thorough changes because that just was part of their personality. Jeno Paulucci, in particular, is one who believed in constant change and betterment. These CEOs were not rethinking because they were indecisive or lacking in forcefulness. Strong egos did not keep them from such open self-criticism and willingness to change. Maybe it was because their powerful self-possession helped them to recover, bounce back from adversities, and move forward better.

They all had strong temperaments. Their tempers varied greatly, ranging from Jeno's self-described "Italian" eruptions to the cool demeanor of Robert Townsend when he faced down dismissive public criticism. One and all they exhibited emotional intelligence, which they put to work in their personal relations. Their work was far from being purely cognitive. It included an emotional underlay. Interestingly, it was the most emotional of the group, Jeno Paulucci, who involved himself the most hands-on in political campaigns, including supporting Republican and Democratic presidential candidates in different election periods.

They were in awe of no one, encountering occasional celebrities with equanimity.

They stood apart.

It's true a few like Yvon, Anita, and Paul formed coalitions to pursue common ecological objectives. Yvon's organizing of the outdoor recreation businesses, which bought full-page newspaper ads in 2017 to oppose Donald Trump's exploitation and shrinking of the public lands, was a recent such initiative, and it was coupled with the filing of follow-up lawsuits.

Even so, in general, they did not close ranks with others to champion causes. Moreover, of the twelve, I cannot count any who were close friends or collaborators with one another, although some formed associations, as Ray Anderson did with Paul Hawken. It is a big country and their respective realms rarely intersected. This illustrates a Lone Ranger dimension. Aside from Yvon, Roddick, and Shallal (locally), they were not keenly attracted to forming movements of like-minded businesses.

It is, of course, exhausting enough to run businesses successfully, as they did, so, as they realized, it would be a drain on their time to steer their companies *and* also work on diffusing their superior practices. The latter might also be a thankless task. They knew better than anyone the deep wells of structural and personal resistance to change, to any serious overhaul, that they would find among business executives. One notable exception is Paul Hawken. He used his businesses chiefly to educate others in adopting the principles articulated in his permanent bestseller, *The Ecology of Commerce*. This book changed Ray Anderson's life work for Planet Earth. In most cases, though, the CEOs didn't proselytize. Some did have a central cause to which they devoted their spare energies; others like Bernard Rapoport, were wildly eclectic. Rapoport put his money behind the fundamentally progressive Institute for Policy Studies but also a program designed to get Jews to marry Jews instead of Gentiles. And he was the chief supporter of the "radical" *Texas Observer*, which was not averse to criticizing him and his industry.

Their relations with the press, if they could be persuaded to talk about it, centered on wonderment. They kept asking why the media wasn't more interested in what they were doing, which seemed to be and was quite extraordinary. Weren't such things newsworthy, like Anderson's Interface moving toward zero environmental impact? The press largely ignored them except when they pulled off some exhibitionistic media event, as Anita and Jeno often did. Bob Townsend was something of an exception as he advanced "outrageous" advice, such as his thought that CEOs shouldn't stay more than six years, which got him featured in the business press for a time.

If the present generation of rising businesspeople read about these CEOs' civically engaged, environmentally attuned company practices, always connected to running a profit-generating business, they may be intrigued by the lack of wide diffusion of knowledge about these leaders in the mass media.

Examining the business world, I can see why, at least in the past, big business had reasons for their complacency. They had no interest in these pioneers because old-style business executives had no place for either civic or environmentalist consciousness. These businesspeople had short-range yardsticks by which they and their companies were measured. They looked especially at quarterly profits and used overly monetized and manipulative accounting. They came up with innovative ways to enrich themselves and circumvent federal prohibitions. Stock options in stock buybacks promoted new metrics that led to staggering increases in executive compensation packages, which now tower over the average worker pay at their companies. The big CEOs had short tenures, which fed their myopia: their urge to "make the most while they can!"

Also encouraging the business world's dismissal of any models that went against the grain by pushing for civic and economic responsibility was the collapse of existing countervailing forces. Labor unions shrunk and became weaker. Shareholders rights and remedies, whether institutional or individual, fell by the wayside, helped by the laws of the state of Delaware and the weak Securities and Exchange Commission. Consumer groups were overwhelmed by fast-growing business lobbies with their own mass media. Automation and leveraged globalization further fed the supremacy of big business. The enlarged and refined expansion of numerous corporate PACs and other political energies matured the modern *corporate state*, which is characterized by its enormous corporate welfare outlays, inflated government contracts and leaseholds, rigid intellectual property protections, and stunning success in monetizing elections. The takeover of the government by corporations went from "elected" politicians to the capture of federal agencies to the corporatized judiciary, right up to the US Supreme Court.

In these rosy (for business executives) environments, where failure means bailouts and golden handshakes, and wars mean enormous contracts, and giant corporate law firms mean destruction of freedom of contracts and essential privacies, and obstructions to the use of the courts by the aggrieved and wrongfully injured masses, what's not to like? The perverse incentives offered no auspicious openings in which might be heard the voice of those like these twelve CEOs, who look to a morality encompassing all, not only themselves but workers, consumers, and nature. In the reigning business climate, the worst became first, and the best remained mostly unto themselves.

Yet it is permissible to wonder how long this gilded party can last, especially as climate catastrophes, pandemics, and other omnicides intensify. History is certainly not on their side, though it has given the plutocrats and the oligarchs far more time to be displaced or tamed than historians might have expected. For sure, the corporate state makes the run much longer for these "malefactors of great wealth," as President Theodore Roosevelt called them, than if they were free to collapse on their own deceptive balance sheets. We saw this with the bailout of incompetent, mismanaged giant banks and other financial behemoths during the 2008 breakdown.

However, is there not a limit to the depletion of public budgets through ever deeper deficits, born of government giveaways to corporations, recently exploited more deeply during the COVID pandemic, and government escape hatches for what is left of corporate taxation? Is there not a limit to their blocking of public, civic voices and their corollary manipulation of public opinion, constructed by the narrow choices of a two-party duopoly marinated in corporate cash?

We know from history that such bloated, corrupt regimes eventually collapse. And we also know from history, the history I am presenting in this book, that business might have gone another way, might have followed the lead of the courageous men and women who, as did the ones profiled here, took a different path. They provided superior or new products and services in the marketplace and complied with and exceeded the laws applicable to their business. They took care to add a civic engagement role and to reduce the external costs of their kind of business activity on innocent third parties and their critical environments.

True, they were more than a little constrained by the strictures of their respective industries, which they struggled to break through. But they did break through, nonetheless, going well beyond their more conforming peers. They tempered the tyrannies of avaricious commercialism, and its expanding concentration of corporate power, with decades of energy, humanity, and respect for those under their governance or attracted by their offerings.

Reading about them must give us pause in these frenetic times of blitzing technologies and shortened attention spans. This pause in which we all, from business education majors and apprentices to the highest echelons of corporate rulers, must ask ourselves this:

The peoples' righteous necessities and dreams have been aborted or dashed for what? The endless accumulation of riches. Greed Inc., destruction of peoples' dreams and our living world so the few can pile up their hoards that they sit on cluelessly.

As one mega-billionaire confessed to me, "We know how to make a lot of money, but we don't have a clue about what to do with it, including me, Ralph."

BIBLIOGRAPHY

Jack Bogle

Arvedlund, Erin, and Art Carey. "John Bogle, Who Founded Vanguard and Revolutionized Retirement Savings, Dies at 89." *The Philadelphia Inquirer,* January 16, 2019.

Berle, Adolph A., Jr., and Gardiner C. Means. *The Modern Corporation and Private Property.* New York: The Macmillan Company, 1932.

Bogle, John C. "Bogle Sounds a Warning on Index Funds." *The Wall Street Journal,* November 29, 2018.

———. "The Supreme Court Had its Say, Now Let Shareholders Decide." *The New York Times,* May 15, 2011.

———. *Enough: True Measures of Money, Business, and Life.* Hoboken, NJ: John Wiley & Sons, 2009.

———. *The Battle for the Soul of Capitalism.* New Haven, CT: Yale University Press, 2005.

Clifford, Steven A. *The CEO Pay Machine: How It Trashes America and How to Stop It.* New York: Blue Rider Press, 2017.

"Don't Let High Costs Eat Your Returns." See "Costs," under "How to Invest" at investor.vanguard.com.

McBride, Elizabeth. "Jack Bogle's Last Warning to the Investment Industry: 'Don't Forget the Little Guy You Serve,'" CNBC, Jan 19, 2019, cnbc.com.

Monks, Robert A. G. *Corpocracy: How CEOs and the Business Roundtable Hijacked the World's Greatest Wealth Machine and How to Get it Back.* Hoboken, NJ: John Wiley & Sons, 2008.

Phillips, Peter M. *Giants: The Global Power Elite.* New York: Seven Stories Press, 2018.

Shaw, Christopher W. *Money, Power, and the People: The American Struggle to Make Banking Democratic.* Chicago: University of Chicago Press, 2019.

Anita Roddick

Costello, Brid. "Body Shop Founder Anita Roddick, 64." *Women's Wear Daily* 194, no. 54 (2007): 18.

Engel, Jonathan. *The Epidemic: A Global History of AIDS.* Washington, D.C.: Smithsonian Books, 2006.

Hecht, Susanna, and Alexander Cockburn. *The Fate of the Forest: Developers, Destroyers, and Defenders of the Amazon.* London: Verso, 1989.

Lagarias, Peter C., and Robert S. Boulter . "The Modern Reality of the Controlling Franchisor: The Case for More, Not Less, Franchisee Protections." *Franchise Law Journal* 29, no. 3 (2010): 139-147, 173.

Nader, Ralph. "The Legacies of Anita Roddick." *Common Dreams,* September 15, 2007.

Roddick, Anita. *Body and Soul: Profits with Principles.* New York: Crown, 1991.

———. *Take it Personally.* Berkeley, CA: Conari Press, 2001.

Schapiro, Mark. *Exposed: The Toxic Chemistry of Everyday Products and What's at Stake for American Power.* White River Junction, VT: Chelsea Green, 2007.

Slavin, Terry. "'The Spirit of Anita Roddick Is Strong with Us': Why Natura Bought The Body Shop." *Reuters,* October 26, 2017.

Vallely, Paul. "Dame Anita Roddick." *The Independent* (London), September 12, 2007.

Ray Anderson

Anderson, Ray C. Speech at "Rethinking Development: Local Pathways to Global Wellbeing" conference, St. Francis Xavier University, Antigonish, Nova Scotia, Canada, June 20 to June 24, 2005.

Anderson, Ray C. *Mid-Course Correction: Toward a Sustainable Enterprise— The Interface Model.* Atlanta, GA: Peregrinzilla Press, 1998.

Anderson, Ray C., with Robin White. *Business Lessons from a Radical Industrialist.* New York: St. Martin's Press, 2010.

Badie, Rick. "Carpet Manufacturer 'Clearly a Visionary.'" *Atlanta Journal-Constitution*, August 11, 2011.

Gore, Albert. *Earth in the Balance: Ecology and the Human Spirit*. Boston: Houghton Mifflin, 1992.

Hawken, Paul G. *The Ecology of Commerce: Doing Good Business*. New York: Harper Collins, 1993.

Hawken, Paul G., Amory B. Lovins, and L. Hunter Lovins. *Natural Capitalism: Creating the Next Industrial Revolution*. Boston: Little, Brown and Company, 1999.

Herndon, G. Melvin. "Hemp in Colonial Virginia." *Agricultural History* 37, no. 2 (1963): 86–93.

Langer, Emily. "Ray Anderson, 'Greenest CEO in America,' Dies at 77." *The Washington Post*, August 10, 2011.

Nader, Ralph. *Unsafe at Any Speed: The Designed-In Dangers of the American Automobile*. New York: Grossman Publishers, 1965.

Herb Kelleher

Blanchard, Kenneth H., and Colleen Barrett. *Lead with LUV: A Different Way to Create Real Success*. Upper Saddle River, NJ: FT Press, 2011.

Economy, Peter. "17 Powerfully Inspiring Quotes from Southwest Airlines Founder Herb Kelleher." *Inc.*, January 4, 2019.

Elliott, Christopher. "What You Need to Know About Ralph Nader's Crusade to Save Southwest's Nuts." *Forbes*, July 24, 2018.

Freiberg, Kevin, and Jackie Freiberg. *Nuts! Southwest Airlines' Crazy Recipe for Business and Personal Success*. Austin, TX: Bard Books, 1996.

Gittell, Jody Hoffer. *The Southwest Airlines Way: Using the Power of Relationships to Achieve High Performance*. New York: McGraw-Hill, 2003.

"Herb Kelleher on the Record." *Business Week*, December 21–23, 2003.

Reingold, Jennifer. "Southwest's Herb Kelleher: Still Crazy After All These Years." *Fortune*, January 14, 2013.

Jeno Paulucci

Kaunonen, Gary. *Flames of Discontent: The 1916 Minnesota Iron Ore Strike*. Minneapolis, MN: University of Minnesota Press, 2017.

Larson, Don W. *Land of the Giants: A History of Minnesota Business*. Minneapolis: Dorn Books, 1979.

Leipold, L. E. *Jeno F. Paulucci: Merchant Philanthropist*. Minneapolis: T. S. Denison & Company, Inc., 1968 .

Paulucci, Jeno F., with Les Rich and James Tills. *Jeno: The Power of the Peddler.* Sanford, FL: Paulucci International, 2005.

Paulucci, Jeno F., with Les Rich. *How It Was to Make $100,000,000 in a Hurry: The Tale of Jeno and the Bean Sprout.* New York: Grosset & Dunlap Publishers, 1969.

Pine, Carol, and Susan Mundale. *Self-Made: The Stories of 12 Minnesota Entrepreneurs.* Minneapolis: Dorn Books, 1982.

Youngblood, Dick, Pamela Miller, and Jim Anderson. "Tycoon Was 'Everything to Duluth and Iron Range.'" *Star Tribune* (Minneapolis), November 25, 2011.

Sol Price

"A Rich Man Wants to Share the Wealth." *Multinational Monitor* 16, no. 12 (1995): 27–28.

Bianco, Anthony. *The Bully of Bentonville: How the High Cost of Wal-Mart's Everyday Low Prices Is Hurting America.* New York: Currency/Doubleday, 2006.

Carnegie, Andrew. *The Gospel of Wealth.* New York: The Century Co., 1901.

Goldsmith, Jan. "Someone San Diego Should Know: Bob Fellmeth." *The San Diego Union-Tribune,* October 14, 2019.

Kupper, Thomas. "Sol Price: Legacy of Generosity." *The San Diego Union-Tribune,* December 15, 2009.

Miller, Stephen. "Developer of Big-Box Stores Supersized the Art of Retail." *The Wall Street Journal,* December 15, 2009.

Nader, Ralph. *Crashing the Party: Taking on the Corporate Government in an Age of Surrender.* New York: Thomas Dunne Books, 2002.

Price, Robert E. *Sol Price: Retail Revolutionary and Social Innovator.* San Diego, CA: San Diego History Center, 2012.

Shannon, David A. *The Socialist Party of America.* New York: The Macmillan Company, 1955.

Walton, Samuel M., with John Huey. *Made in America: My Story.* New York: Bantam Books, 1992.

Robert Townsend

Clifford, Steven A. *The CEO Pay Machine: How it Trashes America and How to Stop It.* New York: Blue Rider Press, 2017.

McGregor, Douglas M. *The Human Side of Enterprise.* New York: McGraw-Hill, 1960.

McWhirter, William A. "The 'Up the Organization' Man." *Life* 68, no. 14 (1970): 61–72.

Nader, Ralph, and William C. Taylor. *The Big Boys: Power and Position in American Business*. New York: Pantheon Books, 1986.

Pace, Eric. "Robert Townsend, 77, Dies, Wrote Up the Organization." The *New York Times*, January 14, 1998.

Townsend, Robert C. *Up the Organization: How to Stop the Corporation from Stifling People and Strangling Profits*, commemorative ed. New York: John Wiley & Sons, 2007.

———. *Further Up the Organization*. New York: Alfred A. Knopf, 1984.

Andy Shallal

Bhattari, Abha. "What Starbucks Could Learn from This Washington Restaurateur About Race at Work." *The Washington Post*, May 18, 2018.

Debonis, Mike. "Andy Shallal Is Running for D.C. Mayor." *The Washington Post*, November 8, 2013.

Green, Mark J., and Ralph Nader. *Fake President: Decoding Trump's Gaslighting, Corruption, and General Bullsh*t*. New York: Skyhorse Publishing, 2019.

McWhorter, John H. Woke *Racism: How a New Religion Has Betrayed Black America*. New York: Penguin Books, 2021.

Michaels, Walter Benn, and Adolph Reed, Jr. *No Politics But Class Politics*. London: Eris, 2023.

Montgomery, David. "Andy Shallal, Owner of Busboys and Poets, Is 'Democracy's Restaurateur.'" *The Washington Post*, December 8, 2011.

Reed, Touré F. *Toward Freedom: The Case Against Race Reductionism*. London: Verso, 2020.

Sani, Christina Studivant. "Andy Shallal on How His Anacostia Busboys and Poets Will Engage Its Neighbors." *Washington City Paper*, March 6, 2019.

Williams, John-John, IV. "Owner of Busboys and Poets Says Columbia Has Embraced His Brand of Diversity." *The Baltimore Sun*, April 13, 2022.

B. Rapoport

Andrews, Nina. "Insurer's Chief Mixes Profit and Social Good." *The New York Times*, September 19, 1988.

Chomsky, Noam. *Fateful Triangle: The United States, Israel, and the Palestinians*, updated ed. New York: Black Rose Books, 1999.

Findley, Paul A. *They Dare to Speak Out: People and Institutions Confront Israel's Lobby*. Westport, CT: Lawrence Hill & Company, 1988.

Green, Mark J. *Selling Out: How Big Business and Corporate Money Buys Elections, Rams Through Legislation, and Betrays Our Democracy*. New York: ReganBooks, 2002.

Leopold, Les. *The Man Who Hated Work and Loved Labor: The Life and Times of Tony Mazzocchi*. White River Junction, VT: Chelsea Green Publishing Company, 2007.

Lewis, Charles. *The Buying of the President*. New York: Avon Book, 1996.

Nader, Ralph, and Donald K. Ross. *Action for a Change: A Student's Manual for Public Interest Organizing*. New York: Grossman Publishers, 1972.

Oltersdorf, Cora. "Bernard Rapoport, B.A. '39." *Texas Alcalde* 86, no. 2 (1997): 34–35.

Rapoport, Bernard, with Don E. Carleton. *Being Rapoport: Capitalist with a Conscience*. Austin, TX: University of Texas Press, 2002.

Schwartz, John. "Bernard Rapoport, Liberal Donor in Texas, Dies at 94." *The New York Times*, April 22, 2012.

Shannon, David A. *The Socialist Party of America*. New York: The Macmillan Company, 1955.

Smith, J. B. "Waco Philanthropist Bernard Rapoport Dies at Age 94." *Waco* (TX) *Tribune-Herald*, April 6, 2012.

Stein, Philip M. *The Best Money Congress Can Buy*. New York: Pantheon Books, 1988.

Yvon Chouinard

Abrams, Rachel, and Ashley Southall. "Douglas Tompkins, 72, Founder of North Face, Dies in Kayak Accident." *New York Times*, December 9, 2015.

Beer, Jeff. "Patagonia Founder Yvon Chouinard Talks About the Sustainability Myth, the Problem with Amazon—and Why It's Not Too Late to Save the Planet." *Fast Company*, October 16, 2019.

Brower, David R., with Steve Chapple. *Let the Mountains Talk, Let the Rivers Run*. New York: Harper Collins, 1995.

Chouinard, Yvon. Let My People Go Surfing: The Education of a Reluctant Businessman. New York: Penguin Press, 2005.

Chouinard, Yvon, and Vincent Stanley. *The Responsible Company: What We've Learned from Patagonia's First 40 Years*. Ventura, CA: Patagonia Books, 2012.

Chouinard, Yvon, and Land Tawney. "Hunters, Hikers Unite to Protect Beloved Public Lands, Waters." *The Denver Post*, July 23, 2018.

Cummings, William. "'The President Stole Your Land' Patagonia Homepage Says." *USA Today*, December 4, 2017.

Gelles, David. "Billionaire No More: Patagonia Founder Gives Away the Company." *The New York Times*, September 14, 2022.

Herndon, G. Melvin. "Hemp in Colonial Virginia." *Agricultural History* 37, no. 2 (1963): 86–93.

Mark, Jason. "The Gift." *Sierra*, September/October 2019, 32–39, 49.

Nader, Ralph. *Unstoppable: The Emerging Left-Right Alliance to Dismantle the Corporate State*. New York: Nation Books, 2014.

Paumgarten, Nick. "Wild Man: Patagonia's Philosopher King." *The New Yorker*, September 19, 2016, 63–73.

Power, Thomas Michael. *Environmental Protection and Economic Well-Being: The Economic Pursuit of Quality*, 2nd ed. Armonk, NY: M. E. Sharpe, 1996.

Robinson, Doug. "The Whole Natural Art of Protection." *Chouinard Catalog*, 1972, 12–25.

Skrabec, Quentin R., Jr. *The Green Vision of Henry Ford and George Washington Carver: Two Collaborators in the Cause of Clean Industry*. Jefferson, NC: McFarland & Company, Inc., Publishers, 2013.

Gordon B. Sherman

Chambers, Edward T., and Michael A. Cowan. *Roots for Radicals: Organizing for Power, Action, and Justice*. New York: Continuum, 2003.

Flagler, J. M. "Man of Parts." *New Yorker*, September 15, 1962, 34–36.

"Gordon Sherman of Midas Muffler." *New York Times*, May 16, 1987.

Hawken, Paul G. *Growing a Business*. New York: Simon & Schuster, 1987.

Heise, Kenan. "Gordon Sherman, Exec and Activist." *Chicago Tribune*, May 15, 1987.

Kusch, Frank. *Battleground Chicago: The Police and the 1968 Democratic National Convention*. Chicago: University of Chicago Press, 2008.

Lagarias, Peter C., and Robert S. Boulter. "The Modern Reality of the Controlling Franchisor: The Case for More, Not Less, Franchisee Protections." *Franchise Law Journal* 29, no. 3 (2010): 139-147, 173.

Morris, Desmond J. *The Naked Ape: A Zoologist's Study of the Human Animal*. New York: McGraw-Hill, 1967.

Nader, Laura. *Culture and Dignity: Dialogs Between the Middle East and the West*. New York: John Wiley & Sons, 2013.

———. "Controlling Processes: Tracing the Dynamic Components of Power." *Current Anthropology* 38, no. 5 (1997): 711–37.

Rice, Berkeley. *The C-5A: An Inside Story of the Military-Industrial Complex.* Boston: Houghton Mifflin Company, 1971.

Sherman, Gordon B. "The Corporate Ethic." Lecture in the Department of Anthropology at the University of California, Berkeley, 1987, archive.org.

Paul Hawken

Commoner, Barry. *Making Peace with the Planet.* New York: Pantheon Books, 1990.

Gunther, Marc. "Paul Hawken's Winning Investment Strategy." *Huffington Post*, April 17, 2010, HuffPost.com.

Hawken, Paul G. *Blessed Unrest: How the Largest Social Movement in History is Restoring Grace, Justice, and Beauty to the World.* New York: Penguin Books, 2007.

———. *The Ecology of Commerce: Doing Good Business.* New York: Harper Collins, 1993.

———. *Growing a Business.* New York: Simon & Schuster, 1987.

———. *The Next Economy.* New York: Henry Holt & Co., 1983.

Hawken, Paul G., ed. *Drawdown: The Most Comprehensive Plan Ever Proposed to Reverse Global Warming.* New York: Penguin Books, 2017.

Hawken, Paul G., Amory B. Lovins, and L. Hunter Lovins. *Natural Capitalism: Creating the Next Industrial Revolution.* Boston: Little, Brown and Company, 1999.

Helvarg, David. *Fifty Ways to Save the Ocean.* Novato, CA.: New World Library, 2006.

ACKNOWLEDGMENTS

I wish to thank Jean Bauer for deciphering my hand-written edits of my Underwood typewriter drafts and conveying the manuscript to a computer. Also, I am grateful to John Richard for his careful scrutiny of the manuscript's later stages of preparation.

It was Dennis Johnson, CEO of Melville House who, unique among his peers, recognized the exemplary and emulative value of these CEO profiles to future business leaders, students, and other citizens who lack frames of reference in evaluating today's Big Business executives rulers. Special thanks go to Carl Bromley, Melville House's executive editor, who suggested improvements but maintained the light touch so desired by possessive authors.

INDEX

Cheney, Dick, 187, 189, 196, 212

Cheshin, Ruth, 213

Children on the Edge, 54

Children's Advocacy Institute (CAI) at University of San Diego School of Law, 148

Chile: Araucaria forests, 230; Cani sanctuary, 230; Estancia Monte Leon, 229; Patagonia land trust, 229–30, 239–40; Valle Chacabuco, 229

Chinese food companies, 116, 117, 121, 122–23, 124, 129

Chippewa people, 132

Chouinard, Claire, 227, 251

Chouinard, Fletcher, 227, 251

Chouinard, Malinda, 219, 237, 251

Chouinard, Yvon, xvi, xx, 219–51, 301–2; early life, 219–21; environmental consciousness, 223–24, 228–32, 234–44, 246–51, 301–2; *Let My People Go Surfing*, 223–24, 227; political endorsements, 243, 247–48, 250; *The Responsible Company*, 242. *See also* Patagonia

Chouinard, Yvonne, 220

Chouinard Equipment, 222, 224

Christian Action Council (CAC), 228

Chrysler, 74, 289–90

Chun King company, 116, 122–23, 124

Church, Frank, 204

Cicero, 280

Cisco, 12, 13

Citigroup, 23

the City (London), 46–47, 51, 54

City Heights Initiative, San Diego, 156–58, 159; Urban Village, 157

Civics for Democracy: A Journey for Teachers and Students (Isaac), 43

Civil Aeronautics Board (CAB), 97

civil rights movement, 279–80

Clay, Lucius, 129–31

Clean Water Act, 285

Clifford, Steve, 12

climate change, 57–58, 61–62, 83, 271, 285–98; Anderson and Interface's "Climate Take Back" mission, 81–82; Anderson and Interface's Mission Zero 2020 initiative, 72, 73–74, 80–81, 303; Anita Roddick's campaign against ExxonMobil, 55; Clinton/Gore report (1993), 61–62, 289; Gordon Roddick's message, 57–58; Hawken's Project Drawdown, 285–86, 287, 288–89; McKibben's work, 290, 292; SEC climate disclosure mandates, 299–300; Trump's climate denial, 192, 293. *See also* environmental consciousness and sustainability policies

Clinton, Bill, 6, 61–62, 75, 204, 214, 289

Clinton, Hillary, 204

Coca-Cola Company, x, 37–38

Cohen, Ben, xiv, 40

Columbia University Business School, 162

Commoner, Barry, 289

Communist Party (US), 112

The Conference Board, 169

Friends of the Ventura River, 231
Frost, Tom, 224–25
Fulbright, J. William, 212
Fuller, Buckminster, 294
Fund for the Replacement of
  Animals in Medical Experiments,
  42–43
Further Up the Organization
  (Townsend), 164, 176
Gannett Peak (Wyoming), 221
Garland, Judy, 112
Gates, Bill, 3
Gateway Marketplace (San Diego),
  156
Gautreaux v. CHA, 259
General Electric (GE), 23, 163
General Foods, 114–15
General Motors (GM), 23, 161,
  164–65, 172–73, 181, 182,
  289–90
The Georgia Conservancy, 74
Georgia Tech, 59
"gig economy," xiii, 272
Givat Gonen High School
  (Jerusalem), 211
Giving Pledge, xi–xii
Global Climate Action Summit in
  San Francisco (September 2018),
  80–81
"Global Power Elite," 28–29
Google, 267, 283
Gore, Al, 61–62, 153, 248, 289
Gottlieb, Robert A., 170, 181
Gould, Jay, 80–81
grand juries, xvii, 143–44, 155
Grand Staircase-Escalante National
  Monument (Utah), 228
Gray, Vincent C., 190

"Great Books Curriculum" at the
  University of Chicago, 254, 276
Great Depression, 13, 154, 168
"Great Recession," 23–24
Green New Deal, 249
Green Party (Brazil), 56–57
Green Party (US), 153, 242, 247
GreenBiz, 74
Greenpeace, 38–39, 55
"greenwashing," 285
Growing a Business (Hawken), 286,
  288
GSD&M (Austin), 88–89
Guardians (Jewish fundraising
  organization), 142
Gurash, John, 149
Hall, Gus, 112
Hardy, Jerry, 166
Harley-Davidson, 233
Harvard Business School, 36
Harvard Law School, x, 37
Harvard Medical School, 209
Hawken, Paul, xv, 60–61, 65, 249,
  279–98, 301–2; *Blessed Unrest*,
  284–85, 286, 287–88; and civil
  rights movement, 279–80;
  commencement speech at
  University of Portland (2009),
  293–97; *Drawdown*, 286, 287,
  288–89; *The Ecology of Commerce*,
  60–61, 280–81, 286, 298, 302;
  environmental and sustainability
  thinking, xv, 60–61, 281–98,
  301–2; foreword to *Dream of a
  Nation* (2011), 290–92; *Growing
  a Business*, 286, 288; Highwater
  Global Fund, 282–83; *The Next
  Economy*, 286; OneSun, 281;

Reebok International, xiii, xv
Rendell, Ed, 6
Republic Steel, 108
Republican Party, 152, 204, 214, 243
Reserve Mining Company, 107, 124
The Responsible Company: What We've Learned from Patagonia's First 40 Years (Chouinard and Stanley), 242
Retail Clerks and Food Handlers Union, 119, 120
A Revolution in Kindness (Roddick), 54
Richards, Ann, 204
Ricks, Ron, 103
Ridgeway, Rick, 240
Ridley, Dillon, 75
Robinson, Doug, 225
Rocky Mountain Institute, 74
Roddick, Anita, xiv, xvi, xviii–xix, xx, 31–58, 301–2, 303; *Body and Soul: Profits with Principles*, 32–33; *Business as Unusual*, 54; on the cosmetics industry, 32–33; death (2007), 55; environmental consciousness, xvi, xix, 34, 37–41, 55, 299, 301–2; feminism, 31; on going public, xviii–xix, 46–47, 51; human rights issues and campaigns, 37, 38, 42, 51–52, 58; *A Revolution in Kindness*, 54; *Take It Personally*, 54–55. *See also* The Body Shop
Roddick, Gordon, xviii–xix, 31, 33–34, 38, 40, 44, 46–47, 50, 53, 56, 57–58. *See also* The Body Shop

Roddick, Justine, 52
Roddick, Samantha, 52
Roddick Foundation, 55–56, 58
Rodino, Peter, 133–34
Rohatyn, Felix, 23
Romanian orphanages, 51–52
Roosevelt, Franklin D., 153, 201
Roosevelt, Theodore, 304
Rules for Radicals (Alinsky), 258
Sam Walton: Made in America: My Story (Walton), 145
Sam's Club, 152, 158
Samuelson, Paul A., 7
San Diego Community College, 156
San Diego High School, 142
San Diego Hospice, 155
San Diego State University, 157
San Francisco Conservatory of Music, 261
Schumpeter, Joseph, 225
Seabra, Antonio Luiz, 56
Seaman, Donna, 284
Sears, Roebuck, 7
Securities and Exchange Commission (SEC), 5, 10, 14, 125–26, 205, 263, 304; "business judgment rule," 22; climate disclosure mandates, 299–300
Service Employees International Union (SEIU), 206
Seventh Generation, 246
Shallal, Andy, xvi, xix, 185–97, 302; Busboys and Poets restaurants, xvi, 185–86, 188, 190–92, 194–97; new employee interviews, 191–92, 194–95; political and social justice activism in